METHUEN'S ENGLISH CLASSICS

Arnold, Matthew: *Selections from Matthew Arnold's Poetry*
Blake, William: *Songs of Innocence and of Experience*
Borrow, George: *Selections from Borrow*
Browning, Robert and E. B.: *Selections from the Brownings*
Bunyan, John S.: *Selections from Bunyan*
Byron, Lord: *Selections from Byron*
Coleridge, Samuel Taylor: *Selections from Coleridge*
Coulton, G. G.: *Pearl: A Fourteenth-century Poem*
Cowper, William: *Selections from Cowper*
Defoe, Daniel: *Selections from Defoe*
Dyson, C. M.: *Victorian Narrative Poems*
Evelyn, J.: *Selections from Evelyn's Diary*
Goldsmith, Oliver: *Selections from Goldsmith*
Hazlitt, W.: *The Best of Hazlitt*
Jonson, Ben: *Every Man in His Humour*
Keats, John: *Selections from Keats*
Kinglake, A. W.: *Eothen*
Lamb, Charles: *The Best of Lamb*
Macaulay, Lord: *Selections from Macaulay*
Marlow, Christopher: *Edward the Second*
    The Tragical History of Doctor Faustus
Mavor, Dorothea: *Elizabethan Lyrics*
Milton, John: *Minor English Poems*
Montagu, Lady Mary Wortley: *Letters from Constantinople*
Pope, Alexander: *The Rape of the Lock*
    An Epistle to Dr Arbuthnot
Segar, Mary C.: *Essays from Eighteenth-century Periodicals*
Spenser, Edmund: *Spenser's Minor Poems*
Swift, J.: *Selections from Swift*
Tennyson, Alfred, Lord: *Select Poems*
Webster, John: *The Duchess of Malfi*
White, Gilbert: *White's Natural History of Selborne*
Wordsworth, William: *Selections from Wordsworth*
Wordsworth, William, and Coleridge, S. T.: *The Lyrical Ballads*
    (1798–1805)

VOLPONE

OR, THE FOX

by Ben Jonson

edited by

DAVID COOK, M.A. (Lond.)

Lecturer in English, University of Southampton;
Formerly English Master, Matthew Arnold
Secondary Modern Boys' School, Staines

LONDON

Methuen & Co Ltd

11 NEW FETTER LANE EC4

First published in this edition in 1962
Reprinted 1964
Introduction and Notes: © 1962 by David Cook
Printed in Great Britain by
Richard Clay and Company Ltd, Bungay, Suffolk
Catalogue No. 2/7455/6
1·2

Contents

Introduction   *page* 7

   JONSON'S LIFE; JONSON'S COMEDY; VOL-
PONE; THE STRUCTURE OF VOLPONE;
SOURCES; THE TEXT; THE NOTES; ACKNOW-
LEDGEMENTS

Volpone   51

Notes   184

   PERSONS OF THE PLAY; DEDICATION; THE
ARGUMENT; PROLOGUE; THE TEXT

Introduction

JONSON'S LIFE

Although we know a great deal more about Jonson than about some of his contemporaries, his biography is only sketchily documented, and many important facts about his life cannot be firmly established. The most reliable account of what is both known and conjectured is to be found in the first volume of Herford and Simpson's full edition of the works (supplemented in the eleventh volume by more recent information). Here I intend to give only the simple outlines of the playwright's career, ignoring the picturesque myths that have persistently clung to his name, and keeping as far as possible to known facts.

Ben Jonson was probably born in 1573 in or near London. His paternal grandfather had been a 'gentleman' from the Scottish border country; but the dramatist's father had 'losed all his estate' in Mary's reign, 'being cast in prison'. Later, presumably under Elizabeth, he became 'a grave minister of the gospel'. He died a month before his son Benjamin was born. Within three years his widow was remarried to a master-builder. Of Jonson's mother we know only that, when he was in the power of the law for satirising the king, she prepared a poison for her son and herself to forestall the carrying out of any extreme sentence.

Ben was 'brought up poorly' at first in a private school in St Martin's Church; but fortunately an unidentified friend stepped in to send him to the great Westminster School, where his master was the renowned Camden, who helped lay the foundations of Jonson's considerable learning. His studies were interrupted, however, and he was put to work, probably as a bricklayer in his stepfather's business. This trade he 'could not endure', so after an undetermined period he abandoned it and went to fight in Flanders. There the campaign was at a stand-still, so Jonson created action by challenging an enemy to single combat between the camps, killing him and bearing back his arms as victor.

Jonson later told Drummond that he soon returned from Flanders and 'betook himself to his wonted studies', though, of course, he must have needed to earn his living. He was married, we believe in 1594, to a woman whom he briefly described as 'a shrew but honest'. She bore him at least two children in their early married life (as we know from their father's epitaphs upon their untimely deaths), probably more; all we know of the marriage otherwise is that Jonson later lived apart from his wife for five years, and that he was unfaithful to her.

Jonson's first known connexion with the theatre was as a member of a strolling company of actors in 1597, one of his parts probably being Hieronimo in Kyd's *Spanish Tragedy*, though there is evidence that he was a poor player. As such he came to London, but it was as a writer that he was picked out by Henslowe, the brilliant manager of London's second company, the Admiral's Men, for whom we find him a playwright in July 1597. Almost at once he was involved in scandal. He was set to finish a play, *The Isle of Dogs*, left incomplete by Nashe; the piece was officially condemned as seditious and slanderous; and several of the company were briefly imprisoned, Jonson among them. This was all part of a dramatist's life, however, and before long he was back writing plays for Henslowe which have not been preserved, so that by autumn of 1598 he could be hailed as among the 'best for tragedie'. But it was in comedy that he was to make his first resounding success with the performance of *Every Man in His Humour*, in September of the same year. This outstanding achievement was likely to have been his last, since only a few days later he quarrelled with an actor in the company, duelled with him, killed his opponent, was arrested for felony, confessed, and escaped the gallows only by pleading the ancient right of benefit of clergy as a literate man, so that his punishment was reduced to confiscation of all his goods and branding on the thumb.

Nothing cowed, Jonson continued to write tragedies, since lost, for Henslowe; while in 1599 or early 1600 he presented the Chamberlain's Men with a companion piece to his first triumph, *Every Man Out of His Humour*, in which he took his innovations further, reducing the narrative interest to a minimum and relying on brilliant, satiric character sketches to carry the play through. Though enthusiasm for his second 'humour' play was not undivided, Jonson's position was firmly established.

Now followed two comedies in which satire, abstraction and moralisation considerably outweighed full-blooded drama. These two plays were also influenced by the part Jonson took in the 'War of the Theatres'. A young admirer of Jonson, John Marston, had rashly attempted a flattering representation of his master in *Histriomastix*, but the result was nearer parody. Perhaps Jonson light-heartedly returned the doubtful compliment in the figure of Clove in *Every Man Out of His Humour*; Marston thought so, took offence, and retaliated with a deliberate caricature of Ben in his *Jack Drum's Entertainment*. So that Jonson included a sharper retort in his next play, *Cynthia's Revels*, a work performed by one of the children's companies (the 'little eyases' of *Hamlet*). Marston now recruited Dekker to his aid; Jonson, hearing of this, speeded his *Poetaster*, also for the Children of Paul's, so that the next salvoes from both sides were eventually fired about the same time in 1601, Jonson's play coming on the heels of Marston's *What You Will* and completely overshadowing it. However, Jonson's satire had many targets besides his rivals, and raised a hornets' nest about his head. He made no reply to Dekker's *Satiromastix*, the opposition's most effective piece, but retired from the arena with an air of injured innocence, and a few months later turned back to writing tragedy for Henslowe.

Soon after James's accession in 1603, the first of the two tragic works which Jonson preserved for posterity was performed. *Sejanus* sought to restore classic loftiness to tragedy, but the groundlings were appalled by its long speeches; admirers were in a minority; there was violent popular protest against the play. Not long after this Jonson joined with Chapman and Marston in writing *Eastward Ho!*; for satire therein against Scots in general, and the king in particular, the two latter were imprisoned, and Jonson voluntarily joined them. There was talk of ears and noses being cut off; but powerful friends intervened, and all three escaped unmutilated.

From the beginning of James's reign Jonson had been engaged to write masques and entertainments. In such works he displayed a rare and delicate vein of lyrical invention, which set him head and shoulders above all his fellows in this special field. He was called on for many such works throughout James's reign; a labour in which he delighted in spite of a protracted animosity between himself and Inigo Jones, chief designer of these fantastically lavish court displays.

The failure of *Sejanus* was to be reversed by the resounding success of *Volpone*, written late in 1605 or early in 1606 and performed soon afterwards by the King's Men (the new name of the Chamberlain's Men of the previous reign). It was presented not only in London, but also successively at the two universities, where it was equally acclaimed, their 'love and acceptance' being recognised some two years later when Jonson added the dedication.

This period was the peak of his dramatic career. His best masques were written now. His other comic masterpieces followed: *Epicoene or the Silent Woman* (1609–10) and *The Alchemist* (1610). Only when Jonson again attempted classic tragedy in *Catiline* (1611) was he faced once more with fiasco.

The years following James's accession were the great period of the Mermaid Tavern, where Jonson was a leading spirit, and where he entered into the renowned wit-combats with Shakespeare, of which we get such tantalisingly inadequate glimpses from contemporary reports. Jonson was a generous if difficult friend, numbering noblemen as well as writers among his exceptionally wide circle of intimates; with a special position in the court and inn alike; bluff, but unnervingly direct 'for he would not flatter though he saw death'.

In 1612–13 Jonson travelled on the continent as a not very successful tutor to Sir Walter Raleigh's sparkish son. Back in England he resumed his stage work with another important play, *Bartholomew Fair* (1614); but two years later *The Devil Is An Ass* marked the beginning of Jonson's decline as a playwright, though he excelled still at masques. Not for nine years did he write another comedy, *The Staple of News* in 1625; though all this time he was a dominant figure in the literary world. His walking tour of Scotland is of particular interest to us, since it included his visit to Drummond of Hawthornden, a Scottish poet who during two or three weeks gleaned a store of information from his great guest.

He made résumés of their conversations, and so left for posterity the most important single record concerning Jonson's career. In 1623 there was a fire in Jonson's library which destroyed for ever works in prose and poetry which he had been engaged on during the previous years.

The story after Charles's accession is often a sad one, not least in having to record a late but unimpressive comedy, *The New Inn* (1628–29); yet his creative genius was not quenched, and in 1632 he produced, in spite of inauspicious circumstances, a not insignificant new work, *The Magnetic Lady*. His last years were overshadowed by sickness and debt, in spite of unbroken friendships and sometimes generous financial relief. This period was, indeed, illuminated by the unfailing devotion displayed by the leading figures of the new generation of writers, the 'Tribe of Ben', who still looked on him as the master spirit: when he was no longer in the public eye, Jonson was still the centre of the world of letters for his literary successors. His fitful sickness was by no means a time of intellectual atrophy or decline.

When Jonson at length died on 6 August 1637, 'all or the greatest part of the nobility and gentry then in town' followed his hearse to the grave in Westminster Abbey. In Herford's words: 'Neglected as his later days had been, the passing of Ben was, for the entire English world of letters, the passing of its king – a king who had perhaps ceased to govern, but who still reigned.'

JONSON'S COMEDY

ON READING JONSON'S PLAYS

It is quite difficult to become good at reading plays; but it is an absorbing and rewarding apprenticeship. Plays are essentially live creations to be acted and seen; but reading them in print is more than a substitute for going to the theatre. A drama like *Volpone*, of course, might remain completely unknown to many of us if we had to wait to see it on the stage, but even if we could go and watch it, the careful, repeated, private thought we can give the work on the printed page would add very greatly to our appreciation and understanding of it as a piece of dramatic art.

Knowing how to play the piano does not enable one to master the violin as a matter of course. In the same way, a wide acquaintance with other fiction does not make one immediately adept at reading drama. In fact, one of the main reasons why many people find plays rather dull to read is that, quite naturally, but quite wrongly, they think of them as if they were very short novels. But plays, like paintings or symphonies, are highly concentrated works of art, much more concentrated than continuous fiction. If we limit ourselves to the story and characters of a novel we may come to appreciate it quite fully (though there are certainly many more things to be considered); but if we think only of the subject of a painting, only of the tunes of a symphony, only of the plot and characters of a play, we may seem to have very little for our money. We have to be affected by the colour and form of a painting, by the development and rhythmic interplay within a symphony, before they become intensely significant to us. In just the same way we need to be influenced by the style and patterning of a play before we can comprehend it as an important work.

A glance at the first act of Shakespeare's *Much Ado About Nothing* will show what I mean. In this act very little actually happens: plot is minimal; and there are only two characters of any complexity, Beatrice and Benedick. Yet it is lively, gripping, vivid and crowded. Interest and movement lie far more in the pattern than in the story; there is a closer analogy with painting than with the novel; the different groups of characters, like boldly contrasted blocks of colour, are set against each other in sharply differentiated dialogues: the witty group, the romantic group, the sinister group.

A failure to understand the dramatic medium can seriously affect our ability to appreciate Ben Jonson. Deplorably limited as such an approach may be, it is possible to derive a good deal from Shakespeare by considering plots and characters alone; and his are probably the first plays we know well. Since Jonson's characters have comparatively little to offer in this purely narrative sense, the first impression they give may be one of flatness, disappointment; just as someone who has delighted in Constable's portrayal of the English countryside might be repelled and bewildered by the works of Turner if he was hoping for the same treatment.

Once style and pattern are recognised as the most essential complements of dramatic action, not the portrayal of 'real characters' (a very dangerous phrase) or telling a romantic tale, one can understand that Jonson's mode of drama is properly and intentionally different from Shakespeare's. Jonson is no more trying to draw complex Shakespearian figures and failing than the later Picasso is trying unsuccessfully to paint Rembrandt faces. Jonson and Shakespeare are composing works as different as those of Bach and Beethoven. If I labour this point, it is because one must grasp it to begin enjoying Ben Jonson; and I am sure he is a playwright with a strong modern appeal, once his qualities are realised.

Jonson's writing is highly stylised, highly disciplined, formalised. He is not in the tradition of intimate, human comedy which links Chaucer, Shakespeare, Fielding, Browning and Dylan Thomas, for instance; but belongs to the more critical and satirical body together with Congreve, Pope, Oscar Wilde, Bernard Shaw and T. S. Eliot.

One of the main difficulties in reading Jonson is that his characters speak so racily and colloquially, and at the same time with such exuberance and zest, that we may be left floundering in our efforts to keep up with the tempo of their unfamiliar vocabulary. On the other hand, to read the plays slowly for the first time is to make them flag, to make them seem bookish and laborious, which they are not.

My advice to someone coming to a play by Jonson for the first time would be to read it as rapidly as is reasonably possible, without worrying at all if there are many details that fly by uncomprehended; get the feel, the speed, the relish of the thing. There will be plenty of time to turn back to incidental points afterwards. If you think it will help, read a little about the play first, but not too much: don't swamp your own appreciation by an overdose of other people's opinions. Above all, remember what Jonson says himself in the prologue to *Volpone*, where he claims that

> In all his poems still hath been this measure,
> To mix profit with your pleasure –

in short, the pleasure must come first, and then other things will be added unto you. So that any reader's first critical, and aesthetic responsibility is to come to know the play in such a way that he or she will enjoy it.

A LIVE TRADITION

The general remarks which now follow are directly relevant to *Volpone*, which cannot be very fully appreciated without some understanding of the playwright's approach. Jonson knew what he was about. He carefully considered the nature of dramatic art; and came to certain definite conclusions about its proper form and treatment. Fortunately, he was ready and eager to discuss these beliefs in the plays themselves, several of which have inductions which are, in fact, skilfully dramatised debates on dramatic theory and practice.

His desire to analyse and think about his writing does not make Jonson a desiccated theorist. A creative artist, whether he is articulate like Jonson or not, must consider and comprehend the medium in which he works. (It would be very foolish to believe that because Shakespeare is critically reticent he was therefore an instinctive genius without any deep interest or concern in his methods and materials: this would be to deny him artistry, which is patently absurd.) Jonson, as Schelling has said, 'believed that there was a professional way of doing things'; professional, that is, in the best sense of the word, implying an acceptance of artistic discipline, a realisation that inspiration will become art only if it is intelligently controlled and channelled.

So when we speak of Jonson as a 'classical' dramatist, we must realise that he was never in any sense adopting a dead tradition on trust. He weighed all matters for himself. The traditional concepts he accepts become his own from free choice. He changes his dramatic mode to suit his own genius, and finally creates something unique, which is anything but a slavish model of Roman (or any other) comedy.

It is worth noting here that the main stream of Elizabethan and Jacobean literary theory and criticism was rigidly and uncompromisingly 'classical', judging contemporary writing by the criteria of another age, and holding an author 'justified' only if he could find a precedent in Greek or Latin for his particular literary manner and practices. The two writers who partake inevitably of this tradition, and yet stand out most unmistakably as liberal and positive thinkers, are Philip Sidney and Ben Jonson. Sidney, perhaps our first dramatic critic, wrote some years before the outset of the Elizabethan–Jacobean dramatic era proper, and so was much more concerned with what ought to be done than with criticising what had been done. The acceptance of artistic discipline and a sense of the high seriousness of poetry and drama so warmly advocated by Sidney were to inform much of the work in the period ahead; but Jonson alone among the dozen or so outstanding dramatists was to follow not only the spirit but much of the precept of Sidney, whose *Apologie for Poetrie*, written in the early 1580s, was first published in 1595, just about the time when Jonson must have been taking up his theatrical career.

Before going into detail, it is wise to stand back and consider the more general effect that this tradition has on Jonson's work. His plays are characterised by a firmness, a solidity, a direct clarity. There is no confusion of style or material. In this Jonson can best be compared (very different though they are in many important respects) not with another English dramatist but with Molière; for in France the purist conception of drama was dominant for a long period. The real strength of this mode is its refusal to intermingle in the same work different kinds of experience. Comedy is comedy: to introduce sentiment, pathos, romance is to diffuse the effect, is to pander to dilettanteism or philistinism. Much as Jonson admired Shakespeare, it was precisely for this that he attacked him, more in sorrow than in anger.

If comedy is to remain unadulterated, its purpose must be to make us laugh. Such a clear-cut definition would exclude the complex pattern of humour, sentiment and serious melancholy which is the groundwork of Shakespeare's early comedies. Sidney and Jonson agree that the immediate aim is to create comic spectacle and situation; but both recognise laughter as a means, not an end. Jonson's comedy is essentially didactic. What we are to laugh at is carefully selected with a satirical eye. The characters live and move in order to create 'an image of the time', and Jonson shares with Middleton and Dekker the ability to portray vividly from first-hand knowledge the teeming life of his London. But, in Jonson's earlier comedies at least, this image itself is created in order to 'sport with human follies', and the playwright hastens to tell us that

> I mean such errors as you'll all confess.

We are to be amused not simply in order to forget our troubles, but to laugh ourselves out of our own follies and affectations. As Sidney has it:

> Comedy is an imitation of the common errors of our life, which he [the dramatist] representeth in the most ridiculous and scornful sort that may be; so as it is impossible that any beholder can be content to be such a one.

This purpose leads to a certain hardness of outline in the dramatis personae, a didactic precision; irrelevant inconsistencies are ironed out, because these would serve only to confuse the mind, and divert the attention. Once the characters are known, their behaviour is largely predictable; they show none of the waywardness or complexity of warring, and often illogical, human motives; though I shall suggest later that if there is one figure in Jonson's works who is a partial exception to this rule, it is Volpone himself. This is the sort of characterisation which Sidney is assuming when he neatly labels his examples of comic types: 'a busy loving courtier, a heartless threatening Thraso, a self-wise-seeming schoolmaster, a awry-transformed traveller' and so forth.

Such essentially 'classical' concentration was implied by critics, Sidney among them, when they described comedy as a 'kind', a clearly defined literary form with its own laws and discipline. Obviously, to compare this (unfavourably or otherwise) with Shakespearian or romantic comedy is irrelevant. It has to be appreciated as a distinct species of drama. For making us laugh, of course, this comic style is not to be bettered. Sentiment is not denied, but simply excluded. All that we are shown is subject for our amusement.

CLASSICISM MODIFIED

It is clear that classical rules were never a strait-jacket for Jonson. He later epitomised his attitude:

I know nothing can conduce more to letters than to examine the writings of the ancients, and not to rest in their sole authority, or take all upon trust from them. . . . For to all the observations of the ancients we have our own experience, which if we will use and apply, we have better means to pronounce. It is true they opened the gates, and made the way that went before us, but as guides, not commanders. . . . Truth lies open to all; it is no man's several.

Here is Jonson's sturdy common sense. Though he was probably the most learned of the Elizabethan–Jacobean playwrights, yet he did not retire to an ivory tower; he took his own advice, and looked around him as keenly as any. If he abjured enchanted islands and impossible sea-coasts; if he refused to make his plays hinge on freaks of circumstance, confusions of identity and misunderstandings; he was not doing so 'upon trust' from the ancients, but because that part of 'our own experience' which activated him was observation of human follies in a familiar London setting, rather than the ethereal reaches of the imagination and the emotions.

One precept Jonson unhesitatingly flouted in most of his plays, namely that virtue should finally be rewarded and vice punished:

> For indeed poetry ever setteth virtue so out in her best colours, making Fortune her well-waiting hand-maid, that one must needs be enamoured of her. . . . And of the contrary part, if evil men come to the stage, they ever go out (as the tragedy writer answered to one that misliked the show of such persons) so manacled, as they little animate folks to follow them. (Sidney, *Apologie for Poetrie*.)

In comedy, however, it was understood that the wicked should receive their just deserts in a manner that would not cast any gloomy cloud over the happy dénouement. In fact, the rogues in the final version of *Every Man In His Humour* and in *Bartholomew Fair* meet either nominal punishment or none at all. In *The Alchemist*, Subtle and Doll, though effectively humiliated (the proper fate of vice in critical comedy), are not formally punished, while Face is left cock of the walk. It might, therefore, seem strange that it is the ending of the more conventionally moral *Volpone* which Jonson feels called upon to defend on the grounds

B

that 'it is the office of the comic poet to imitate justice, and instruct to life'. Why should Jonson apologise for ending the play with the guilty cast down? The reason is clear. True the evil are properly arraigned and 'go out manacled', but there is no display of virtue triumphant to conclude the play on the joyous note demanded by convention. None of Jonson's comedies has an ending compatible with strict neo-classical theory; it is simply that *Volpone* breaks a different 'rule'.

THE UNITIES

Neo-classic critics attributed the first definition of the unities of time, place and action to Aristotle. In fact, Aristotle never (in his extant writings) formulated these concepts in such a way or used this phraseology. He did not discuss 'place' in this sense at all, and his two brief comments on 'time' are not altogether consistent. Nevertheless the sixteenth century tended to talk of the unities as received truth, and they were often regarded as the centre-piece of the whole design of theoretical criticism.

Characteristically Jonson did not accept the unities as laws, but welcomed them as optional aids to artistic discipline. He scorned dramatists who rejected restraint, and rebuked Shakespeare among others for what he regarded as wanton licence:

> To make a child now swaddled, to proceed
> Man, and then shoot up, in one beard and weed,
> Past threescore years; or, with three rusty swords
> And help of some few foot and half-foot words,
> Fight over York and Lancaster's long jars,
> And in the tiring-house bring wounds to scars.
> He rather prays you will be pleased to see
> One such today as other plays should be;
> Where neither chorus wafts you o'er the seas,
> Nor creaking throne comes down the boys to please.

But he finds no virtue in following precept simply for its own sake. The prologue to *Volpone* declares:

> The laws of time, place, persons he observeth,
> From no needful rule he swerveth.

The word 'needful' is crucial.

Volpone gains in concentration from the restriction of the action to one day, a time-span which Jonson carefully points out. The play opens after sunrise: 'Good-morrow to the day'; and Voltore makes 'early visitation'. At the end of Act I Lady Politic Would-be is put off for three hours, and returns in the afternoon (Act III, scene iv). Volpone tells Celia that he had played the mountebank 'but this morning'. And the first trial scene promises that judgement will be given 'before night', which thus sets the time for the final action of the play. There is one apparent inconsistency: we learn that Volpone has appeared to Celia in 'several shapes', though at the beginning of the play he knew nothing of her (and even Mosca discovered her 'but yesterday'), so that there has hardly been time for Volpone to have adopted other disguises. We might argue that he is here talking at random to impress Celia. But, in any case, one should not approach drama like a Sherlock Holmes. Slight contradictions are common in great plays; would pass unnoticed on the stage; and have no real significance.

Jonson can claim 'unity of place' for *Volpone* according to the scope allowed by neo-classic convention, which demanded that everything should take place in one town. Our play passes entirely within Venice, in three houses, the street and the Scrutineo. It is, perhaps, an arbitrary distinction to allow that a stage may represent successively scenes in different houses, but not in different cities or countries; but such a limitation helps to bind together certain plays, this among them.

Jonson himself echoes Aristotle quite closely with regard to what became known as 'unity of action' when he says of a play that one 'should not be able to remove a part without troubling the whole'. It is generally true that he himself observes this most fundamental of the three principles. *Volpone* is an exception. The passages between Sir Politic and Peregrine are not in the strictest sense necessary to the whole structure, and are sometimes cut in performance, an amputation which would be impossible elsewhere in the design. But, as I shall argue later, this part of the play is, in fact, needed for proper balance, as Jonson was able to understand, since he was a great playwright rather than an ardent purist.

What might seem to be a more fundamental irregularity lies in the apparent break in the chain of causation between Acts IV and

V, since the cause of the catastrophe is not to be found in the preceding events: disaster is not imminent. Jonson's concern here, and the true logic of the action, lie deeper. The play demonstrates the inexorable course of successful vice, which cannot come to rest when prudence and reason dictate. Sheer impetus and the intoxication of triumph carry the protagonists inevitably forward to self-induced disaster. The evil carries the seeds of its own destruction.

ACTION

Jonson is one of the masters of dramatic structure in our language. Yet the unity which each of his comedies possesses is different in kind from that conceived by Aristotle, who envisaged a straightforward progression of events, each developing directly out of what preceded it. Jonson's pattern is more complex. There are many interlocking parts, more like a jig-saw than a chain. Each character has his or her own miniature action, which is nevertheless an integral part of the whole. The separate scenes with the legacy-hunters in the first act of *Volpone* cannot be said to develop one from the other: yet they are not merely a succession. The three interests are related, and become interwoven as the action advances.

For Jonson's comedies are not simply static patterns. There is also a progression, a steady increase in tempo. The separate elements in the design become more and more likely to swamp each other, to collide and destroy the whole framework. It is particularly Mosca's function in *Volpone* to try to keep the threads apart while they are, nevertheless, irrevocably twining together. The increasing tempo is related to the mounting difficulty of this task. There is growing suspense as Mosca's efforts to steer the schemes clear of disaster become more desperate. The final momentum, in the last act, derives from the eventual splitting-up of the previously combined interests and actions of Volpone and Mosca; this now complicates the pattern beyond the control of either of them, so that after some hair-breadth escapes the whole structure inevitably crashes.

HUMOURS

Most of us get a general idea of the physiological theory of the four humours from our study of Chaucer, who makes frequent reference to this system of diagnosing temperament. The whole conception derives ultimately from Hippocrates. It is part of an important classical and mediaeval theory of the universe which understands everything to exist as a combination of the four elementary qualities: hotness and coldness, wetness and dryness. These combine in pairs to form the basis of the inorganic universe – earth, air, water and fire. In man they combine in the four liquids or humours which determine each individual's disposition; blood (hot and moist); phlegm (cold and moist); yellow bile (hot and dry); black bile (cold and dry). If one can suppose an average or typical man, he would then be said to have all four humours in perfect balance. If we now conceive of a man with three humours balanced at this perfect mean, but one in excess, then if the excessive humour is blood he would be exceptionally sanguine and cheerful; if it were phlegm, he would be exceptionally calm; if yellow bile, abnormally choleric; and if black bile, particularly melancholy. However, there is no need to assume that only one humour deviates from the mean, or that any humour will be in excess rather than in default, or that there is a single degree of increase or decrease; there will be an infinite number of possible combinations and complexities, corresponding with the infinitely varied characters of mankind.

Ben Jonson appeals directly to this conception in the induction to *Every Man Out of His Humour*:

> So in every human body,
> The choler, melancholy, phlegm, and blood,
> By reason that they flow continually
> In some one part and are not continent,
> Receive the name of humours. Now thus far
> It may, by metaphor, apply itself
> Unto the general disposition.

There is a great danger of our unconsciously patronising those who lived at a time when this concept held sway. As physiology the whole structure may naturally seem to us a primitive and amusing myth. But we may go on from there to assume that an analysis of human conduct which refers to this framework of ideas is also, by definition, elementary and to be discounted. This, however, in no way follows. For the ordinary man, or for the poet or playwright, the humours theory did little more than provide a vocabulary for interpreting his assessment of personality and behaviour. And in this sense it is precisely parallel with our own use of twentieth century psychological jargon. When we adopt the language of complexes, subconscious motivation, compensation, and so forth, we are discussing the same human nature as formed the material for Chaucer or Ben Jonson, who certainly had as full a degree of insight into the workings of the mind as the modern layman, and no doubt a great deal more than most of us. Indeed, very few of us have any fuller understanding of what we are saying in alluding to the endocrine glands than had they in supposing that black bile and yellow bile, blood and phlegm control our private destinies. In the lines quoted above Jonson actually acknowledges that this is nothing more than 'a way of putting it': 'now thus far it may, *by metaphor*, apply itself unto the general disposition', he says. This is very important; until we can see his terminology in perspective we shall be unable to set a true value on his analyses of experience.

COMEDY OF HUMOURS

We are now in a position to see what, in dramatic terms, Jonson meant by 'humours', and what he is attempting in his so-called comedy of humours. Just as Bernard Shaw simplifies the psychological make-up of his characters for dramatic emphasis, thereby making complicated ideas relatively easy to understand, so Jonson simplifies the 'humorous' make-up of his figures to achieve concentration. He is, as it were, presenting us with such theoretical figures as I described just now, with only one humour out of balance. We find characters in Jonson's comedies who have simply an overdose of jealousy, or of stubbornness, of piety, or of avarice; so that these qualities can be seen in isolation for what they are, as they cannot be seen in a complex, living human being.

This again is clearly described by Jonson in the induction to *Every Man Out of His Humour*:

> As when some one peculiar quality
> Doth so possess a man, that it doth draw
> All his affects, his spirits, and his powers,
> In their confluctions, all to run one way,
> This may be truly said to be a humour.

Such are Voltore, Corvino and Corbaccio in *Volpone*, who are to be discussed more fully later. Celia and Bonario are shadows of virtuous humours. More than this, Volpone himself can be seen as a compound of humours. His disguises emphasise his shape-shifting: he is the dying miser, the nimble-witted mountebank or quack; and when dressed as commandator to delight in the discomfiture of the legacy-hunters, he is what the 'character' writers of the period might have called 'the taunting man'. Again, with Celia he is the passionate lover; in the first court scene he is the maltreated invalid. The essential Volpone himself – and there is one, for he is no mere bundle of personifications – is the guiding spirit who delights in his own energy and variety. It is thus that he ultimately eludes the humour framework, and becomes a figure unique in Jonson's drama.

AFFECTED HUMOURS

Jonson considers obsessive humours very seriously indeed, and even extends a degree of compassion to those who are swept away by their destructive force; this is true, I think, in the case of Kitely, the jealous man, in *Every Man In His Humour*.

On the other hand there is the large group of 'humours' for whom Jonson feels nothing but contempt. These are the poseurs, who, far from being seized by an inner compulsion, affect to be what they are not in order to satisfy a foolish vanity. Such cannot be 'truly said to be a humour':

> that a rook, by wearing a pied feather,
> The cable hat-band, or the three-piled ruff,
> A yard of shoe-tie, or the Switzer's knot
> On his French garters, should affect a humour!
> O, 'tis more than most ridiculous.

These figures are particularly characterised by the idle foppery of their dress, believing that they can make themselves of some account in the world by applying themselves to the externals of appearance and speech, and by fashionable attitudinising. Jonson promises tersely to 'scourge these apes'. Those against whom he felt particularly bitter were the gallants who debased poetry by dabbling in rhyming and plagiarism.

Such affectations were the stock-in-trade of the early *Humour* plays. In *Volpone* the Politic Would-be's provide a lighter vein of mere folly as contrast to the more sinister humours at the centre of the play. Lady Would-be is a naïve outsider in the struggle for Volpone's fortune, never really understanding the dark world in which she finds herself a somewhat cumbersome butterfly.

STOCK CHARACTERS

There is another way of grouping Jonson's actors. The whole design is sufficiently stylised for many of the names to be constantly played on in the text – Volpone (fox); Mosca (fly); Voltore (vulture); Corbaccio (raven); Corvino (crow). Such figures not only constitute the comedy of humours, but also readily partake of the classical tradition of stock characters, the stereotyped dramatis personae of the plays of Terence and Plautus.

Some parallel to this repetitive pattern may be found, perhaps, in modern comedy programmes on television and radio, in so many of which appear the same types – the twittering secretary, the raucous charwoman, the blustering but cowardly friend, the defiant but ineffectual husband and so on. The same thing was true of classical comedy: the son sowing his wild oats, the disapproving father, the bragging, mock-valiant soldier, the scheming servant and many other such figures reappear in play after play. Works of this genre and their characters exerted a major influence on English critics, and, rather differently, on English playwrights, by way of sixteenth-century Italian drama, which became very fashionable throughout Europe, especially for performance among groups of lawyers, students and schoolboys. The stock characters of Plautus and Terence made an important mark not only on writers like Lyly, but also on Shakespeare, who absorbed part of all available dramatic traditions. Unique as they are, the Gobbos, the nurse in *Romeo and Juliet*, Falstaff (to mention a few at random) all have a strain of Roman blood in them.

Jonson knew these models at first hand as well as at one remove. But although in his plays the classical influence is much more direct and conscious, it is none the less true that he borrowed nothing directly from anywhere without its passing through a remoulding process in his hands. The crafty servant is already a new being in Brainworm of *Every Man In His Humour*. By the time he came to create Mosca, he made something as distinct from any Latin slave or parasite as Falstaff is from the stock braggart.

Humours and stock characters mingle in particular figures. The birds of prey in *Volpone*, while clearly being 'possessed' by 'one particular quality', are not unrelated to the misers of classic comedy.

Thus for Jonson these figures do not remain Roman types, any more than 'humours' are mere psychopathic curiosities. They derive gusto and exuberance from their immediate contact with contemporary reality. Whatever their antecedents, these are no abstractions of an academic; Volpone and Mosca, as we shall see, can so outrun all precedent as to transcend their supposedly prescribed personalities.

JONSON'S COMIC WORLD

In his great plays Jonson creates a new comic world. Though this is not our world, it is related to our own, in something of the same way that Lilliput or (apter in ratio) Brobdingnag are related to our reality without being the same. In the same manner, Jonson's world, while being exaggerated, is exaggerated in proper proportions, so that we see a magnified version of part of our daily experience, and we are startled by this new vision of the commonplace.

Jonson accomplishes this technically by stylisation and concentration. It is his achievement that he understood his medium very well indeed, and accepted a strict dramatic discipline in full realisation of what he was doing. As with any artistic discipline, its mastery represented not a fettering but a liberation, an ability to convey with great intensity what would otherwise be vague and undefined; and, also, what could not have been said in any other way.

T. S. Eliot has written of Jonson's dramatic manner with great insight:

> The simplification consists largely in reduction of detail. . . . This stripping is essential to the art . . .; it is an art of caricature, of great caricature. . . . It is a great caricature, which is beautiful; and a great humour, which is serious. The 'world' of Jonson is sufficiently large; it is a world of poetic imagination. . . . He did not get the third dimension, but he was not trying to get it.

The environment that Jonson creates is divided mainly between rogues and fools; though the fools may be vicious, silly or affected. We are presented with no complacent morality – a simple goodness opposing a simple evil. We find our sympathies tending towards the rogues, whose wit, dexterity and zest for life appeal to us. And so we are drawn into the complex moral pattern of the play; we cannot stand aside, Pharisee-like, crying, 'I thank thee, Lord, I am not such as these.' We have become involved; we are implicated. If when the play is over we pass judgement, we must partly judge ourselves; if we are alarmed, we are alarmed partly by what we have found in ourselves.

VOLPONE

With *Volpone* Ben Jonson returned to comedy after several years spent on other writing, including his interesting rather than successful tragedy, *Sejanus*. He returned with fiery ideas and high aspirations. The solemn dedication to the universities was added two years later, when the play had already been widely acclaimed, but it is fully in keeping with the work. Here his deeper seriousness is heard as he defends 'so divine a skill' as writing poetry against the debasement to which it is subjected as a result 'of the too much licence of the poetasters of this time'. It is with a characteristic combination of idealism and haughtiness that he declares 'the impossibility of any man's being the good poet, without first being a good man'; and proceeds to set forth the proper functions of the poet:

> He that is said to be able to inform young men to all good disciplines, inflame grown men to all great virtues, keep old men in their best and supreme state or, as they decline to childhood, recover them to their first strength; that comes forth the interpreter and arbiter of nature, a teacher of things divine no less than human, a master in manners; and can alone (or with a few) effect the business of mankind.

He continues with a rejection of profanity, bawdry and personal allusion (although in the last matter he had not been altogether innocent himself during the war of the theatres, even if the first provocation was not his). He attacks the present degradation of drama, perhaps with some side glances at Shakespeare (who, Jonson would have said, should have known better) in his references to 'so bold prolepses, so racked metaphors, with brothelry able to violate the ear of a pagan'. His conclusion to this great declaration of fellowship with two seats of learning he had never attended is a self-dedication:

> if my muses be true to me, I shall raise the despised head of poetry again, and, stripping her out of those rotten and base rags wherewith the times have adulterated her form, restore her to her primitive habit, feature, and majesty, and render her worthy to be embraced and kissed by all the great and master spirits of the world.

This is the man who wrote *Volpone*. Even allowing for the extravagance of language normal in dedications, it is evident that no shy and humble apprentice poet is speaking: but mock modesty never made a satirist. From this declaration it is clear that we shall not be falsifying Jonson's intentions if we take *Volpone* very seriously indeed.

Certainly we find in this play something fundamentally different in many ways from his first and last comedies. True, like others of his plots, this is constructed on the basis of a practical joke, and ultimate downfall comes through over-reaching, so that the biter is bit, and, in a sense, his humour is exposed; but the scale is now increased beyond recognition. His earlier comedy aimed to 'sport with human follies, not with crimes'. This cannot be said of *Volpone*. As in *The Alchemist* and *Bartholomew Fair*, the framework is now one of organised humbug and corruption; but neither of these other plays has a ground-bass of the same sombre intensity. Legacy-hunting proved to be the ideal subject for Jonson's serious satire.

The theme has only one fault – its un-Englishness. The trafficker in bequests or *captator* existed in Rome, and in Roman literature, but this was not a form of avariciousness specifically known to be prevalent in Jacobean London society. It might seem that Jonson was thus deprived of a powerful spring of realism. In fact, unlike all the important comedies that followed *Volpone*, no one of his plays up to this time had had a native setting; the original *Every Man In His Humour* was nominally Italianate. The same is true of *Volpone*. While superficially taking advantage of the current fascination of Italy as a land of supposedly exotic and sensational crime, the play is nevertheless in essentials as English as it is Venetian, and in fundamentals is universal. The greed, cunning and credulity here displayed are peculiar to no place or age. The most ephemeral characters are specifically English. Even though Jonson is characteristically meticulous about details, Volpone as mountebank is international in the prices he asks, settling finally for 'sixpence it will cost you, or six hundred pounds'. Jonson, then, loses little in immediacy because of the setting; and it might even be argued that the very slight distancing which does result from the foreign mise-en-scène partly explains why the satiric sweep is bolder and larger in *Volpone* even than in that tremendous comedy *The Alchemist*, which is so vividly localised in London.

A PREDOMINANT HUMOUR

The 'humours' of the duped characters are more closely related in *Volpone* than in any other of Jonson's plays. In *The Alchemist*, the only comedy that is comparable in scale, the pattern of ideas is more complex. *Volpone* is supremely concentrated. Sir Politic alone is independent of the dominating corruption, and this is an important reason why the necessary relief he brings to the play is outside the main design – he never appears with Volpone and

Mosca except as bystander. For the rest, every other action in the play is determined directly or indirectly by greed. Even Volpone's love scene depends on Corvino's cupidity, and his final manoeuvres in the last act would be pointless but for the frustrated avarice of his victims. It is no blind acquisitiveness that is pilloried. Each step is calculated. With sure dramatic sense Jonson projects into clear-cut action a total and final unscrupulousness. The raven, the crow, the vulture, differ in circumstance, not in bent. The senile Corbaccio clings to his ardent worldliness, and is willing to imperil or sacrifice his son's right in order to feed his flickering life with futile new possessions. Corvino is ready, eager indeed, to make a mockery of the equally fundamental human tie of marriage by prostituting his own wife; an abdication ironically emphasised by his previous obsessive jealousy. Voltore, the man of law and therefore supposedly of justice, debases his profession by his cynical defence of his own and his clients' crimes, demanding that the innocent shall be punished in their place. We see, on consideration, that Jonson has deliberately dramatised acts which represent the extremities of blatant and savagely selfish materialism. We see our whole scale of values inverted. When in the last act Voltore makes an abortive attempt to declare the truth, Corvino cries, 'The devil has entered him.' Family, marriage, law are not just disregarded; they are made the very instruments of destructive greed. And in the person of Lady Would-be folly incompetently trails at the skirts of crime. The caricature of individuals becomes in *Volpone* caricature of society, an intensely serious caricature. A recognisable aspect of our lives is frighteningly enlarged and clarified.

The moral disease which the play exposes is mirrored in the plot and the imagery by reference to physical disease and bodily corruption:

> Now, my feigned cough, my phthisic, and my gout,
> My apoplexy, palsy, and catarrhs,
> Help, with your forced functions, this my posture.

The infirmity which Volpone acts is all too real beneath the skin.

How then can we watch or read this play without horror and disgust? How can it be termed a comedy? How, if Jonson was really concerned about moral issues, could he bring himself to make people laugh at such a spectacle? Let me try to answer the last question first. Jonson wanted us to contemplate this aspect of the world, and of ourselves, in all its starkness. But simply to fill us with loathing would have been a futile task. Repulsion is blind and unconstructive. What Jonson wished was to allow us to watch evil in action, so that we might emerge understanding it a great deal better, having experienced its power. Plato preached that to understand evil is to combat it, and Jonson was a sound classicist.

To this end he employed the insulating power of laughter. For all its enormity, the viciousness in *Volpone* is presented objectively. A grand literary detachment born of indignation informs the whole play.

One of the chief means of achieving this was his creation of characters who not only interest us, but whom we can actually admire and enjoy following. As Una Ellis-Fermor has said of them:

> Cruel and ruthless as they are, repulsive and contemptible as they are all intended to appear, the very solidity of the evil atmosphere lends . . . a greatness to their tenacity and their resolution.

This, clearly, is especially true of Volpone and, after him, of Mosca. We must turn now to consider these characters. Clearly they contribute to the sombre impressions we have just been discussing. But Volpone and Mosca are no petty, small-minded criminals. There is a splendour in the scale on which they work, and an elegance in their skill and sophistication.

MOSCA

Mosca is descended from the parasites and crafty servants of Roman comedy; but what a rapid process of evolution has taken place in the species! Volpone's lieutenant is no common trickster. He has consummate adroitness of mind and spirit; and is distinguished from his lesser predecessors by an awareness of his art as an exacting calling:

> O! your parasite
> Is a most precious thing, dropped from above . . .
> I muse the mystery was not made a science.

He becomes a representative and universal figure, at once both typical and yet something more than the average self-seeker:

> All the wise world is little else, in nature,
> But parasites or sub-parasites.

The great boasting speech which opens Act III lends this relatively uncomplex stage figure conviction and vitality. He seeks his own fulfilment even before his own interest. Mosca thus shares something of Volpone's joy in their feats. He is carried away by zest for the game:

> I fear I shall begin to grow in love
> With my dear self and my most prosperous parts,
> They do so spring and burgeon.

Both the delight and the self-consciousness are beyond any mechanical necessity of plot or character. He is no mere automaton in a scheme of humours.

VOLPONE

This is doubly true of Volpone himself. Far from being restricted to his position within a prescribed framework, he has a direct and unpredictable influence on the plot in the last act.

The strength of Volpone's imposture is that it is grounded on fact. He really is wealthy and without family, with an established reputation, and these facts entrap the gulls more easily and make the Avocatori more reluctant to recognise his deceits.

Even more than Mosca, he is a virtuoso, exulting in the easy dexterity with which he carries off his sleights. The artist in him is stronger than the money-spinner. He takes active pleasure in his contrivances, embroidering upon them for his private satisfaction rather than for greater gain. He glories

> More in the cunning purchase of my wealth,
> Than in the glad possession.

What he deftly acquires he does not hoard. Mosca's praise of his open-handedness is no mere flattery:

> You are not like the thresher that doth stand
> With a huge flail, watching a heap of corn,

> And, hungry, dares not taste the smallest grain,
> But feeds on mallows, and such bitter herbs. . . .
> You will not lie in straw whilst moths and worms
> Feed on your sumptuous hangings and soft beds;
> You know the use of riches, and dare give now,
> From that bright heap, to me, your poor observer,
> Or to your dwarf, or your hermaphrodite. . . .

When their plans prosper, Volpone heaps reward upon Mosca:

> O, there spoke
> My better angel. Mosca, take my keys,
> Gold, plate and jewels, all's at thy devotion;
> Employ them how thou wilt.

Indeed, a common miser could never have laid himself open to being cheated by his own officer as does Volpone when he puts Mosca's name to the will, simply in order to enjoy the last drops of his triumph.

There are two lines of imagery which are significant in comprehending Volpone, and the whole play. First, consider the persistent dual emphasis on gold. It obviously engenders ruthless possessiveness and meanness throughout: Corbaccio even haggles over the reward to be given to Voltore for his false pleading during the first court scene. The metaphor is intensified when Mosca whispers to Voltore on the same occasion, 'I'd have your tongue, sir, tipped with gold for this', or when Mosca, accepting Corbaccio's chequeens on behalf of the figure on the sick-bed, declares,

> This is true physic, this your sacred medicine:
> No talk of opiates to this great elixir!

But further still than this, gold takes on for Volpone and Mosca the glamour of an ideal. Mosca describes the beauty of Celia to his master as

> flesh that melteth in the touch to blood –
> Bright as your gold, and lovely as your gold!

Here we pass on naturally to the second line of imagery, related to the first, which constantly implies the sacredness of riches, gold in particular; at once setting them beyond mere material considerations, and yet finally embodying the total inversion of values

in the play. This idolatrous but dazzling elevation opens the first
act:

> Good morning to the day; and next, my gold!
> Open the *shrine*, that I may see my *saint*.
> *Hail, the world's soul, and mine!* . . .
>   . . . O thou son of Sol,
> (But brighter than thy father) *let me kiss,*
> *With adoration, thee,* and *every relic*
> Of *sacred* treasure in this *blessed* room . . .
>   . . . far transcending
> All style of joy in children, parents, friends,
> Or any other waking dream on earth. . . .
>   . . . Dear *saint,*
> Riches, the *dumb god* that giv'st all men *tongues;*
> That canst do nought and yet mak'st men do all things;
> The price of *souls; even hell, with thee to boot,*
> *Is made worth heaven.* Thou are virtue, fame,
> Honour, and all things else. Who can get thee,
> He shall be noble, valiant, honest, wise.

It would be possible to follow this concept throughout the play.
The passage I quoted just now, in which Volpone declares that his
riches are at Mosca's 'devotion', is characteristic.

Volpone is a sensualist but no vulgarian. When the bed-ridden
old man is suddenly transformed into Celia's ravisher, he is no
crude, lustful animal, but a lyrical voluptuary, attempting to capture her imagination with the splendour not only of lavish promises, but of his own magnetic and soaring personality. Only
when his words fail to move her does he abandon this exotic display, with which he has certainly transported himself.

Such grandeur makes it easy for us to suspend moral judgement, at least during the course of the play, until we can see the
whole pattern in perspective. As I have already suggested, the
partial distancing from every-day reality, especially during the
wooing, contributes to this temporary reservation of judgement.

Volpone is too active and creative to be satisfied with sitting by
and watching his plans mature. He adopts three different disguises, and whenever the tempo of his endeavours flags, he must
whip up his fortunes and compel them in the desired direction.
And he must for ever be going beyond his previous successes. He

c

quits the sham sick-room to ensnare Celia himself in another role; and when all goes well his restless spirit cannot be content, but he must dress up as commandator to put the crowning, though strictly unnecessary, touches to his achievement.

After Mosca has determined on his coup challenging Volpone for an equal share in their accumulated booty, we can watch with ironic detachment as Volpone unknowingly advances towards being hoist with his own petard, till Mosca is spurred into making a bid for the entire fortune. But the magnifico at last proves to be no easy prey to a fellow being, and no pawn in the hands of fate. Samson-like, he pulls down the whole construction of falsehood on the heads of victims and would-be victors alike, leaving himself supreme still amid the ruins.

Some important critics have felt that this catastrophe warps the conclusion. Una Ellis-Fermor calls it a 'last terrific gesture, utterly unbefitting a comedy', and explains the shift in dramatic manner as a result of a 'passionate obsession in the author with the figure of his own creating', Jonson being mesmerised by 'the high insolence with which he has himself fallen in love'. Herford and Simpson, in their monumental edition of the plays, say of *Volpone*: 'In the sternness of the catastrophe, as Jonson felt, it approached tragedy.' This is, perhaps, to over-interpret the words of the dedication, which simply admits that the play 'takes the more liberty' with comic form.

I do not myself feel that the effect of the conclusion is near-tragedy. Though as a character Volpone is allowed to take the law into his own hands more than any other of Jonson's creations, he does not thereby pervert the larger purpose of the play. There is, no doubt, a slight shift of sympathy away from Volpone in the last act, as his callous victimisation of Bonario and Celia becomes more naked: he is transported to realise that they will 'quite divert the torrent Upon the innocent'. But this is incidental. The real nature of the finale depends on Volpone's unflinchingly sardonic tone. His last line: 'This is called the mortifying of the fox', shows no shift of mood. Part of our consciousness remains detached. Laughter still acts as an emotional buffer. For the characters are never intended to be taken too seriously as individuals. In so far as it is about particular figures the play remains a comedy; but as com-

ment on society it is in deadly earnest. The ending is not ponder-
ous; but nor on the other hand is it flippant: we may not dismiss
the whole work as an enormous joke. On the contrary, the final
piece takes its place in the pattern as the curtain falls, and only
then can we consider the play as a whole, and only as a whole is it
serious.

CELIA AND BONARIO

Coleridge complained that, though Jonson's comedies (*Volpone* in
particular) are 'noble efforts of intellectual power' yet they excite
only 'faint interest' because they lack 'any character with whom
you can morally sympathise'. 'Bonario and Celia should have been
made in some way or other principals in the plot. . . . If it were
possible to lessen the paramountcy of Volpone himself, a most
delightful comedy might be produced, by making Celia the ward
or niece of Corvino, instead of his wife, and Bonario her lover.' It
seems that Coleridge is here making the mistake which he himself
elsewhere deplores as 'A fondness for judging one work by comparison with others, perhaps altogether of a different class'. The
changes he suggests would transform *Volpone* into a romantic
comedy, and this it makes no pretence to be. To introduce an elementary opposition between good and evil was no part of the
plan. Jonson seeks no explicit moralisation; he is engaged in a
more subtle and penetrating examination. If Celia and Bonario
were to steal our sympathies, evil would simply be condemned,
not examined as it must inevitably be when it is set only against
gayer or weaker forms of moral failure; and the complex implications of finding ourselves identified, in part at least, with Volpone
and Mosca, would be lost. The shadowiness of the virtuous characters is a necessary part of the design.

Nevertheless, the spectacle of the condemnation of the innocent
victims in the first trial scene makes the audience ready to accept
with satisfaction the downfall of Volpone and Mosca when it
comes about. As when we experience Falstaff's power over the
recruits in *Henry IV, Part II*, we here realise that unqualified admiration for the rogues' panache would lead us to condone the
judicial martyrdom of the guiltless; we see what lies behind the

witty and daring bravado, and we are shocked. For this effect it does not matter that Celia and Bonario do not greatly move us: innocence and justice do. Though Volpone's spell over us is never fully broken, this calculated cruelty, even to such colourless beings, causes a revulsion which convinces us of the rightness, aesthetic as well as moral, of the dénouement.

THE POLITIC WOULD-BE'S

The intensity of *Volpone* requires relief. This it gains in some degree from Lady Would-be, who is however still part of the main design. Sir Politic alone gives us any diversion from the central motif; and so, by definition, his must be a separate action. Not only does this provide some relaxation; but his relatively harmless folly makes the corruption of the main characters stand out in still darker silhouette.

STYLE

Jonson's verse is first and foremost a dramatic instrument, carefully attuned to the task in hand, abjuring any form of self-display. It is interesting to consider his style in relation to T. S. Eliot's discussion of his own attempt to develop an unobtrusive yet flexible medium, which could move easily and rapidly from the trivial to the intense. It is just such a measure which Jonson had perfected by the time he came to write *Volpone*. Speaking so, his characters can be at the same time pleasantly familiar and universally significant.

The effect of his poetry is cumulative. There are few 'quotable' short passages. Jewelled beauty gives place to the paragraphic sweep of his long speeches. We shall learn more by comparing his writing with Marlowe's than with Shakespeare's. Such a comparison will, I think, show that a major characteristic of Jonson's manner, for all his Marlovian reach and energy, is firmness, a solidity which attaches the most voluptuous passages of Volpone's love-making or the most savage caricature of the carrion birds to a familiar reality, a reality which for all its magnification we recognise only too clearly.

JONSON AND THE ACTORS

Jonson was a man of the theatre. His plays are admirably accommodated to the actors, offering splendid opportunities for striking performances. Volpone is something of a Proteus; Mosca is all things to all men; while the birds of prey and the Would-be's are all splendid parts. Ben Jonson's comedies must have been as popular with the players as with the audience.

THE STRUCTURE OF *VOLPONE*

ACT I

Jonson's complete control over his material is already demonstrated fully in the first act. The slow opening shows clearly that the play exists as a pattern to which the plot contributes, not as plot alone. The story, as such, does not get under way until Voltore knocks, after some 170 lines. By this time three things have been effected. First, the preliminary circumstances have been plainly stated. Jonson is very anxious for us to grasp the essential facts. Volpone is explicit:

> I have no wife, no parent, child, ally,
> To give my substance to; but whom I make
> Must be my heir: and this makes men observe me;
> This draws new clients daily to my house,
> Women and men of every sex and age,
> That bring me presents, send me plate, coin, jewels,
> With hope that when I die (which they expect
> Each greedy minute) it shall then return
> Ten-fold upon them.

And Mosca repeats the whole idea in different words while he is helping Volpone on with his gown. But, before this, in the opening speeches already discussed, the mere circumstances of the play have been set in context of the wider *idea* of the accumulation of wealth, particularly of gold, with all its complex significance. Further, there is the strange interlude of the dwarf, the eunuch and the hermaphrodite. The drama of the warping of men's minds is preluded by this quizzical and faintly pathetic display of warped bodies, wedded to the timeless morality theme:

> No, 'tis your fool wherewith I am so taken,
> The only one creature that I can call blessed;
> For all other forms I have proved most distressed.

This sets the play off on its subject, while emphasising that the joke is ultimately a very serious one, since a jester is privileged to speak out with impunity: 'he speaks truth free from slaughter.'

Jonson now presents three precisely parallel scenes with Vulture, Raven and Crow. Only a master could carry off such a first act, so slow to begin with and so simplified thereafter. But because the three visits are not just similar in pattern but are carefully graded in intensity; because Jonson has exerted himself to express a dramatic idea, not just a story; before the act closes it achieves remarkable concentration and power.

The first of the visitations is presented without complexity. In the second, Corbaccio's gloating on Volpone's 'sickness' is made the more macabre and, at the same time, more farcical by his own senile deafness:

> *Mosca.* His speech is broken, and his eyes are set;
>   His face drawn longer than 'twas wont—
> *Corbac.*   How? how?
>   Stronger than he was wont?
> *Mosca.*   No, sir: his face
>   Drawn longer than 'twas wont.
> *Corbac.*   O, good!

Finally Corvino shouts his frenzied taunts in the ear of the supposedly comatose and dying Volpone:

> *Mosca.*   cheeks . . .
>   That look like frozen dish-clouts set on end!
> *Corvino.* Or like the smoked wall, on which the rain
>   Ran down in streaks.
> *Mosca.*   Excellent, sir, speak out . . .

The pitch has risen constantly and has already reached an alarmingly high note.

ACT II

The great hoax is running perfectly to plan. The second act introduces the complication, the one element that has no part in the
original scheme, but which is capable of undermining and destroy-
ing it – Volpone's passion for Celia. However, Act II gives no
hint of disaster. Volpone and Mosca are still in supreme command.
Everything falls right for them.

Structurally this act develops what is to be a recurrent pattern,
with tension relatively low at first, rising progressively to a peak
higher than that of the previous act. Sir Politic relieves us tem-
porarily from the fever at the close of the previous scene, neatly
reversing in his talk with Peregrine the earlier interviews: far from
being another's dupe he invents material for his own self-satisfied
gullibility to work upon. This duologue introduces naturally the
impersonation of the mountebank, during which Volpone shows
his paces, being at his most racy and light-hearted, obviously enjoying himself, and sharing part of this enjoyment with the audience. His energy, wit and resourcefulness are dramatically displayed, issuing at length in his first outburst of lyric extravagance
to Celia. Jonson has ingeniously relieved the possible monotony of
his chief protagonist being tied to a sham death-bed. At the same
time Volpone's performance provides a telling parallel with the
antics of the unnatural trio in Act I; while the charade of sickness
and healing is further elaborated.

With Corvino's entrance the plot offers a natural transition back
to more savage comedy. The structure is brilliantly integrated, as
we see again when we realise how convincingly Volpone's desire
for Celia is related to Corvino's desire for the legacy. It is Volpone's presence in disguise which whips up Corvino's jealousy,
till he sees a phantasmagoria of Celia's depravity. His moral degradation is reflected in the imagery:

> thy restraint before was liberty
> To what I now decree: and therefore mark me.
> First, I will have this bawdy light dammed up;
> And, till it be done, some two or three yards off
> I'll chalk a line, o'er which if thou but chance
> To set thy desperate foot, more hell, more horror,

> More wild, remorseless rage shall seize on thee
> Than on a conjuror that had heedless left
> His circle's safety ere his devil was laid.

This is, however, no more than a prelude to Corvino's offering up Celia as a sacrifice to his greed. What greater reversal is possible than when he finally urges Mosca to report that the idea was spontaneous and unhesitating:

> swear it was
> On the first hearing, as thou mayst do truly –
> Mine own free motion.

The scene closes on Corvino swearing to Celia that his jealousy had been feigned – because he now intends to act as her pander himself.

ACT III

Act I opens with Volpone's hymn to gold; Act III with Mosca's great boasting speech in praise of parasites. This is the act in which the plotting reaches its first climax and its first crisis: discovery is averted only by Mosca's nimble-wittedness.

Bonario's suspicions strike the earliest jarring note. Mosca pacifies him with blatant lies, and then proceeds to draw him into new snares; though now for the first time we are left in suspense by Mosca's scheming, not knowing straight away what outcome he intends.

We then arrive at the expected interlude, introduced by the trio of grotesque figures, 'all the known delicates of a rich man', giving another glimpse of Volpone's private existence; but mainly comprising the visit of Lady Politic Would-be, which is set in an altogether less serious key.

> In the room the women come and go,
> Talking of Michelangelo –

though in Lady Would-be's case the chatter is about Montaigne, Petrarch and Aretine. But her silliness is not entirely innocent. As a legacy-hunter, however ineffectual, she is closely related to the more sinister predators; avarice acquires a new dimension; it reaches down into what is commonplace and seemingly trivial.

Further, her vapid yet grasping femininity stands out in strong contrast to Celia's patient meekness.

Mosca now carefully prepares his pieces for a master stroke. The issue of Volpone's wooing is reached in a scene which, as we have already said, is primarily sensual and passionate. It is important to notice how flat and wooden are the speeches of Celia and Bonario, contrasted with the ringing crescendi of Volpone:

> Forbear, foul ravisher! libidinous swine!
> Free the forced lady, or thou diest, impostor.

Our attention is not to be diverted into romantic side issues. Dramatic interest centres on the imminent ruin of Volpone and Mosca:

> *Volpone*. Fall on me, roof, and bury me in ruin:
> Become my grave, that wert my shelter. O!
> I am unmasked, unspirited, undone,
> Betrayed to beggary, to infamy . . .

Mosca despairs, but is resolute:

> Let's die like Romans,
> Since we have lived like Grecians.

So he is still fully active, ready to make a desperate bid when his wits suggest an opportunity. With a flash of illumination he sees his chance, and converts disaster into new achievement. At one stroke he discredits Bonario, and redoubles Corbaccio's determination to disinherit him. It is characteristic of Jonson's dramatic construction that at this moment the various parts of the rogues' schemes begin to catch up on each other, so that a series of crises develops. Voltore enters, overhears Mosca's parrying of Corbaccio, and in turn needs to be mollified:

> Come,
> Put not your foists upon me: I shall scent them.

But there is now no holding Mosca; and he soon has Voltore by the nose again:

> *Mosca*. Truth be my comfort, and my conscience,
> My only aim was to dig you a fortune
> Out of these two old, rotten sepulchres –
> *Voltore*. I cry thee mercy, Mosca.

Thus the scene ends with everything under control more perfectly than before, provided Volpone and Mosca can impudently maintain their deceits when publicly challenged.

ACT IV

It is this public trial which in Act IV exculpates the rogues, leaving them in final control of the situation, with no further obstacles to enjoying the fruits of their dishonesty.

After the tense finale to the previous act, we again turn to Sir Politic, and later his wife. Their foolishness is the norm against which crime is measured. In particular, Lady Would-be's ridiculous jealousy is in stark contrast to Corvino's wilful bargaining with his wife's virtue.

The false trial is technically a *tour de force* in the opportunity it offers to exhibit all the dupes together. It is the expected climax, the natural coda to the sequence of events, fully satisfying the dramatic idea of the partnership between Volpone and Mosca; and thus forming in advance the perfect foil to the conclusion during which the whole framework is to be destroyed.

Mosca in the Scrutineo is seen manipulating his puppets one after the other. Truth is deliberately perverted in the court. We know, point by point, the successful case to be built on calculated, unscrupulous lying, though the ingenuity still tempers our immediate revulsion. Corbaccio disowns his son publicly; Corvino perjures himself to incriminate his wife, whispering aside to Mosca, 'There is no shame in this now, is there?' Folly is made to serve vice: Lady Politic is brought in to give her vital piece of false evidence: her role is an organic part of the plot. With superb judgement the entry of Volpone on his couch is made the crux of the scene: he is kept at the dramatic centre. The innocent are convicted and await only their sentence:

> 2 *Avoc.* Their shame, even in their cradles, fled their faces.
> 4 *Avoc.* (*To Voltore*) You have done a worthy service to the state, sir,
>   In their discovery.

So at last, as has been said, some protest stirs in the audience against this debauching of justice.

Not in this act, however, do we see the master minds glorying in their victory. For this is, in fact, no ending, but, ironically, the last success before the fall: structurally, the triumph must form the preface to the catastrophe in the last act.

ACT V

Accordingly, the final act opens in exultation. This is the highest point in the partnership's achievements. Mosca recognises that they must now stay or over-reach themselves:

> Here we must rest; this is our master-piece:
> We cannot think to go beyond this.

The speech has a double value. As from the dramatist to the audience it makes a true estimate of the situation, so that we cannot miss the rogues' error; as an utterance by Mosca, it reveals how he sees and approves what is prudent, while submitting to what is rash. The confederacy has surmounted every external difficulty only to be betrayed by what is false within. Since the contributors have founded their actions on selfishness, the league has no firm basis in moderation or trust. Volpone is still not satisfied; he cannot pause; he must try to achieve still more. Mosca, in fact, has no hand in the fatal and superfluous piece of planning; he seizes the chance to build on Volpone's mistake; but he does not engineer the opportunity. Nevertheless his vision too is eventually found wanting: when Mosca estimates Volpone's reactions by his own standards, he disastrously underestimates his master.

The first scene in this act is a fine instance of Jonson's keen dramatic imagination. How could this pair reach further? In any case, how could an extension of their power and skill be presented on the stage? This technical impasse is mastered with such ease that it may not occur to us to stop and consider what a difficult problem it was. Yet out of an unpromising situation Jonson makes one of the finest passages in the play, clearly projected in dramatic terms – a comic climax, and at the same time a final epitome of the central motifs, as the dismayed fortune seekers find Mosca himself is Volpone's heir:

> Are not you he that have today in court
> Professed the disinheriting of your son?

> Perjured yourself? Go home, and die, and stink:
> If you but croak a syllable, all comes out.
> Away, and call your porters . . .

Every hit is scored. The ideas are satisfyingly rounded out without in any degree being laboured.

Briefly and farcically Sir Politic and his lady are disposed of. Sir Politic is betrayed by his own folly, as Volpone and Mosca are betrayed by their own cleverness.

Volpone is blithe in his self-undoing. He sets out with zest, dressed as commandator, to torment the disappointed scavengers. He is too intoxicated to stop and consider that dog is, in fact, as likely to eat dog when Mosca can devour Volpone, as when Volpone consumed Corbaccio and his son, or Corvino and his wife. The 'flesh-fly' takes the simple, inevitable decision, and for once Volpone is a vital move behind.

Our picture of Volpone has altered somewhat. We have seen him jeering at justice itself, not simply at his gulls; which is very different from the infectious mirth of the first act. Now we cease to hear of his wealth being gained in 'no common way'; but of deriving, for instance, from 'A handsome, pretty, customed bawdy-house'.

A new series of crises begins, longer and more dangerous even than those at the end of Act III. First the disillusioned Voltore defects and offers to speak the truth. Volpone rescues the situation in a final performance, as he reveals to Voltore that he still lives, and at the same time the court is almost made to see the escaping blue devil to which the lawyer's dangerous confession is attributed.

However, the Avocatori must now know whether Volpone is alive or not. Mosca is the key witness. The moment has come to betray his superior by insisting that he is dead and that his will is valid. Mosca does not hesitate. Volpone is dumbfounded. But the fly will at first only sting the fox: 'Will you give me half?' Volpone's instantaneous, proud reply is fateful: 'First I'll be hanged,' he whispers. Too late Volpone abandons a hopeless position and offers the half share. Now it is Mosca's turn to make his unfaltering, over-reaching, crucial rejection: 'I cannot now afford it you so cheap.' This is the point of no return. The rising confusion must now break one way or the other. The former partners are now at each other's throats, and all is chaos.

Events move rapidly. We have no time to foresee the inevitable. It seems as if Mosca is successful; he adopts a high-handed tone. Momentarily Volpone alone is degraded: 'Let him be whipped.' However, Volpone is not the figure to exit meekly. He prefers to lose all rather than be outwitted, belittled:

> *Volpone.*   Nay, now
> My ruins shall not come alone. Your match
> I'll hinder sure: my substance shall not glue you,
> Nor screw you into a family.
> *Mosca.*   Why, patron!
> *Volpone.* I am Volpone, and this is my knave . . .

The punishments are uncompromising. The characters are not to be considered merely as exposed jokers. Mosca will be 'perpetual prisoner in our gallies', and Volpone 'cramped with irons', the birds of prey banished or disgraced. The judgement is formal: Jonson's purpose is to wind up the play quickly without anticlimax. The finale rests with Volpone and Mosca, and they have in effect, destroyed themselves.

SOURCES

The plot of *Volpone* is original. However, the picture that Jonson draws of would-be heirs fawning and at the same time preying on wealthy sickness and senility is no macabre invention of his own. This is a theme which could be illustrated from Horace, Juvenal or Pliny; but I have chosen rather to quote some particularly apt passages from Lucian and Petronius. In Lucian the legacy-hunters or *captatores* are often young, and usually get the worst of the bargain. His *Dialogues of the Dead* is a series of conversations among the shades of those who have recently died. One young man complains to Pluto that he has perished at thirty while an old man of ninety, whose fortune he coveted, is still alive. Pluto asks:

> What right have you young fellows got to be prying after other men's goods, and thrusting yourselves upon your childless

elders? . . . It has become quite a profession lately, this amorous devotion to old men and women, – childless, of course; children destroy the illusion.

Callimedes, another young man who has just entered Hades, describes to a friend how he has been caught in his own trap:

Callidemides. I suppose you know that old Ptoeodorus?
Zenophantus. The rich man with no children, to whom you gave most of your company?
Callidemides. That is the man; he had promised to leave me his heir, and I used to show my appreciation. However, it went on such a time . . . so I found a short cut to my property. I bought a potion, and agreed with the butler that the next time his master called for wine . . . he should have this ready in a cup and present it; . . . but by some blunder he handed me the poisoned cup . . .

In the ninth dialogue Polystratus, who has just died at ninety-eight, relates to Simylus how he had beguiled the *captatores*:

Simylus. And what sort of life have you had of it, these thirty years? you were about seventy when I died.
Polyst. Delightful, though you may find it hard to believe.
Simylus. It *is* surprising that you could have any joy of your life – old, weak, and childless, moreover; . . . you were very economical in my day.
Polyst. Ah, but my simple friend, these good things were presents – came in streams. From dawn my doors were thronged with visitors, and in the day it was a procession of the fairest gifts of earth . . .
Simylus. . . . what, you, an old man with hardly a tooth left in your head!
Polyst. Certainly; the first of our townsmen were in love with me. Such as you see me, old, bald, blear-eyed, rheumy, they delighted to do me honour; happy was the man on whom my glance rested for a moment . . .
Simylus. And how did you dispose of your fortune in the end?
Polyst. I gave each an express promise to make him my heir; he believed, and treated me to more attentions than ever; meanwhile I had another genuine will, which was the one I left, with a message to them all to go hang;

he has left his wealth to a Phrygian slave.

In Petronius's *The Satyricon* a party of shipwrecked voyagers is addressed thus by a local inhabitant:

> Strangers, if you are merchants, let me advise you to change your plans and look for some other way of earning your living there. If, however, you belong to that class of cultured men-of-the-world who can sustain with ease a life-time of lying, the road you are walking runs right to riches. In that town literature and the arts go utterly unhonoured; eloquence there has no prestige; and those who live the good and simple life find no admirers. Any man you meet in that town you may be certain belongs to one of two classes: the makers of wills and those who pursue the makers of wills. You will find no fathers there, for those with natural heirs of their own are regarded as pariahs. A father is someone who is never invited to dinner, never entertained, who, in short, is compelled to spend his life, outcast and excluded, among the poor and obscure. Those, however, who remained bachelors in perpetuity and have no close relatives are held in the highest honour and esteem: they and they alone are men of honour and courage, brave as lions, paragons without spot or flaw. In short, sirs, you are going to a place which is like a countryside ravaged by the plague, a place in which you will see only two things: the bodies of those who are eaten, and the carrion crows who eat them (xiii).

The travellers decide to take advantage of this information by pretending that Eumolpus is a wealthy, childless landowner:

> . . . next morning we set out to find quarters a little more in keeping with the grandeur of our pretensions. On the way, however, we ran into a crowd of legacy-hunters who promptly asked us who we were and where we came from. As prearranged, we answered with such a flood of information that they were quickly satisfied on both counts and accepted our story without further question. Immediately a great struggle broke out among them to see which could shower Eumolpus with the most money. . . . All of them did their best to curry favour with Eumolpus by heaping him with presents (xv). (Translation by William Arrowsmith, Ann Arbor, 1959).

THE TEXT

Jonson was the first English dramatist to take his own work so seriously as to see it through the press with scrupulous care, and to prepare his own collected works for publication – they appeared in 1616. The present text of *Volpone* is based on Herford and Simpson's exhaustive collation of copies of the 1607 quarto and the 1616 folio. Punctuation and spelling have been modernised.

Elizabethan punctuation was regulated on principles different from our own. Jonson used stops carefully but heavily; so that his pointing is often of little help to a twentieth-century reader in following his complex constructions. My aim has been to punctuate in such a way as to make Jonson's intentions relatively clear to the modern eye, indicating as far as possible the structure of the sentences and so making the meaning plainer. This has often involved using commas selectively rather than at every reasonable pause.

Archaic conventions in spelling have been abandoned where these do not influence pronunciation: for instance 'happen'd' is printed 'happened' since a reader today is not likely to treat the 'ed' as a separate syllable. The same applies to many printed elisions which do not alter the way we would say a phrase: as an example, 'this's' becomes 'this is', which does not significantly differ in sound or rhythm but is easier to read.

In these respects a completely new departure has been made, without reference to Gifford's 1816 edition, which has served as the basis for most subsequent texts.

The stage directions have also been fully reconsidered, though in some cases it has seemed to me that Gifford is not to be bettered. Directions without any form of precedent in Quarto or Folio are enclosed in square brackets.

The original printings provide scene divisions according to the classical or French system, beginning a new scene whenever characters enter or exit. Naturally, in an edition such as the present the modern English system is substituted. However, changes have been made in the divisions adopted by Gifford and his imitators. It is clear that what appears below as Act III, scene ii is a single action; various personages certainly occupy particular sections of the stage and are unable for a time to hear what is passing elsewhere; but there is no break in continuity. I have therefore swept away Gifford's numerous scene changes which here obscure both the nature of the drama and the manner in which it would certainly have been staged in the Jacobean theatre. A similar but less important division has been removed from the last act.

THE NOTES

The primary aim of the notes is to elucidate the text. Wherever possible difficult words are glossed briefly at the foot of the page. The longer annotations, printed after the play, include only a small amount of ancillary information and comment. Echoes of specific passages from classical authors have not been recorded: these are given in some detail in the notes to Herford and Simpson's great Oxford edition.

ACKNOWLEDGEMENTS

My thinking about *Volpone* is deeply indebted to Mrs Barbara Hardy of Birkbeck College, University of London, who set many of my ideas about the play in train; and to T. S. Eliot and Professor Una Ellis-Fermor, whose writings on Jonson in *Collected Essays* and *Jacobean Drama* respectively I have found of particular value. As any serious study of Jonson in our time is bound to do, this edition owes much in innumerable ways to the scholarship and criticism of C. H. Herford and Percy and Evelyn Simpson.

In the preparation of the present volume I have been greatly helped by Dr Harold Brooks, Senior Lecturer, Birkbeck College, University of London, co-editor of the New Arden Shakespeare, and by Mr John Swannell of the University of Southampton, both of whom have been generous with their time and advice. And I would like to thank Mr Charles Whittaker, also of the University of Southampton, for his help with certain translations from the Greek. My father and Mr Anthony Manser have given painstaking assistance with the proof-reading.

D

VOLPONE

THE PERSONS OF THE PLAY

VOLPONE, *a magnifico*
MOSCA, *his parasite*
VOLTORE, *an advocate*
CORBACCIO, *an old gentleman*
CORVINO, *a merchant*
BONARIO, *Corbaccio's son*
SIR POLITIC WOULD-BE, *a knight*
PEREGRINE, *a gentleman traveller*
NANO, *a dwarf*
CASTRONE, *a eunuch*
ANDROGYNO, *a hermaphrodite*
AVOCATORI, *four magistrates*
NOTARIO, *a notary*

CELIA, *Corvino's wife*
LADY WOULD-BE, *Sir Politic's wife*

Merchants; Commandatori (officers); Servants; Waiting-women;
    a Crowd

The Scene: *Venice*

NOTES: pp. 184–5

VOLPONE

or

THE FOX

A Comœdie

Acted in the yeere 1605. By
the K. MAIESTIES
SERVANTS

The Author B.I.

HORAT

Simul & iucunda, & idonea dicere vita.

TO
THE MOST
NOBLE AND
MOST EQUAL
SISTERS
THE TWO FAMOUS
UNIVERSITIES
FOR THEIR LOVE
AND
ACCEPTANCE
SHOWN TO HIS POEM IN THE
PRESENTATION
BEN. JONSON
THE GRATEFUL ACKNOWLEDGER
DEDICATES
BOTH IT AND HIMSELF

Never, most equal sisters, had any man a wit so presently excellent as that it could raise itself, but there must come both matter, occasion, commenders and favourers to it. If this be true, and that the fortune of all writers doth daily prove it, it behoves the careful to provide well toward these accidents; and, having acquired them, to preserve that part of reputation most tenderly wherein the benefit of a friend is also defended. Hence is it that I now render myself grateful, and am studious to justify the bounty of your act; to which, though your mere authority were satisfying, yet (it being an age wherein poetry 10 and the professors of it hear so ill on all sides) there will a reason be looked for in the subject.

It is certain, nor can it with any forehead be opposed, that the too-much licence of poetasters in this time hath much deformed their mistress, that every day their manifold and

13 *forehead:* confidence.   13 *opposed:* contradicted.

NOTES: pp. 185–6

manifest ignorance doth stick unnatural reproaches upon her.
But for their petulancy, it were an act of the greatest injustice
either to let the learned suffer, or so divine a skill (which indeed should not be attempted with unclean hands) to fall
under the least contempt. For, if men will impartially and not   20
asquint look toward the offices and function of a poet, they
will easily conclude to themselves the impossibility of any
man's being the good poet without first being a good man. He
that is said to be able to inform young men to all good dis-
ciplines, inflame grown men to all great virtues, keep old men
in their best and supreme state or, as they decline to childhood, recover them to their first strength; that comes forth
the interpreter and arbiter of nature, a teacher of things divine
no less than human, a master in manners; and can alone (or
with a few) effect the business of mankind: this, I take him, is   30
no subject for pride and ignorance to exercise their railing
rhetoric upon.

But it will here be hastily answered that the writers of these
days are other things; that not only their manners, but their
natures, are inverted, and nothing remaining with them of the
dignity of poet but the abused name, which every scribe
usurps; that now, especially in dramatic or, as they term it,
stage poetry, nothing but ribaldry, profanation, blasphemy,
all licence of offence to God and man is practised. I dare not
deny a great part of this – and am sorry I dare not – because   40
in some men's abortive features (and would they had never
boasted the light) it is over true. But that all are embarked in
this bold adventure for hell is a most uncharitable thought,
and, uttered, a more malicious slander. For my particular I
can, and from a most clear conscience, affirm that I have ever
trembled to think toward the least profaneness; have
loathed the use of such foul and unwashed bawdry as is now
made the food of the scene. And, howsoever I cannot escape
from some the imputation of sharpness, but that they will say
I have taken a pride or lust to be bitter, and not my youngest   50
infant but hath come into the world with all his teeth; I
would ask of these supercilious politics, what nation,

56VOLPONE

society, or general order, or state I have provoked; what public person; whether I have not in all these preserved their dignity, as mine own person, safe. My works are read, allowed – I speak of those that are entirely mine. Look into them: what broad reproofs have I used? Where have I been particular? Where personal, except to a mimic, cheater, bawd, or buffoon, creatures for their insolencies worthy to be taxed? Yet to which of these so pointingly as he might not either ingenuously have confessed, or wisely dissembled his disease?   60

But it is not rumour can make men guilty, much less entitle me to other men's crimes. I know that nothing can be so innocently writ or carried, but may be made obnoxious to construction. Marry, whilst I bear mine innocence about me, I fear it not. Application is now grown a trade with many; and there are that profess to have a key for the deciphering of everything: but let wise and noble persons take heed how they be too credulous, or give leave to these invading inter-   70 preters to be over familiar with their fames, who cunningly and often utter their own virulent malice under other men's simplest meanings. As for those that will, by faults which charity hath raked up or common honesty concealed, make themselves a name with the multitude; or, to draw their rude and beastly claps, care not whose living faces they entrench with their petulant styles; may they do it without a rival, for me. I choose rather to live graved in obscurity, than share with them in so preposterous a fame.

Nor can I blame the wishes of those severe and wiser   80 patriots who, providing the hurts these licentious spirits may do in a state, desire rather to see fools and devils and those antique relics of barbarism retrieved, with all other ridiculous and exploded follies, than behold the wounds of private men, of princes, and nations. For, as Horace makes Trebatius speak, among these

– *Sibi quisque timet, quanquam est intactus, et odit.*

76 *claps:* applause.   81 *providing:* foreseeing.
NOTES: pp. 186–7

And men may justly impute such rages, if continued, to the
writer, as his sports. The increase of which lust in liberty,
together with the present trade of the stage in all their mis- 90
cellane interludes, what learned or liberal soul doth not already abhor? – where nothing but the filth of the time is
uttered, and that with such impropriety of phrase, such
plenty of solecisms, such dearth of sense, so bold prolepses,
so racked metaphors, with brothelry able to violate the ear of
a pagan, and blasphemy to turn the blood of a Christian to
water. I cannot but be serious in a cause of this nature,
wherein my fame and the reputations of divers honest and
learned are the question; when a name so full of authority,
antiquity and all great mark is, through their insolence, be- 100
come the lowest scorn of the age; and those men subject to
the petulancy of every vernaculous orator, that were wont to
be the care of kings and happiest monarchs.

  This it is that hath not only rapt me to present indignation,
but made me studious heretofore, and by all my actions, to
stand off from them; which may most appear in this my latest
work, which you, most learned arbitresses, have seen, judged
and, to my crown, approved; wherein I have laboured, for
their instruction and amendment, to reduce not only the ancient forms, but manners of the scene – the easiness, the pro- 110
priety, the innocence, and last the doctrine, which is the principal end of poesie: to inform men in the best reason of
living. And though my catastrophe may, in the strict rigour
of comic law, meet with censure as turning back to my promise, I desire the learned and charitable critic to have so
much faith in me to think it was done of industry; for
with what ease I could have varied it nearer his scale (but
that I fear to boast my own faculty) I could here insert.
But my special aim being to put the snaffle in their mouths
that cry out we never punish vice in our interludes &c., 120
I took the more liberty; though not without some lines
of example drawn even in the ancients themselves, the

94 *prolepses:* anachronisms.   102 *vernaculous:* scurrilous.
113 *catastrophe:* dénouement.   118 *faculty:* facility, ability.

NOTES: pp. 186–7

goings out of whose comedies are not always joyful,
but oft-times the bawds, the servants, the rivals, yea, and
the masters are mulcted; and fitly, it being the office of
a comic poet to imitate justice and instruct to life, as well
as purity of language, or stir up gentle affections. To which
I shall take the occasion elsewhere to speak.

For the present, most reverenced sisters, as I have cared to
be thankful for your affections past, and here made the under-   130
standing acquainted with some ground of your favours, let me
not despair their continuance to the maturing of some
worthier fruits; wherein, if my muses be true to me, I shall
raise the despised head of poetry again, and, stripping her out
of those rotten and base rags wherewith the times have adulterated her form, restore her to her primitive habit, feature,
and majesty, and render her worthy to be embraced and
kissed of all the great and master spirits of our world. As for
the vile and slothful, who never effected an act worthy of
celebration, or are so inward with their own vicious natures as   140
they worthily fear her and think it a high point of policy to
keep her in contempt with their declamatory and windy in-
vectives, she shall out of just rage incite her servants (who are
genus irritabile) to spout ink in their faces, that shall eat
farther than their marrow into their fames; and not Cinnamus, the barber, with his art, shall be able to take out
the brands, but they shall live and be read
till the wretches die, as things worst
deserving of themselves in
chief, and then of all   150
mankind.

From my house in the Black-Friars
this 11. of February. 1607.

123 *goings out:* endings.

NOTES: p. 188

Volpone *or* The Fox

The Argument

VOLPONE, childless, rich, feigns sick, despairs,
O ffers his state to hopes of several heirs,
L ies languishing; his parasite receives
P resents of all, assures, deludes; then weaves
O ther cross-plots, which ope themselves, are told.
N ew tricks for safety are sought; they thrive: when, bold,
E ach tempts the other again, and all are sold.

Prologue

Edifying + delightf...

Now, luck yet send us, and a little wit
   Will serve to make our play hit;
According to the palates of the season,
   Here is rhyme, not empty of reason.
This we were bid to credit from our poet,
   Whose true scope, if you would know it,
In all his poems still hath been this measure,
   To mix profit with your pleasure;
And not as some, whose throats their envy failing,
   Cry hoarsely, 'All he writes is railing':   10
And, when his plays come forth, think they can flout them,
   With saying, 'He was a year about them'.
To these there needs no lie, but this his creature,
   Which was two months since no feature;
And though he dares give them five lives to mend it,
   'Tis known, five weeks fully penned it,
From his own hand, without a coadjutor,
   Novice, journeyman, or tutor.

NOTES: p. 188

Yet thus much I can give you as a token
  Of his play's worth: no eggs are broken,   *not a farce*   20
Nor quaking custards with fierce teeth affrighted,
  Wherewith your rout are so delighted;   *not going to*
Nor hales he in a gull, old ends reciting,   *say something*
  To stop gaps in his loose writing;   *used before*
With such a deal of monstrous and forced action,
  As might make Bedlam a faction;
Nor made he his play for jests, stolen from each table,
  But makes jests to fit his fable;
And so presents quick comedy, refined
  As best critics have designed;   30
The laws of time, place, persons he observeth,   *the unities to*
  From no needful rule he swerveth.   *Venice*
All gall and copperas from his ink he draineth;
  Only a little salt remaineth,
Wherewith he'll rub your cheeks, till, red with laughter,
  They shall look fresh a week after.

in Venice in streets + his house

persons — unity of action — Everything must read
on the same plot. Disrupted

Plot — Volpone. decieves the others

Not a part — this catking

Two units of action
5th act does not stem

Main theme or controlling force — Is the humor
of peoples actions. (Greed).

NOTES: pp. 189–90

Act I

Scene I. [*In* VOLPONE'S *house.*

Enter VOLPONE *and* MOSCA.

Volpone. Good morning to the day; and next, my gold!
    Open the shrine, that I may see my saint.
    [MOSCA *draws a curtain, and reveals piles of gold,* plate
        jewels etc.]
    Hail, the world's soul, and mine! More glad than is
    The teeming earth to see the longed-for sun
    Peep through the horns of the celestial Ram,
    Am I, to view thy splendour, darkening his;
    That, lying here amongst my other hoards,
    Show'st like a flame by night, or like the day
    Struck out of chaos, when all darkness fled
    Unto the centre. O thou son of Sol   10
    (But brighter than thy father), let me kiss,
    With adoration, thee, and every relic
    Of sacred treasure in this blessed room.
    Well did wise poets by thy glorious name
    Title that age which they would have the best –
    Thou being the best of things, and far transcending
    All style of joy in children, parents, friends,
    Or any other waking dream on earth.
    Thy looks when they to Venus did ascribe,
    They should have given her twenty thousand Cupids: 20
    Such are thy beauties and our loves! Dear saint,
    Riches, the dumb god that giv'st all men tongues;
    That canst do nought and yet mak'st men do all things;
    The price of souls; even hell, with thee to boot,
    Is made worth heaven. Thou art virtue, fame,
    Honour, and all things else. Who can get thee,
    He shall be noble, valiant, honest, wise —

Mosca. And what he will, sir. Riches are in fortune
    A greater good than wisdom is in nature.
Volpone. True, my beloved Mosca. Yet I glory   30
    More in the cunning purchase of my wealth,
    Than in the glad possession, since I gain
    No common way: I use no trade, no venture;
    I wound no earth with ploughshares; fat no beasts
    To feed the shambles; have no mills for iron,
    Oil, corn, or men, to grind them into powder;
    I blow no subtle glass; expose no ships
    To threatenings of the furrow-faced sea;
    I turn no monies in the public bank,
    Nor usure private —
Mosca.   No, sir, nor devour   40
    Soft prodigals. You shall have some will swallow
    A melting heir as glibly as your Dutch
    Will pills of butter, and ne'er purge for it;
    Tear forth the fathers of poor families
    Out of their beds, and coffin them alive
    In some kind, clasping prison, where their bones
    May be forth-coming when the flesh is rotten:
    But your sweet nature doth abhor these courses;
    You loathe the widow's or the orphan's tears
    Should wash your pavements, or their piteous cries   50
    Ring in your roofs, and beat the air for vengeance.
Volpone. Right, Mosca; I do loathe it.
Mosca.   And besides, sir,
    You are not like the thresher that doth stand
    With a huge flail, watching a heap of corn,
    And, hungry, dares not taste the smallest grain,
    But feeds on mallows, and such bitter herbs;
    Nor like the merchant who hath filled his vaults
    With Romagnía, and rich Candian wines,
    Yet drinks the lees of Lombard's vinegar.
    You will not lie in straw whilst moths and worms   60

31 *purchase:* gaining.   35 *shambles:* slaughter-house.
        40 *private:* privately.
NOTES: pp. 190–1

Feed on your sumptuous hangings and soft beds:
You know the use of riches, and dare give now,
From that bright heap, to me, your poor observer,   *Being Greedy too*
Or to your dwarf, or your hermaphrodite,
Your eunuch, or what other household trifle
Your pleasure allows maintenance —

Volpone.   Hold thee, Mosca;
                          [*Gives him money.*]
Take of my hand; thou strik'st on truth in all,   *trying to put him back in his place*
And they are envious term thee parasite.
Call forth my dwarf, my eunuch, and my fool,
And let them make me sport. [*Exit* MOSCA.] What
    should I do   70
But cocker up my genius, and live free
To all delights my fortune calls me to?   *his power; money.*
I have no wife, no parent, child, ally,
To give my substance to; but whom I make
Must be my heir: and this makes men observe me;
This draws new clients daily to my house,
Women and men of every sex and age,
That bring me presents, send me plate, coin, jewels,   *Illusion Bible*
With hope that when I die (which they expect
Each greedy minute) it shall then return   80
Tenfold upon them; whilst some, covetous
Above the rest, seek to engross me whole,
And counter-work the one unto the other,   *trying to outdo each other.*
Contend in gifts, as they would seem in love:
All which I suffer, playing with their hopes,
And am content to coin them into profit,
And look upon their kindness, and take more,
And look on that; still bearing them in hand,
Letting the cherry knock against their lips,
And draw it by their mouths, and back again. How now! 90

74 *substance:* possessions.

they Make offerings to Valpone
Valpone gets his gold by taking advantage of humans (wealthy, selfish type)

Enter MOSCA *with* NANO, ANDROGYNO *and* CASTRONE

Nano.   *Now, room for fresh gamesters, who do will you to know,*
     They do bring you neither play nor university show;
   And therefore do entreat you that whatsoever they rehearse
     May not fare a whit the worse for the false pace of the verse.
   If you wonder at this, you will wonder more ere we pass,
     For know, here is enclosed the soul of Pythagoras,
   That juggler divine, as hereafter shall follow;
     Which soul (fast and loose, sir) came first from Apollo,
   And was breathed into Æthalides, Mercurius his son,
     Where it had the gift to remember all that ever was done.   100
   From thence it fled forth, and made quick transmigration
     To goldilocked Euphorbus, who was killed in good fashion
   At the siege of old Troy, by the cuckold of Sparta.
     Hermotimus was next (I find it in my charta)
   To whom it did pass, where no sooner it was missing
     But with one Pyrrhus of Delos it learned to go a-fishing;
   And thence did it enter the sophist of Greece.
     From Pythagore, she went into a beautiful piece
   Hight Aspasia, the meretrix; and the next toss of her
     Was again of a whore – she became a philosopher,   110
   Crates the cynic. As itself doth relate it,
     Since kings, knights, and beggars, knaves, lords, and fools gat it,
   Besides ox and ass, camel, mule, goat, and brock,
     In all which it hath spoke as in the cobbler's cock.
   But I come not here to discourse of that matter,
     Or his one, two, or three, or his great oath, 'By quater!'
   His musics, his trigon, his golden thigh,
     Or his telling how elements shift; but I
   Would ask how of late thou hast suffered translation,
     And shifted thy coat in these days of reformation.   120

Androg.   *Like one of the reformed, a fool, as you see,*
     Counting all old doctrine heresy.

Nano.   *But not on thine own forbid meats hast thou ventured?*

Androg.   *On fish, when first a Carthusian I entered.*

Nano.   *Why, then thy dogmatical silence hath left thee?*

Androg.   *Of that an obstreperous lawyer bereft me.*

Nano.   *O wonderful change! When sir lawyer forsook thee,*
     For Pythagore's sake, what body then took thee?

Androg.   *A good dull mule.* Nano. *And how! by that means*
     Thou wert brought to allow of the eating of beans?   130

Androg.   *Yes.* Nano. *But from the mule into whom didst thou pass?*

---

97 *juggler:* trickster.   104 *charta:* charter, record.
109 *meretrix:* prostitute.   112 *gat it:* bore it.   113 *brock:* badger.

NOTES: pp. 191–4

Androg.   *Into a very strange beast, by some writers called an ass;*
          By others a precise, pure, illuminate brother
            Of those devour flesh, and sometimes one another;
            And will drop you forth a libel, or a sanctified lie,
            Betwixt every spoonful of a Nativity pie.

Nano.   *Now quit thee, for heaven, of that profane nation,*
          And gently report thy next transmigration.

Androg. *To the same that I am.* Nano. *A creature of delight –*
          And, what is more than a fool, an hermaphrodite?   140
          Now prithee, sweet soul, in all thy variation,
          Which body wouldst thou choose to take up thy station?

Androg. *Troth, this I am in: even here would I tarry.*

Nano.   *'Cause here the delight of each sex thou canst vary?*

Androg. *Alas, those pleasures be stale and forsaken;*
          No, 'tis your fool wherewith I am so taken,
          The only one creature that I can call blessed;
          For all other forms I have proved most distressed.

Nano.   *Spoke true, as thou were in Pythagoras still.*
          This learned opinion we celebrate will,   150
          Fellow eunuch, as behoves us, with all our wit and art,
          To dignify that whereof ourselves are so great and special a part.

Volpone. Now, very, very pretty! Mosca, this
   Was thy invention?

Mosca.   If it pleases my patron:
   Not else.

Volpone.   It doth, good Mosca.

Mosca.   Then it was, sir.

SONG

   Fools, they are the only nation
   Worth men's envy or admiration;
   Free from care or sorrow-taking,
   Selves, and others, merry making:
   All they speak or do is sterling.   160
   Your fool, he is your great man's darling,
   And your lady's sport and pleasure;
   Tongue and bauble are his treasure.
   E'en his face begetteth laughter,
   And he speaks truth free from slaughter;

   137 *nation:* sect.   163 *bauble:* jester's sceptre.
                 NOTES: p. 194

E

He's the grace of every feast,
And, sometimes, the chiefest guest;
Hath his trencher and his stool
When wit waits upon the fool.
　　O, who would not be　　　　　　　　　　170
　　　　He, he, he?　　　　　　　(*Knocking.*)
Volpone. Who's that? Away! [*Exeunt* NANO *and* CASTRONE.]
　　Look, Mosca.
Mosca. 　　　　　　　Fool, begone! 　[*Exit* ANDROGYNO.]
　　'Tis Signor Voltore, the advocate:
　　I know him by his knock.
Volpone. 　　　　　　　Fetch me my gown,
　　My furs, and night-caps; say my couch is changing;
　　And let him entertain himself awhile
　　Without in the gallery. [*Exit* MOSCA.] Now, now my
　　　　clients
　　Begin their visitation! Vulture, kite,
　　Raven, and gorcrow, all my birds of prey
　　That think me turning carcass, now they come: 　　180
　　I am not for them yet.

　　　　　　[*Enter* MOSCA, *with the gown, &c.*]

　　　　　　　How now? the news?
Mosca. A piece of plate, sir.
Volpone. 　　　　　　Of what bigness?
Mosca. 　　　　　　　　　　Huge,
　　Massy, and antique, with your name inscribed,
　　And arms engraven.
Volpone. 　　　　　　Good! and not a fox
　　Stretched on the earth, with fine delusive sleights,
　　Mocking a gaping crow – ha, Mosca?
Mosca. 　　　　　　　　　　Sharp, sir.
Volpone. Give me my furs. [*Puts on his sick dress.*] Why dost
　　thou laugh so, man?
Mosca. I cannot choose, sir, when I apprehend
　　What thoughts he has without now, as he walks:

168 *trencher:* platter.　　　182 *plate:* gold plate.

NOTES: p. 194

That this might be the last gift he should give;　　190
That this would fetch you; if you died today,
And gave him all, what he should be tomorrow;
What large return would come of all his ventures;
How he should worshipped be, and reverenced;
Ride with his furs and foot-cloths; waited on
By herds of fools and clients; have clear way
Made for his mule, as lettered as himself;
Be called the great and learned advocate:
And then concludes, there's nought impossible.
Volpone. Yes, to be learned, Mosca.
Mosca.　　　　　　　　　　O, no: rich　　　200
Implies it. Hood an ass with reverend purple
So you can hide his two ambitious ears,
And he shall pass for a cathedral doctor.
Volpone. My caps, my caps, good Mosca. Fetch him in.
Mosca. Stay, sir: your ointment for your eyes.
Volpone.　　　　　　　　　　　That's true;
Dispatch, dispatch: I long to have possession
Of my new present.
Mosca.　　　　　　That, and thousands more,
I hope to see you lord of.
Volpone.　　　　　　　Thanks, kind Mosca.
Mosca. And that, when I am lost in blended dust,
And hundred such as I am, in succession —　　210
Volpone. Nay, that were too much, Mosca.
Mosca.　　　　　　　　　　You shall live
Still to delude these harpies.
Volpone.　　　　　　　　Loving Mosca!
'Tis well: my pillow now, and let him enter.
　　　　　　　　　　　[*Exit* MOSCA.]
Now, my feigned cough, my phthisic, and my gout,
My apoplexy, palsy, and catarrhs,
Help, with your forced functions, this my posture,
Wherein, this three year, I have milked their hopes.

197 *lettered:* learned.
216 *posture:* imposture.
NOTES: p. 194

He comes; I hear him. [*He coughs*:] Uh! uh! uh!
uh! O —

Scene III *Enter* MOSCA *with* VOLTORE. lawyer

Mosca. You still are what you were, sir. Only you,
Of all the rest, are he commands his love;   220
And you do wisely to preserve it thus   — Working in
With early visitation, and kind notes   conjunction with
Of your good meaning to him, which, I know,   Volpone
Cannot but come most grateful. Patron! sir!
Here's Signor Voltore is come —
Volpone.   What say you?
Mosca. Sir, Signor Voltore is come this morning
To visit you.
Volpone.   I thank him.
Mosca.   And hath brought
A piece of antique plate, bought of St Mark,
With which he here presents you.
Volpone.   He is welcome.
Pray him to come more often.
Mosca.   Yes.
Voltore.   What says he?   230
Mosca. He thanks you, and desires you see him often.
Volpone. Mosca.
Mosca.   My patron?
Volpone.   Bring him near. Where is he?
I long to feel his hand.
Mosca.   The plate is here, sir.
Voltore. How fare you, sir?
Volpone.   I thank you, Signor Voltore.
Where is the plate? Mine eyes are bad.
Voltore [*putting it into his hands*].   I'm sorry
To see you still thus weak.
Mosca [*aside*].   That he's not weaker.
Volpone. You are too munificent.
Voltore.   No, sir; would to heaven

222 *notes:* indications.
NOTES: p. 195

I could as well give health to you as that plate.

Volpone. You give, sir, what you can. I thank you. Your love
　　Hath taste in this, and shall not be unanswered.　　240
　　I pray you see me often.

Voltore.　　　　　　　Yes, I shall, sir.

Volpone. Be not far from me.

Mosca.　　　　　　　Do you observe that, sir?

Volpone. Hearken unto me still; it will concern you.

Mosca. You are a happy man, sir; know your good.

Volpone. I cannot now last long —

Mosca.　　　　　　　You are his heir, sir.

Voltore. Am I?

Volpone.　　　I feel me going: uh! uh! uh! uh!
　　I'm sailing to my port: uh! uh! uh! uh!
　　And I am glad I am so near my haven.

Mosca. Alas, kind gentleman! Well, we must all go —

Voltore. But, Mosca —

Mosca.　　　　　　Age will conquer.

Voltore.　　　　　　　　　Pray thee, hear me: 250
　　Am I inscribed his heir for certain?

Mosca.　　　　　　　　　　Are you?
　　I do beseech you, sir, you will vouchsafe
　　To write me in your family. All my hopes
　　Depend upon your worship. I am lost
　　Except the rising sun do shine on me.

Voltore. It shall both shine, and warm thee, Mosca.

Mosca.　　　　　　　　　　　Sir,
　　I am a man that hath not done your love
　　All the worst offices: here I wear your keys,
　　See all your coffers and your caskets locked,
　　Keep the poor inventory of your jewels,　　260
　　Your plate, and monies; am your steward, sir,
　　Husband your goods here.

Voltore.　　　　　　　But am I sole heir?

Mosca. Without a partner, sir; confirmed this morning:
　　The wax is warm yet, and the ink scarce dry
　　Upon the parchment.

NOTES: p. 195

Voltore.   Happy, happy me!
    By what good chance, sweet Mosca?
Mosca.   Your desert, sir;
    I know no second cause.
Voltore.   Thy modesty
    Is loath to know it; well, we shall requite it.
Mosca. He ever liked your course, sir: that first took him.
    I oft have heard him say how he admired   270
    Men of your large profession, that could speak
    To every cause, and things mere contraries,
    Till they were hoarse again, yet all be law;
    That, with most quick agility, could turn,
    And re-turn; make knots, and undo them;
    Give forked counsel; take provoking gold
    On either hand, and put it up: these men,
    He knew, would thrive with their humility.
    And, for his part, he thought he should be blest
    To have his heir of such a suffering spirit,   280
    So wise, so grave, of so perplexed a tongue,
    And loud withal, that would not wag, nor scarce
    Lie still, without a fee; when every word
    Your worship but lets fall is a chequeen!

                                   (*Knocking.*)
    Who's that? One knocks; I would not have you seen, sir.
    And yet – pretend you came, and went in haste;
    I'll fashion an excuse. And, gentle sir,
    When you do come to swim in golden lard,
    Up to the arms in honey, that your chin
    Is borne up stiff with fatness of the flood,   290
    Think on your vassal; but remember me:
    I have not been your worst of clients.
Voltore.   Mosca!—
Mosca. When will you have your inventory brought, sir?
    Or see a copy of the will? — Anon!
    I'll bring them to you, sir. Away, begone,
    Put business in your face.

                                   [*Exit* VOLTORE.]

                    NOTES: pp. 195–6

Volpone [*springing up*]. Excellent, Mosca!
Come hither, let me kiss thee.

Mosca. Keep you still, sir.
Here is Corbaccio.

Volpone. Set the plate away:
The vulture's gone, and the old raven's come.

Mosca. Betake you to your silence, and your sleep. 300
[*Addresses the plate*] Stand there and multiply. Now we
    shall see
A wretch who is indeed more impotent
Than this can feign to be; yet hopes to hop
Over his grave.

Enter CORBACCIO.

Signor Corbaccio!
You're very welcome, sir.

Corbac. How does your patron?

Mosca. Troth, as he did, sir; no amends.

Corbac. What! mends he?

Mosca. No, sir: he's rather worse.

Corbac. That's well. Where is he?

Mosca. Upon his couch, sir, newly fallen asleep.

Corbac. Does he sleep well?

Mosca. No wink, sir, all this night,
Nor yesterday, but slumbers.

Corbac. Good! he should take 310
Some counsel of physicians. I have brought him
An opiate here from mine own doctor.

Mosca. He will not hear of drugs.

Corbac. Why? I myself
Stood by while it was made, saw all the ingredients,
And know it cannot but most gently work:
My life for his, 'tis but to make him sleep.

Volpone [*aside*]. Aye, his last sleep, if he would take it.

Mosca. Sir,
He has no faith in physic.

Corbac. Say you? say you?

NOTES: p. 196

Mosca. He has no faith in physic. He does think
    Most of your doctors are the greater danger,   320
    And worse disease to escape. I often have
    Heard him protest that your physician
    Should never be his heir.
Corbac.   Not I his heir?
Mosca. Not your physician, sir.
Corbac.   O, no, no, no,
    I do not mean it.
Mosca.   No, sir, nor their fees
    He cannot brook: he says they flay a man
    Before they kill him.
Corbac.   Right; I do conceive you.
Mosca. And then, they do it by experiment,
    For which the law not only doth absolve them,
    But gives them great reward; and he is loath   330
    To hire his death so.
Corbac.   It is true, they kill
    With as much licence as a judge.
Mosca.   Nay, more;
    For he but kills, sir, where the law condemns,
    And these can kill him too.
Corbac.   Aye, or me;
    Or any man. How does his apoplex?
    Is that strong on him still?
Mosca.   Most violent.
    His speech is broken, and his eyes are set;
    His face drawn longer than 'twas wont —
Corbac.   How? how?
    Stronger than he was wont?
Mosca.   No, sir: his face
    Drawn longer than 'twas wont.
Corbac.   O, good!
Mosca.   His mouth   340
    Is ever gaping, and his eyelids hang.

326 *brook:* endure.   327 *conceive:* understand.
335 *apoplex:* apoplexy.

NOTES: p. 196

Corbac.   Good.

Mosca. A freezing numbness stiffens all his joints,
    And makes the colour of his flesh like lead.

Corbac.   'Tis good.

Mosca. His pulse beats slow, and dull.

Corbac.   Good symptoms still.

Mosca. And from his brain —

Corbac.   Ha? How? Not from his brain?

Mosca. Yes, sir, and from his brain —

Corbac.   I conceive you; good.

Mosca. Flows a cold sweat, with a continual rheum
    Forth the resolved corners of his eyes.

Corbac. Is't possible? Yet I am better, ha!
    How does he with the swimming of his head?   350

Mosca. O, sir, 'tis past the scotomy; he now
    Hath lost his feeling, and hath left to snort:
    You hardly can perceive him that he breathes.

Corbac. Excellent, excellent! Sure I shall outlast him:
    This makes me young again a score of years.

Mosca. I was a-coming for you, sir.

Corbac.   Has he made his will?
    What has he given me?

Mosca.   No, sir.

Corbac.   Nothing, ha?

Mosca. He has not made his will, sir.

Corbac.   Oh, oh, oh!
    What then did Voltore, the lawyer, here?

Mosca. He smelt a carcass, sir, when he but heard   360
    My master was about his testament –
    As I did urge him to it for your good —

Corbac. He came unto him, did he? I thought so.

Mosca. Yes, and presented him this piece of plate.

Corbac. To be his heir?

Mosca.   I do not know, sir.

Corbac.   True;
    I know it too.

347 *rheum:* mucous discharge.   348 *resolved:* drooping.
NOTES: p. 196

Mosca [*aside*].   By your own scale, sir.

Corbac.   Well,
I shall prevent him yet. See, Mosca, look:
Here I have brought a bag of bright chequeens,
Will quite weigh down his plate.

Mosca [*taking the bag*].   Yea, marry, sir.   370
This is true physic, this your sacred medicine:
No talk of opiates to this great elixir!

Corbac. 'Tis aurum palpabile, if not potabile.

Mosca. It shall be ministered to him in his bowl?

Corbac. Aye, do, do, do.

Mosca.   Most blessed cordial!
This will recover him.

Corbac.   Yes, do, do, do.

Mosca. I think it were not best, sir.

Corbac.   What?

Mosca.   To recover him.

Corbac. O, no, no, no; by no means.

Mosca.   Why, sir, this
Will work some strange effect, if he but feel it.

Corbac. 'Tis true, therefore forbear; I'll take my venture:
Give me it again.

Mosca.   At no hand; pardon me: 380
You shall not do yourself that wrong, sir. I
Will so advise you, you shall have it all.

Corbac. How?

Mosca.   All, sir; 'tis your right, your own; no man
Can claim a part: 'tis yours without a rival,
Decreed by destiny.

Corbac.   How? How, good Mosca?

Mosca. I'll tell you, sir. This fit he shall recover —

Corbac. I do conceive you.

Mosca.   And, on first advantage
Of his gained sense, will I re-importune him

---

367 *prevent:* forestall.   369 *weigh down:* outweigh.
387 *advantage:* opportunity.
388 *gained sense:* regained consciousness.

NOTES: pp. 196–7

 Unto the making of his testament:
 And show him this.   [*Pointing to the money.*]
Corbac.   Good, good.
Mosca.   'Tis better yet, 390
 If you will hear, sir.
Corbac.   Yes, with all my heart.
Mosca. Now would I counsel you, make home with speed;
 There, frame a will, whereto you shall inscribe
 My master your sole heir.
Corbac.   And disinherit
 My son?
Mosca. O, sir, the better: for that colour *— the pretense will make it much more tempting*
 Shall make it much more taking.
Corbac.   O, but colour?
Mosca. This will, sir, you shall send it unto me.
 Now, when I come to enforce, as I will do,
 Your cares, your watchings, and your many prayers,
 Your more than many gifts, your this day's present, 400
 And last, produce your will, where, without thought
 Or least regard unto your proper issue, *own offspring*
 A son so brave and highly meriting,
 The stream of your diverted love hath thrown you
 Upon my master, and made him your heir;
 He cannot be so stupid, or stone dead,
 But, out of conscience and mere gratitude —
Corbac. He must pronounce me his? *(hen)*
Mosca.   'Tis true.
Corbac.   This plot
 Did I think on before.
Mosca.   I do believe it. *(ironic)*
Corbac. Do you not believe it?
Mosca,   Yes, sir.
Corbac.   Mine own project. 410
Mosca. Which, when he hath done, sir —
Corbac.   Published me his heir?
Mosca. And you so certain to survive him —

     396 *but:* only.
     NOTES: p. 197

Corbac.   Aye.
Mosca. Being so lusty a man —
Corbac.   'Tis true.
Mosca.   Yes, sir —
Corbac. I thought on that too. See, how he should be
      The very organ to express my thoughts!
Mosca. You have not only done yourself a good —
Corbac. But multiplied it on my son?
Mosca.   'Tis right, sir.
Corbac. Still my invention.
Mosca.   Alas, sir! heaven knows,
      It hath been all my study, all my care,
      (I e'en grow grey withal) how to work things —   420
Corbac. I do conceive, sweet Mosca.
Mosca.   You are he
      For whom I labour here.
Corbac.   Aye, do, do, do:
      I'll straight about it.
Mosca [*aside*].   Rook go with you, raven!
Corbac. I know thee honest.
Mosca [*aside*].   You do lie, sir —
Corbac.   And —
Mosca [*aside*]. Your knowledge is no better than your ears,
      sir.
Corbac. I do not doubt to be a father to thee.
Mosca [*aside*]. Nor I to gull my brother of his blessing.
Corbac. I may have my youth restored to me – why not?
Mosca [*aside*]. Your worship is a precious ass —
Corbac.   What sayst thou?
Mosca. I do desire your worship to make haste, sir.   430
Corbac. 'Tis done, . . . 'tis done; I go.   [*Exit.*]
Volpone [*rising from the sick bed*].   O, I shall burst!
      Let out my sides, let out my sides —
Mosca.   Contain
      Your flux of laughter, sir. You know this hope
      Is such a bait, it covers any hook.

433 *flux:* flow.
NOTES: p. 197

Volpone. O, but thy working and thy placing it!
    I cannot hold; good rascal, let me kiss thee:
    I never knew thee in so rare a humour.
Mosca. Alas, sir, I but do as I am taught;
    Follow your grave instructions; give them words;
    Pour oil into their ears, and send them hence.   440
Volpone. 'Tis true, 'tis true. What a rare punishment
    Is avarice to itself!
Mosca.   Aye, with our help, sir.
Volpone. So many cares, so many maladies,
    So many fears attending on old age;
    Yea, death so often called on, as no wish
    Can be more frequent with them; their limbs faint,
    Their senses dull; their seeing, hearing, going,
    All dead before them; yea, their very teeth,
    Their instruments of eating, failing them:
    Yet this is reckoned life! Nay, here was one   450
    Is now gone home, that wishes to live longer!
    Feels not his gout, nor palsy; feigns himself
    Younger by scores of years; flatters his age
    With confident belying it; hopes he may
    With charms, like Æson, have his youth restored;
    And with these thoughts so battens, as if fate
    Would be as easily cheated on as he,
    And all turns air! (*Knocking.*) Who's that there, now? a
        third?
Mosca. Close; to your couch again: I hear his voice.
    It is Corvino, our spruce merchant.
Volpone [*lying down*].   Dead.   460
Mosca. Another bout, sir, with your eyes. [*Anointing them.*]
    Who's there?

              Enter CORVINO.

    Signor Corvino! come most wished for! O,
    How happy were you, if you knew it, now!

435 *working:* manipulating.   447 *going:* power of movement.
456 *battens:* thrives, grows fat.   457 *cheated on:* cheated, deceived.

Corvino. Why? what? wherein?
Mosca.   The tardy hour is come, sir.
Corvino. He is not dead?
Mosca.   Not dead, sir, but as good;
 He knows no man.
Corvino.   How shall I do, then?
Mosca.   Why, sir?
Corvino. I have brought him here a pearl.
Mosca.   Perhaps he has
 So much remembrance left as to know you, sir:
 He still calls on you; nothing but your name
 Is in his mouth. Is your pearl orient, sir?   470
Corvino. Venice was never owner of the like.
Volpone. Signior Corvino!
Mosca.   Hark!
Volpone.   Signior Corvino!
Mosca. He calls you. Step and give it him.
  [*To* VOLPONE] He's here, sir,
 And he has brought you a rich pearl.
Corvino.   How do you, sir?
 Tell him it doubles the twelfth carat.
Mosca.   Sir,
 He cannot understand: his hearing's gone;
 And yet it comforts him to see you —
Corvino.   Say
 I have a diamond for him too.
Mosca.   Best show it, sir;
 Put it into his hand: 'tis only there
 He apprehends. He has his feeling yet.   480
 See how he grasps it!
Corvino.   Alas, good gentleman!
 How pitiful the sight is!
Mosca.   Tut, forget, sir.
 The weeping of an heir should still be laughter
 Under a visor.
Corvino.   Why, am I his heir?

Mosca. Sir, I am sworn: I may not show the will
　　　Till he be dead; but here has been Corbaccio,
　　　Here has been Voltore, here were others too –
　　　I cannot number 'em, they were so many –
　　　All gaping here for legacies; but I,
　　　Taking the vantage of his naming you,　　　　　490
　　　'Signor Corvino, Signor Corvino,' took
　　　Paper, and pen, and ink, and there I asked him
　　　Whom he would have his heir! 'Corvino.' Who
　　　Should be executor? 'Corvino.' And
　　　To any question he was silent to,
　　　I still interpreted the nods he made,
　　　Through weakness, for consent; and sent home the
　　　　others,
　　　Nothing bequeathed them but to cry and curse.
Corvino. O, my dear Mosca. (*They embrace.*) Does he not per-
　　　ceive us?
Mosca. No more than a blind harper. He knows no man,　　500
　　　No face of friend, nor name of any servant,
　　　Who 'twas that fed him last, or gave him drink;
　　　Not those he hath begotten, or brought up,
　　　Can he remember.
Corvino. 　　　　　　　Has he children?
Mosca. 　　　　　　　　　　　　　　Bastards,
　　　Some dozen or more that he begot on beggars,
　　　Gypsies, and Jews, and black-moors, when he was
　　　　drunk.
　　　Knew you not that, sir? 'Tis the common fable
　　　The dwarf, the fool, the eunuch, are all his;
　　　He's the true father of his family,
　　　In all save me – but he has given them nothing.　　510
Corvino. That's well, that's well! Art sure he does not hear
　　　us?
Mosca. Sure, sir? Why, look you, credit your own sense.
　　　[*Shouting in* VOLPONE'S *ear:*] The pox approach and
　　　　add to your diseases,

　　490 *the vantage:* advantage.　　　509 *family:* household.
NOTES: p. 198

If it would send you hence the sooner, sir.
For your incontinence, it hath deserved it
Throughly and throughly, and the plague to boot!
[*To* CORVINO] You may come near, sir.

    [*To* VOLPONE] Would you would once close
Those filthy eyes of yours, that flow with slime
Like two frog-pits; and those same hanging cheeks,
Covered with hide instead of skin —

    [*To* CORVINO] Nay, help, sir —   520
That look like frozen dish-clouts set on end!
Corvino. Or like an old smoked wall, on which the rain
    Ran down in streaks!
Mosca.   Excellent, sir, speak out;
    You may be louder yet: a culverin
    Discharged in his ear would hardly bore it.
Corvino. His nose is like a common sewer, still running.
Mosca. 'Tis good! And what his mouth?
Corvino.   A very draught.
Mosca. O, stop it up —
Corvino.   By no means.
Mosca.   Pray you, let me.
    Faith, I could stifle him rarely with a pillow
    As well as any woman that should keep him.   530
Corvino. Do as you will, but I'll begone.
Mosca.   Be so;
    It is your presence makes him last so long.
Corvino. I pray you use no violence.
Mosca.   No, sir? Why?
    Why should you be thus scrupulous, pray you, sir?
Corvino. Nay, at your discretion.
Mosca.   Well, good sir, be gone.
Corvino. I will not trouble him now to take my pearl.
Mosca. Pooh! Nor your diamond. What a needless care
    Is this afflicts you? Is not all here yours?
    Am not I here, whom you have made: your creature? –

---

516 *to boot:* besides.   537 *needless care:* unnecessary concern.
        539 *your creature:* your dependant.

NOTES: p. 198

That owe my being to you?

Corvino.   Grateful Mosca!   540
    Thou art my friend, my fellow, my companion,
    My partner, and shalt share in all my fortunes.

Mosca. Excepting one.

Corvino.   What's that?

Mosca.   Your gallant wife, sir. *(cilia).*

               [*Exit* CORVINO.]

    Now he is gone: we had no other means
    To shoot him hence but this.

Volpone.   My divine Mosca!
    Thou hast to-day outgone thyself. (*Knocking*.)   Who's
      there?
    I will be troubled with no more. Prepare
    Me music, dances, banquets, all delights;
    The Turk is not more sensual in his pleasures
    Than will Volpone. [*Exit* MOSCA.] Let me see; a pearl!   550
    A diamond! plate! chequeens! Good morning's pur-
      chase.
    Why, this is better than rob churches yet;
    Or fat by eating, once a month, a man.

             [*Enter* MOSCA.]

    Who is't?

Mosca.   The beauteous Lady Would-be, sir,
    Wife to the English knight, Sir Politic Would-be,
    (This is the style, sir, is directed me)
    Hath sent to know how you have slept tonight,
    And if you would be visited.

Volpone.   Not now:
    Some three hours hence —

Mosca.   I told the squire so much.

Volpone. When I am high with mirth and wine, then, then.   560
    'Fore heaven, I wonder at the desperate valour
    Of the bold English, that they dare let loose
    Their wives to all encounters!

          551 *purchase:* gain.
          NOTES: p. 198

F

Mosca.   Sir, this knight
   Had not his name for nothing: he is politic,
   And knows, howe'er his wife affect strange airs,
   She hath not yet the face to be dishonest;
   But had she Signor Corvino's wife's face —
Volpone. Hath she so rare a face?
Mosca.   O, sir, the wonder,
   The blazing star of Italy! a wench
   Of the first year! a beauty ripe as harvest!   570
   Whose skin is whiter than a swan all over,
   Than silver, snow, or lilies; a soft lip,
   Would tempt you to eternity of kissing!
   And flesh that melteth in the touch to blood —
   Bright as your gold, and lovely as your gold!
Volpone. Why had not I known this before?
Mosca.   Alas, sir,
   Myself but yesterday discovered it.
Volpone. How might I see her?
Mosca.   O, not possible;
   She's kept as warily as is your gold;
   Never does come abroad, never takes air   580
   But at a window. All her looks are sweet
   As the first grapes or cherries, and are watched
   As near as they are.
Volpone.   I must see her.
Mosca.   Sir,
   There is a guard of ten spies thick upon her,
   All his whole household; each of which is set
   Upon his fellow, and have all their charge,
   When he goes out, when he comes in, examined.
Volpone. I will go see her, though but at her window.
Mosca. In some disguise, then.
Volpone.   That is true. I must
   Maintain mine own shape still the same: we'll think.   590
                       [Exeunt.]

NOTES: pp. 198–9

Act II

Scene I. [*Outside* CORVINO'S *house.*]

Enter SIR POLITIC WOULD-BE, *and* PEREGRINE.

Sir P. W. Sir, to a wise man, all the world's his soil.
　　It is not Italy, nor France, nor Europe
　　That must bound me, if my fates call me forth.
　　Yet, I protest, it is no salt desire
　　Of seeing countries, shifting a religion,
　　Nor any disaffection to the state
　　Where I was bred, and unto which I owe
　　My dearest plots, hath brought me out; much less
　　That idle, antique, stale, grey-headed project
　　Of knowing men's minds and manners, with Ulysses;　10
　　But a peculiar humour of my wife's,
　　Laid for this height of Venice, to observe,
　　To quote, to learn the language, and so forth —
　　I hope you travel, sir, with licence?
Peregr.　　　　　　　　　　　　Yes.
Sir P. W. I dare the safelier converse — How long, sir,
　　Since you left England?
Peregr.　　　　　　　　　Seven weeks.
Sir P. W.　　　　　　　　　　　　So lately?
　　You have not been with my lord ambassador?
Peregr. Not yet, sir.
Sir P. W.　　　　　Pray you, what news, sir, vents our
　　climate?
　　I heard last night a most strange thing reported
　　By some of my lord's followers, and I long　　　　20
　　To hear how 'twill be seconded.
Peregr.　　　　　　　　　　　What was 't, sir?

　　4 *salt:* wanton.　　8 *plots:* plans.　　11 *humour:* whim.
　　13 *quote:* take note.　　　21 *seconded:* followed up.

NOTES: p. 199

83

Sir P. W. Marry, sir, of a raven that should build
In a ship royal of the king's.
Peregr. [*aside*].   This fellow,
Does he gull me, trow? or is gulled? Your name, sir?
Sir P. W. My name is Politic Would-be.
Peregr. [*aside*].   O, that speaks him.
A knight, sir?
Sir P. W.   A poor knight, sir.
Peregr.   Your lady
Lies here in Venice, for intelligence
Of tires and fashions, and behaviour,
Among the courtesans? the fine Lady Would-be?
Sir P. W. Yes, sir; the spider and the bee oftimes   30
Suck from one flower.
Peregr.   Good Sir Politic,
I cry you mercy! I have heard much of you:
'Tis true, sir, of your raven.
Sir P. W.   On your knowledge?
Peregr. Yes, and your lion's whelping in the Tower.
Sir P. W. Another whelp?
Peregr.   Another, sir.
Sir P. W.   Now heaven!
What prodigies be these? The fires at Berwick!
And the new star! These things concurring, strange,
And full of omen! Saw you those meteors?
Peregr. I did, sir.
Sir P. W.   Fearful! Pray you, sir, confirm me,
Were there three porpoises seen above the bridge,   40
As they give out?
Peregr.   Six, and a sturgeon, sir.
Sir P. W. I am astonished.
Peregr.   Nay, sir, be not so;
I'll tell you a greater prodigy than these —
Sir P. W. What should these things portend?
Peregr.   The very day
(Let me be sure) that I put forth from London,

24 *gull:* make a fool of.
NOTES: pp. 200–1

There was a whale discovered in the river
As high as Woolwich, that had waited there
(Few know how many months) for the subversion
Of the Stode fleet. *see bottom page 201*
Sir P. W.   Is't possible? Believe it,
'Twas either sent from Spain, or the Archdukes: 50
Spinola's whale, upon my life, my credit! *202*
Will they not leave these projects? Worthy sir,
Some other news.
Peregr.   Faith, Stone, the fool, is dead,
And they do lack a tavern fool extremely.
Sir P. W. Is Mass Stone dead?
Peregr.   He's dead, sir; why, I hope
You thought him not immortal. [*Aside*] O, this knight,
Were he well known, would be a precious thing
To fit our English stage: he that should write
But such a fellow, should be thought to feign
Extremely, if not maliciously.
Sir P. W.   Stone dead!   60
Peregr. Dead. Lord! how deeply, sir, you apprehend it!
He was no kinsman to you?
Sir P. W.   That I know of.
Well, that same fellow was an unknown fool.
Peregr. And yet you knew him, it seems.
Sir P. W.   I did so. Sir,
I knew him one of the most dangerous heads
Living within the state, and so I held him.
Peregr. Indeed, sir?
Sir P. W.   While he lived, in action.
He has received weekly intelligence,
Upon my knowledge, out of the Low Countries,
For all parts of the world, in cabbages;   70
And those dispensed again to ambassadors,
In oranges, musk-melons, apricots,
Lemons, pome-citrons, and suchlike; sometimes
In Colchester oysters, and your Selsey cockles.

61 *apprehend:* feel.   63 *unknown:* under-estimated.
NOTES: pp. 201–2

Peregr. You make me wonder.

Sir P. W.   Sir, upon my knowledge.
    Nay, I have observed him, at your public ordinary,
    Take his advertisement from a traveller
    (A concealed statesman) in a trencher of meat;
    And instantly, before the meal was done,
    Convey an answer in a tooth-pick.

Peregr.   Strange!   80
    How could this be, sir?

Sir P. W.   Why, the meat was cut
    So like his character, and so laid, as he
    Must easily read the cypher.

Peregr.   I have heard
    He could not read, sir.

Sir P. W.   So 'twas given out,
    In polity, by those that did employ him:
    But he could read, and had your languages,
    And to 't, as sound a noddle —

Peregr.   I have heard, sir,
    That your baboons were spies, and that they were
    A kind of subtle nation near to China.

Sir P. W. Aye, aye, your Mamaluchi. Faith, they had   90
    Their hand in a French plot or two; but they
    Were so extremely given to women, as
    They made discovery of all; yet I
    Had my advices here, on Wednesday last,
    From one of their own coat, they were returned,
    Made their relations, as the fashion is,
    And now stand fair for fresh employment.

Peregr. [*aside*].   Heart!
    This Sir Poll will be ignorant of nothing.
    It seems, sir, you know all.

Sir P. W.   Not all, sir; but
    I have some general notions. I do love   100

---

77 *advertisement:* instructions.   78 *trencher:* platter.
93 *made discovery of:* disclosed.   96 *relations:* reports.
                 97 *fair:* ready.
NOTES: pp. 202–3

To note and to observe; though I live out,
Free from the active torrent, yet I'd mark
The currents and the passages of things
For mine own private use; and know the ebbs
And flows of state.

Peregr.　　　　　　　Believe it, sir, I hold
Myself in no small tie unto my fortunes *Thank my lucky stars*
For casting me thus luckily upon you,
Whose knowledge, if your bounty equal it,
May do me great assistance in instruction
For my behaviour, and my bearing, which　　　　　110
Is yet so rude and raw.

Sir P. W.　　　　　　Why, came you forth
Empty of rules for travel? *satire on making mysteries out of ordinary things*

Peregr.　　　　　　　Faith, I had
Some common ones from out that vulgar grammar
Which he that cried Italian to me taught me.

Sir P. W. Why, this it is that spoils all our brave bloods,
Trusting our hopeful gentry unto pedants,
Fellows of outside, and mere bark. You seem
To be a gentleman of ingenuous race — *noble birth*
I not profess it, but my fate hath been
To be where I have been consulted with, *says he is a master at travel* 120
In this high kind, touching some great men's sons,
Persons of blood and honour —

Enter MOSCA *and* NANO, *disguised.*

Peregr.　　　　　　　Who be these, sir?
Mosca. Under that window, there 't must be. The same.
　　　　　[MOSCA *and* NANO *set up a small platform.*]
Sir P. W. Fellows, to mount a bank. Did your instructor
In the dear tongues never discourse to you
Of the Italian mountebanks?

Peregr.　　　　　　　Yes, sir.
Sir P. W.　　　　　　　　Why,
Here shall you see one.
Peregr.　　　　　　　They are quacksalvers,

NOTES: pp. 203–4

Fellows that live by venting oils and drugs.

Sir P. W. Was that the character he gave you of them?

Peregr. As I remember.

Sir P. W.   Pity his ignorance.   130
They are the only knowing men of Europe:
Great general scholars, excellent physicians,
Most admired statesmen, professed favourites,
And cabinet counsellors to the greatest princes;
The only languaged men of all the world!

Peregr. And I have heard they are most lewd impostors;
Made all of terms and shreds; no less beliers
Of great men's favours than their own vile med'cines,
Which they will utter upon monstrous oaths;
Selling that drug for twopence, ere they part,   140
Which they have valued at twelve crowns before.

Sir P. W. Sir, calumnies are answered best with silence.
Yourself shall judge. Who is it mounts, my friends?

Mosca. Scoto of Mantua, sir.

Sir P. W.   Is't he? Nay, then
I'll proudly promise, sir, you shall behold
Another man than has been phant'sied to you.
I wonder yet, that he should mount his bank
Here in this nook, that has been wont to appear
In face of the Piazza. Here he comes.

[*Enter* VOLPONE, *disguised as a mountebank, and followed
by a crowd.*]

Volpone [*to* NANO]. Mount, zany.

Crowd.   Follow, follow, follow,
follow, follow.   150

Sir P. W. See how the people follow him! He's a man
May write ten thousand crowns in bank here. Note;
Mark but his gesture: I do use to observe
The state he keeps in getting up.

---

128 *venting:* vending, selling.   136 *lewd:* ignorant.
137 *beliers:* fabricators.   149 *in face of:* opposite.
152 *may write:* is good for.

NOTES: pp. 204–5

[VOLPONE *mounts the platform.*]

Peregr.   'Tis worth it, sir.

Volpone. *Most noble gentlemen, and my worthy patrons, it*
may seem strange that I, your Scoto Mantuano, who was
ever wont to fix my bank in face of the public Piazza,
near the shelter of the Portico to the Procuratia, should
now, after eight months' absence from this illustrious city of
Venice, humbly retire myself into an obscure nook of the 160
Piazza.

Sir P. W. Did not I now object the same?

Peregr.   Peace, sir.

Volpone. *Let me tell you: I am not, as your Lombard proverb*
saith, cold on my feet; or content to part with my commodi-
ties at a cheaper rate than I accustomed: look not for it.
Nor that the calumnious reports of that impudent detractor
and shame to our profession (Alessandro Buttone, I mean)
who gave out, in public, I was condemned a sforzato to the
galleys for poisoning the Cardinal Bembo's – cook, hath at
all attached, much less dejected me. No, no, worthy gentle- 170
men; to tell you true, I cannot endure to see the rabble of
these ground ciarlitani, that spread their cloaks on the pave-
ment as if they meant to do feats of activity, and then
come in lamely with their mouldy tales out of Boccacio, like
stale Tabarine, the fabulist; some of them discoursing their
travels, and of their tedious captivity in the Turks' galleys,
when, indeed, were the truth known, they were the Chris-
tians' galleys, where very temperately they ate bread and
drunk water, as a wholesome penance, enjoined them by
their confessors, for base pilferies. 180

Sir P. W. Note but his bearing, and contempt of these.

Volpone. *These turdy-facy-nasty-paty-lousy-fartical rogues,*
with one poor groatsworth of unprepared antimony, finely
wrapped up in several scartoccios, are able, very well, to
kill their twenty a week, and play; yet these meagre,
starved spirits, who have half stopped the organs of their

170 *attached:* arrested, restrained.

NOTES: p. 205

minds with earthy oppilations, want not their favourers
among your shrivelled salad-eating artisans, who are over-
joyed that they may have their hap'orth of physic; though it
purge them into another world, it makes no matter.   190

Sir P. W. Excellent! Have you heard better language, sir?

Volpone. Well, let them go. And, gentlemen, honourable gentlemen, know, that for this time, our bank, being thus removed
from the clamours of the canaglia, shall be the scene of pleasure and delight; for I have nothing to sell, little or nothing
to sell.

Sir P. W. I told you, sir, his end.

Peregr.   You did so, sir.

Volpone. I protest, I, and my six servants, are not able to make
of this precious liquor so fast as it is fetched away from my
lodging by gentlemen of your city; strangers of the Terra- 200
firma; worshipful merchants; aye, and senators too, who,
ever since my arrival, have detained me to their uses by their
splendidous liberalities. And worthily: for what avails
your rich man to have his magazines stuffed with moscadelli, or of the purest grape, when his physicians prescribe
him, on pain of death, to drink nothing but water cocted
with aniseeds? O, health! health! the blessing of the rich!
the riches of the poor! who can buy thee at too dear a rate,
since there is no enjoying this world without thee? Be not
then so sparing of your purses, honourable gentlemen, as to 210
abridge the natural course of life —

Peregr. You see his end.

Sir P. W.   Aye; is't not good?

Volpone. For when a humid flux, or catarrh, by the mutability
of air, falls from your head into an arm or shoulder, or any
other part, take you a ducat, or your chequeen of gold, and
apply to the place affected: see what good effect it can work.
No, no; 'tis this blessed unguento, this rare extraction,
that hath only power to disperse all malignant humours
that proceed either of hot, cold, moist, or windy causes —

194 *canaglia:* rabble, canaille.   204 *magazines:* storehouses.
206 *cocted:* boiled.   217 *unguento:* ointment.

NOTES: pp. 205–6

Peregr. I would he had put in dry too.

Sir P. W.   Pray you observe.   220

*Volpone. To fortify the most indigest and crude stomach; aye,
were it of one that, through extreme weakness, vomited blood,
applying only a warm napkin to the place, after the unction
and fricace; for the vertigine in the head, putting but a
drop into your nostrils, likewise behind the ears; a most
sovereign and approved remedy – the mal caduco, cramps,
convulsions, paralysies, epilepsies, tremor-cordia, retired
nerves, ill vapours of the spleen, stoppings of the liver, the
stone, the strangury, hernia ventosa, iliaca passio; stops a
dysenteria immediately; easeth the torsion of the small guts;   230
and cures melancholia hypocondriaca, being taken and applied according to my printed receipt. For this* (Holding up
the instructions) *is the physician, this* (Holding up the
liquid) *the medicine; this counsels, this cures; this gives the
direction, this works the effect; and, in sum, both together
may be termed an abstract of the theoric and practic in the
Æsculapian art. 'Twill cost you eight crowns.* [To NANO]
*And, Zan Fritada, pray thee sing a verse extempore in
honour of it.*

Sir P. W. How do you like him, sir?

Peregr.   Most strangely, I!

Sir P. W. Is not his language rare?

Peregr.   But alchemy –   240
I never heard the like – or Broughton's books.

SONG.

*Had old Hippocrates, or Galen,
That to their books put med'cines all in,
But known this secret, they had never
(Of which they will be guilty ever)
Been murderers of so much paper,
Or wasted many a hurtless taper;*

221 *crude:* unable to digest.   224 *fricace:* massage.
224 *vertigine:* giddiness.   230 *torsion:* twisting.
                    240 *but alchemy:* sheer alchemy.

NOTES: p. 206

No Indian drug had e'er been famed,
Tobacco, sassafras not named;
Ne yet of guacum one small stick, sir,   250
Nor Raymond Lully's great elixir;
Ne had been known the Danish Gonswart,
Or Paracelsus, with his long sword.

Peregr. All this, yet, will not do. Eight crowns is high.

Volpone. *No more. Gentlemen, if I had but time to discourse to
you the miraculous effects of this my oil, surnamed Oglio del
Scoto; with the countless catalogue of those I have cured of
the aforesaid, and many more diseases; the patents and pri-
vileges of all the princes and commonwealths of Christen-
dom; or but the depositions of those that appeared on my*   260
*part, before the signory of the Sanita and most learned Col-
lege of Physicians, where I was authorised, upon notice taken
of the admirable virtues of my medicaments and mine own
excellency in matter of rare and unknown secrets, not only
to disperse them publicly in this famous city, but in all the
territories that happily joy under the government of the
most pious and magnificent states of Italy. But may some
other gallant fellow say, 'O, there be divers that make profession to have as good and as experimented receipts as
yours'; indeed, very many have assayed, like apes, in imita-*   270
*tion of that which is really and essentially in me, to make
of this oil; bestowed great cost in furnaces, stills, alembics,
continual fires, and preparation of the ingredients (as indeed there goes to it six hundred several simples, besides
some quantity of human fat, for the conglutination, which
we buy of the anatomists), but when these practitioners come
to the last decoction – blow, blow, puff, puff, and all
flies in fumo: ha, ha, ha! Poor wretches! I rather pity their
folly and indiscretion than their loss of time and money; for
those may be recovered by industry, but to be a fool born*   280
is a disease incurable. For myself, I always from my youth

269 *experimented:* tested.
272 *alembics:* ancient distilling apparatus.
275 *conglutination:* binding.

NOTES: pp. 206–7

*have endeavoured to get the rarest secrets, and book
them, either in exchange, or for money: I spared nor cost
nor labour where anything was worthy to be learned. And,
gentlemen, honourable gentlemen, I will undertake, by virtue of chemical art, out of the honourable hat that covers
your head, to extract the four elements; that is to say, the fire,
air, water, and earth, and return you your felt without burn
or stain. For, whilst others have been at the balloo, I have
been at my book; and am now past the craggy paths of* 290
*study, and come to the flowery plains of honour and reputa-
tion.*

Sir P. W. I do assure you, sir, that is his aim.

Volpone. *But to our price.*

Peregr.   And that withal, Sir Poll.

Volpone. *You all know, honourable gentlemen, I never valued
this ampulla, or vial, at less than eight crowns; but for this
time, I am content to be deprived of it for six: six crowns is
the price, and less, in courtesy, I know you cannot offer me.
Take it or leave it, howsoever, both it and I am at your service. I ask you not as the value of the thing, for then I* 300
*should demand of you a thousand crowns: so the Cardinals
Montalto, Fernese, the great Duke of Tuscany, my gossip,
with divers other princes, have given me; but I despise
money. Only to show my affection to you, honourable gentlemen, and your illustrious state here, I have neglected the
messages of these princes, mine own offices; framed my jour-
ney hither, only to present you with the fruits of my travels.*
[To NANO and MOSCA] *Tune your voices once more to the
touch of your instruments, and give the honourable assem-
bly some delightful recreation.*   310

Peregr. What monstrous and most painful circumstance
       Is here, to get some three or four gazetts,
       Some threepence in the whole – for that 'twill come to!

---

282 *book them:* record them.   294 *withal:* too.
306 *offices:* affairs.   311 *circumstance:* ado.
           312 *gazetts:* Venetian small coins.

NOTES: p. 207

SONG.

You that would last long, list to my song:
Make no more coil, but buy of this oil.
Would you be ever fair and young?
Stout of teeth, and strong of tongue?
Tart of palate? quick of ear?
Sharp of sight? of nostril clear?
Moist of hand? and light of foot?　　　　　　　　320
Or I will come nearer to't —
Would you live free from all diseases?
Do the act your mistress pleases,
Yet fright all aches from your bones?
Here's a med'cine for the nones.

Volpone. *Well, I am in a humour, at this time, to make a present*
of the small quantity my coffer contains – to the rich in cour-
tesy, and to the poor for God's sake. Wherefore now mark:
I asked you six crowns, and six crowns, at other times,
you have paid me. You shall not give me six crowns, nor　330
five, nor four, nor three, nor two, nor one; nor half a ducat;
no, nor a moccenigo. Sixpence it will cost you, or six hun-
dred pound – expect no lower price, for, by the banner of my
front, I will not bate a bagatine. That I will have only, a
pledge of your loves, to carry something from amongst you to
show I am not contemned by you. Therefore, now, toss your
handkerchiefs cheerfully, cheerfully; and be advertised,
that the first heroic spirit that deigns to grace me with a
handkerchief, I will give it a little remembrance of some-
thing beside, shall please it better than if I had presented　340
it with a double pistolet.

Peregr. Will you be that heroic spark, Sir Poll?

　　　(CELIA, *at a window, throws down her handkerchief.*)
　　　O, see! The window has prevented you.

Volpone. *Lady, I kiss your bounty; and, for this timely grace*
you have done your poor Scoto of Mantua, I will return

314 *list:* listen.	315 *coil:* fuss, commotion.
326 *humour:* mood.	343 *prevented:* forestalled.

*you, over and above my oil, a secret of that high and inesti-
mable nature shall make you for ever enamoured on that
minute wherein your eye first descended on so mean, yet not
altogether to be despised, an object. Here is a powder concealed in this paper of which, if I should speak to the worth,* 350
*nine thousand volumes were but as one page, that page as a
line, that line as a word, so short is this pilgrimage of man
(which some call life) to the expressing of it. Would I reflect
on the price, why, the whole world were but as an empire, that
empire as a province, that province as a bank, that bank as a
private purse, to the purchase of it. I will only tell you: it is
the powder that made Venus a goddess (given her by Apollo),
that kept her perpetually young, cleared her wrinkles, firmed
her gums, filled her skin, coloured her hair; from her derived
to Helen, and at the sack of Troy unfortunately lost; till* 360
*now, in this our age, it was as happily recovered by a studi-
ous antiquary, out of some ruins of Asia, who sent a moiety
of it to the court of France (but much sophisticated), wherewith the ladies there now colour their hair. The rest, at this
present, remains with me; extracted to a quintessence, so
that, wherever it but touches, in youth it perpetually pre-
serves, in age restores the complexion; seats your teeth, did
they dance like virginal jacks, firm as a wall; makes them
white as ivory, that were black as —*

Enter CORVINO.

Corvino. Spite of the devil, and my shame! come down, here. 370
Come down. No house but mine to make your scene?
Signior Flaminio, will you down, sir? down!
What, is my wife your Franciscina, sir?
No windows on the whole piazza here
To make your properties, but mine? – but mine?
          (*He beats away* VOLPONE *and his followers.*)
Heart! ere tomorrow I shall be new christened
And called the Pantalone di Besogniosi,
About the town.

363 *sophisticated:* adulterated.

Peregr.   What should this mean, Sir Poll?

Sir P. W. Some trick of state, believe it. I will home.

Peregr. It may be some design on you.

Sir P. W.   I know not.   380

I'll stand upon my guard.

Peregr.   It is your best, sir.

Sir P. W. This three weeks, all my advices, all my letters,
They have been intercepted.

Peregr.   Indeed, sir!

Best have a care.

Sir P. W.   Nay, so I will.

Peregr.   This knight,
I may not lose him, for my mirth, till night. [*Exeunt.*]

Scene II. [*In* VOLPONE'S *house.*]

Enter VOLPONE *and* MOSCA.

Volpone. O, I am wounded!

Mosca.   Where, sir?

Volpone.   Not without;
Those blows were nothing: I could bear them ever.
But angry Cupid, bolting from her eyes,
Hath shot himself into me like a flame,
Where now he flings about his burning heat –
As in a furnace an ambitious fire
Whose vent is stopped. The fight is all within me.
I cannot live except thou help me, Mosca;
My liver melts, and I, without the hope
Of some soft air from her refreshing breath,   10
Am but a heap of cinders.

Mosca.   Alas, good sir,
Would you had never seen her!

Volpone.   Nay, would thou
Hadst never told me of her!

3 *bolting:* discharging an arrow.

NOTES: p. 209

Mosca.   Sir, 'tis true;
    I do confess I was unfortunate
    And you unhappy; but I'm bound in conscience,
    No less than duty, to effect my best
    To your release of torment, and I will, sir.
Volpone. Dear Mosca, shall I hope?
Mosca.   Sir, more than dear,
    I will not bid you to despair of aught
    Within a human compass.
Volpone.   O, there spoke   20
    My better angel. Mosca, take my keys:
    Gold, plate, and jewels, all's at thy devotion;
    Employ them how thou wilt. Nay, coin me too,
    So thou in this but crown my longings, Mosca.
Mosca. Use but your patience.
Volpone.   So I have.
Mosca.   I doubt not
    To bring success to your desires.
Volpone.   Nay, then,
    I not repent me of my late disguise.
Mosca. If you can horn him, sir, you need not.
Volpone.   True.
    Besides, I never meant him for my heir.
    Is not the colour of my beard and eyebrows   30
    To make me known?
Mosca.   No jot.
Volpone.   I did it well.
Mosca. So well, would I could follow you in mine
    With half the happiness! And yet, I would
    Escape your epilogue.
Volpone.   But were they gulled
    With a belief that I was Scoto?
Mosca.   Sir,
    Scoto himself could hardly have distinguished!
    I have not time to flatter you now. We'll part,
    And as I prosper, so applaud my art.   [*Exeunt.*]

          34 *gulled:* taken in, fooled.
           NOTES: pp. 209–10

G

Scene III. [*In* CORVINO'S *house.*]

Enter CORVINO *and* CELIA.

Corvino. Death of mine honour, with the city's fool,
    A juggling, tooth-drawing, prating mountebank?
    And at a public window, where, whilst he
    With his strained action and his dole of faces
    To his drug-lecture draws your itching ears,
    A crew of old, unmarried, noted lechers
    Stood leering up like satyrs? And you smile
    Most graciously, and fan your favours forth,
    To give your hot spectators satisfaction!
    What, was your mountebank their call, their whistle?   10
    Or were you enamoured on his copper rings,
    His saffron jewel with the toad-stone in it,
    Or his embroidered suit with the cope-stitch,
    Made of a hearse-cloth? – or his old tilt-feather,
    Or his starched beard? Well, you shall have him, yes!
    He shall come home and minister unto you
    The fricace for the mother. Or, let me see,
    I think you'd rather mount; would you not mount?
    Why, if you'll mount, you may; yes truly, you may.
    And so you may be seen down to the foot.   20
    Get you a cittern, Lady Vanity,
    And be a dealer with the virtuous man:
    Make one. I'll but protest myself a cuckold,
    And save your dowry. I'm a Dutchman, I!
    For if you thought me an Italian,
    You would be damned ere you did this, you whore!
    Thou'dst tremble to imagine that the murder
    Of father, mother, brother, all thy race,
    Should follow, as the subject of my justice.
Celia. Good sir, have patience.
Corvino.   What couldst thou propose   30
    Less to thyself than, in this heat of wrath

Get upon the platform to be treated? [margin annotation]

2 *prating:* prattling.   10 *call:* summons.

NOTES: pp. 210–11

And stung with my dishonour, I should strike
This steel into thee, with as many stabs
As thou wert gazed upon with goatish eyes?

Celia. Alas, sir, be appeased! I could not think
My being at the window should more now
Move your impatience than at other times.

Corvino. No? Not to seek and entertain a parley
With a known knave? Before a multitude
You were an actor, with your handkerchief,   40
Which he most sweetly kissed in the receipt,
And might, no doubt, return it with a letter,
And point the place where you might meet – your sister's,
Your mother's, or your aunt's might serve the turn.

Celia. Why, dear sir, when do I make these excuses,
Or ever stir abroad, but to the church?
And that so seldom —

Corvino.   Well, it shall be less;
And thy restraint before was liberty
To what I now decree: and therefore mark me.
First, I will have this bawdy light dammed up;   50
And, till it be done, some two or three yards off
I'll chalk a line, o'er which if thou but chance
To set thy desperate foot, more hell, more horror,
More wild, remorseless rage shall seize on thee
Than on a conjuror that had heedless left
His circle's safety ere his devil was laid.
Then, here's a lock which I will hang upon thee;
And, now I think on't, I will keep thee backwards:
Thy lodging shall be backwards; thy walks backwards;
Thy prospect, all, be backwards; and no pleasure   60
That thou shalt know, but backwards. Nay, since you
    force
My honest nature, know it is your own
Being too open makes me use you thus,

34 *goatish:* licentious.   38 *entertain a parley:* hold conference.
43 *point:* appoint.   50 *light:* window.
57 *lock:* chastity belt.   60 *prospect:* view, outlook.
NOTES: p. 211

Since you will not contain your subtle nostrils
In a sweet room, but they must snuff the air
Of rank and sweaty passengers — (*Knocking*.) One knocks.
Away, and be not seen, pain of thy life;
Not look toward the window: if thou dost –
Nay, stay, hear this – let me not prosper, whore,
But I will make thee an anatomy,   70
Dissect thee mine own self, and read a lecture
Upon thee to the city, and in public.
Away!

> [*Exit* CELIA.]

> [*Enter* Servant.]
           Who's there?
Servant.   'Tis Signor Mosca, sir.
Corvino. Let him come in. [*Exit* Servant.] His master's dead:
     there's yet
     Some good to help the bad.

> *Enter* MOSCA.

                                   My Mosca, welcome!
     I guess your news.
Mosca.   I fear you cannot, sir.
Corvino. Is't not his death?
Mosca.   Rather the contrary.
Corvino. Not his recovery?
Mosca.   Yes, sir.
Corvino.   I am cursed;
     I am bewitched; my crosses meet to vex me.
     How? how? how? how?
Mosca.   Why, sir, with Scoto's oil.   80
     Corbaccio and Voltore brought of it
     Whilst I was busy in an inner room —
Corvino. Death! that damned mountebank! But for the law,
     Now I could kill the rascal. It cannot be
     His oil should have that virtue. Have not I
     Known him, a common rogue, come fiddling in

66 *passengers:* passers-by.

To the osteria with a tumbling whore,
And, when he has done all his forced tricks, been glad
Of a poor spoonful of dead wine, with flies in it?
It cannot be. All his ingredients   90
Are a sheep's gall, a roasted bitch's marrow,
Some few sod earwigs, pounded caterpillars,
A little capon's grease, and fasting spittle:
I know them to a dram.

Mosca.   I know not, sir;
But some on't, there, they poured into his ears,
Some in his nostrils, and recovered him,
Applying but the fricace.

Corvino.   Pox o' that fricace!

Mosca. And since, to seem the more officious
And flattering of his health, there they have had,
At extreme fees, the college of physicians   100
Consulting on him, how they might restore him;
Where one would have a cataplasm of spices,
Another a flayed ape clapped to his breast,
A third would have it a dog, a fourth an oil
With wild cats' skins. At last they all resolved
That, to preserve him was no other means
But some young woman must be straight sought out,
Lusty, and full of juice, to sleep by him;
And to this service, most unhappily,
And most unwillingly, am I now employed,   110
Which here I thought to pre-acquaint you with
For your advice, since it concerns you most;
Because I would not do that thing might cross
Your ends, on whom I have my sole dependence, sir;
Yet if I do it not, they may dilate
My slackness to my patron, work me out
Of his opinion; and there all your hopes,

87 *osteria:* inn, hostelry.
92 *sod:* boiled (from 'seethe').
98 *officious:* helpful.
107 *straight:* immediately.
114 *ends:* purposes.

89 *dead wine:* stale wine.
97 *fricace:* massage.
102 *cataplasm:* poultice.
113 *cross:* run counter to.
117 *opinion:* good opinion.

NOTES: p. 212

Ventures, or whatsoever, are all frustrate.
I do but tell you, sir. Besides, they are all
Now striving who shall first present him. Therefore —   120
I could entreat you, briefly conclude somewhat:
Prevent them if you can.

Corvino.   Death to my hopes!
This is my villainous fortune. Best to hire
Some common courtesan.

Mosca.   Aye, I thought on that, sir.
But they are all so subtle, full of art –
And age again doting and flexible —
So as (I cannot tell) we may, perchance,
Light on a quean may cheat us all.

Corvino.   'Tis true.

Mosca. No, no: it must be one that has no tricks, sir,
Some simple thing, a creature made unto it;   130
Some wench you may command. Have you no kins-
    woman?
Godso — Think, think, think, think, think, think, think,
    sir.
One o' the doctors offered there his daughter.

Corvino. How!

Mosca.   Yes, Signor Lupo, the physician.

Corvino. His daughter?

Mosca.   And a virgin, sir. Why, alas,
He knows the state of his body, what it is —
That nought can warm his blood, sir, but a fever;
Nor any incantation raise his spirit;
A long forgetfulness hath seized that part.
Besides, sir, who shall know it? Some one or two —   140

Corvino. I pray thee give me leave. [*Aside*] If any man
But I had had this luck – The thing in itself,
I know, is nothing – Wherefore should not I
As well command my blood and my affections
As this dull doctor? In the point of honour,
The cases are all one of wife and daughter.

122 *prevent:* forestall.   138 *incantation:* magical chanting.
NOTES: pp. 212–13

Mosca [*aside*]. I hear him coming.
Corvino [*aside*].   She shall do it: 'tis done.
    Slight! if this doctor, who is not engaged
    Unless it be for his counsel (which is nothing)
    Offer his daughter, what should I, that am   150
    So deeply in? I will prevent him, wretch!
    Covetous wretch! Mosca, I have determined.
Mosca. How, sir?
Corvino.   We'll make all sure. The party you wot of
    Shall be mine own wife, Mosca.
Mosca.   Sir, the thing
    (But that I would not seem to counsel you)
    I should have motioned to you at the first.
    And, make your count, you have cut all their throats.
    Why, 'tis directly taking a possession!
    And in his next fit, we may let him go.
    'Tis but to pull the pillow from his head,   160
    And he is throttled: it had been done before
    But for your scrupulous doubts.
Corvino.   Aye, a plague on't.
    My conscience fools my wit. Well, I'll be brief,
    And so be thou, lest they should be before us.
    Go home, prepare him, tell him with what zeal
    And willingness I do it: swear it was
    On the first hearing, as thou mayst do truly —
    Mine own free motion.
Mosca.   Sir, I warrant you
    I'll so possess him with it, that the rest
    Of his starved clients shall be banished all,   170
    And only you received. But come not, sir,
    Until I send, for I have something else
    To ripen for your good; you must not know it.
Corvino. But do not you forget to send now.

          152 *determined:* made up my mind.
          156 *motioned:* proposed, suggested.
          157 *make your count:* rest assured.
          168 *warrant:* assure.
          169 *possess:* impress, inspire.
              NOTES: p. 213

Mosca.   Fear not.

                    [*Exit.*]

Corvina. Where are you, wife? My Celia! wife!

         Enter CELIA.

                 – What, blubbering?
    Come, dry those tears. I think thou thought'st me in
      earnest.
    Ha! by this light, I talked so but to try thee.
    Methinks the lightness of the occasion
    Should have confirmed thee. Come, I am not jealous.
Celia. No.
Corvino.   Faith I am not, I, nor never was: 180
    It is a poor, unprofitable humour.
    Do not I know, if women have a will
    They'll do 'gainst all the watches of the world,
    And that the fiercest spies are tamed with gold?
    Tut, I am confident in thee, thou shalt see it;
    And see, I'll give thee cause too, to believe it.
    Come, kiss me. Go, and make thee ready straight
    In all thy best attire, thy choicest jewels:
    Put them all on, and with them thy best looks.
    We are invited to a solemn feast   190
    At old Volpone's, where it shall appear
    How far I am free from jealousy or fear.   [*Exeunt.*]

     181 *humour:* state of mind.   187 *straight:* immediately.

NOTES: p. 213

Act III

Scene I. [*A Street.*]

Enter MOSCA.

Mosca. I fear I shall begin to grow in love
With my dear self and my most prosperous parts,
They do so spring and burgeon. I can feel
A whimsy in my blood. I know not how,
Success hath made me wanton. I could skip
Out of my skin now, like a subtle snake,
I am so limber. O! your parasite
Is a most precious thing, dropped from above,
Not bred amongst clods and clotpoles here on earth.
I muse the mystery was not made a science,   10
It is so liberally professed. Almost
All the wise world is little else, in nature,
But parasites or sub-parasites. And yet
I mean not those that have your bare town-art,
To know who's fit to feed them; have no house,
No family, no care, and therefore mould
Tales for men's ears, to bait that sense; or get
Kitchen-invention, and some stale receipts
To please the belly, and the groin; nor those,
With their court-dog tricks, that can fawn and fleer,   20
Make their revenue out of legs and faces,
Echo my lord, and lick away a moth:
But your fine, elegant rascal, that can rise
And stoop almost together, like an arrow;
Shoot through the air as nimbly as a star;

2 *parts:* talents.   3 *burgeon:* bud, grow, flourish.
4 *whimsy:* capriciousness, whirling.   7 *limber:* lithe and nimble.
10 *I muse:* I am surprised.   18 *kitchen-invention:* back-stairs gossip.
18 *stale receipts:* unoriginal ideas.

NOTES: p. 214

Turn short, as doth a swallow; and be here,
And there, and here, and yonder, all at once –
Present to any humour, all occasion;
And change a visor swifter than a thought.
This is the creature had the art born with him;   30
Toils not to learn it, but doth practise it
Out of most excellent nature: and such sparks
Are the true parasites, others but their zanies.

Enter BONARIO.

Who's this? Bonario, old Corbaccio's son?
The person I was bound to seek. Fair sir,
You are happily met.
Bonario.   That cannot be by thee.
Mosca. Why, sir?
Bonario.   Nay, pray thee know thy way, and leave me.
I would be loath to interchange discourse
With such a mate as thou art.
Mosca.   Courteous sir,
Scorn not my poverty.
Bonario.   Not I, by heaven;   40
But thou shalt give me leave to hate thy baseness.
Mosca. Baseness?
Bonario.   Aye; answer me, is not thy sloth
Sufficient argument? thy flattery?
Thy means of feeding?
Mosca.   Heaven be good to me!
These imputations are too common, sir,
And easily stuck on virtue when she's poor.
You are unequal to me; and however
Your sentence may be righteous, yet you are not,
That, ere you know me, thus proceed in censure:
St Mark bear witness 'gainst you, 'tis inhuman.   50
                                        [*Weeping.*]
Bonario [*aside*]. What, does he weep? The sign is soft and
          good.

26 *turn short:* double back.   39 *mate:* fellow, companion.
NOTES: pp. 214–15

　　I do repent me that I was so harsh.
Mosca. 'Tis true that, swayed by strong necessity,
　　I am enforced to eat my careful bread
　　With too much obsequy; 'tis true, beside,
　　That I am fain to spin mine own poor raiment
　　Out of my mere observance, being not born
　　To a free fortune: but that I have done
　　Base offices in rending friends asunder,
　　Dividing families, betraying counsels,　　　　　　　60
　　Whispering false lies, or mining men with praises,
　　Trained their credulity with perjuries,
　　Corrupted chastity, or am in love
　　With mine own tender ease, but would not rather
　　Prove the most rugged and laborious course
　　That might redeem my present estimation,
　　Let me here perish, in all hope of goodness.
Bonario. This cannot be a personated passion.
　　I was to blame so to mistake thy nature.
　　Prithee forgive me, and speak out thy business.　　　70
Mosca. Sir, it concerns you; and though I may seem
　　At first to make a main offence in manners,
　　And in my gratitude unto my master,
　　Yet for the pure love which I bear all right
　　And hatred of the wrong, I must reveal it.
　　This very hour your father is in purpose
　　To disinherit you —
Bonario.　　　　　　　How!
Mosca.　　　　　　　　　　And thrust you forth,
　　As a mere stranger to his blood: 'tis true, sir.
　　The work no way engageth me, but as
　　I claim an interest in the general state　　　　　　80
　　Of goodness and true virtue, which I hear
　　To abound in you, and for which mere respect,
　　Without a second aim, sir, I have done it.

---

54 *careful:* hard-won.　　　　　55 *obsequy:* obsequiousness.
57 *observance:* dutiful service.　　76 *in purpose:* planning.
　　　　　79 *engageth:* concerns.

NOTES: p. 215–16

Bonario. This tale hath lost thee much of the late trust
          Thou hadst with me: it is impossible.
          I know not how to lend it any thought,
          My father should be so unnatural.
Mosca. It is a confidence that well becomes
          Your piety; and formed, no doubt, it is
          From your own simple innocence, which makes   90
          Your wrong more monstrous and abhorred. But, sir,
          I now will tell you more. This very minute
          It is, or will be, doing; and if you
          Shall be but pleased to go with me, I'll bring you –
          I dare not say where you shall see, but – where
          Your ear shall be a witness of the deed;
          Hear yourself written bastard, and professed
          The common issue of the earth.
Bonario.   I'm mazed!
Mosca. Sir, if I do it not, draw your just sword,
          And score your vengeance on my front and face;   100
          Mark me your villain. You have too much wrong,
          And I do suffer for you, sir. My heart
          Weeps blood in anguish —
Bonario.   Lead. I follow thee.
                                        [*Exeunt.*]

Scene II. [*In* VOLPONE'S *house.*]

Enter VOLPONE, *followed by* NANO, ANDROGYNO *and*
CASTRONE.

Volpone. Mosca stays long, methinks. Bring forth your sports
          And help to make the wretched time more sweet.
Nano. Dwarf, fool, and eunuch, well met here we be.
          A question it now were whether of us three,
          Being all the known delicates of a rich man,
          In pleasing him claim the precedency can.

98 *mazed:* amazed, bewildered.   100 *front:* brows, forehead.
          5 *delicates:* amusements, playthings.
                    NOTES: p. 216

Castro. *I claim for myself.* Andro. *And so doth the fool.*
Nano.   *'Tis foolish indeed: let me set you both to school.*
            First for your dwarf: he's little and witty
                And everything, as it is little, is pretty,   10
            Else why do men say to a creature of my shape,
                So soon as they see him, 'It's a pretty little ape'?
            And why a pretty ape but for pleasing imitation
                Of greater men's action, in a ridiculous fashion?
            Beside, this feat body of mine doth not crave
                Half the meat, drink and cloth one of your bulks
                will have.
            Admit your fool's face be the mother of laughter,
                Yet, for his brain, it must always come after;
            And though that do feed him, it's a pitiful case,
                His body is beholding to such a bad face.   20
                                        (*Knocking.*)
Volpone. Who's there? My couch! Away! Look, Nano, see!
      Give me my caps first—Go, inquire!

            [*Exuent* NANO, ANDROGYNO *and* CASTRONE.]

                                    Now, Cupid
      Send it be Mosca, and with fair return.
Nano [*at the door*].   It is the beauteous madam —
Volpone.   Would-be – is it?
Nano. The same.
Volpone.   Now torment on me! Squire her in,
      For she will enter, or dwell here for ever.
      Nay, quickly. [*Retiring to his couch.*] That my fit were
          past! I fear
      A second hell too, that my loathing this
      Will quite expel my appetite to the other.
      Would she were taking now her tedious leave.   30
      Lord, how it threats me, what I am to suffer!

            Enter NANO *with* LADY POLITIC WOULD-BE.

Lady P. W. I thank you, good sir. Pray you signify
            15 *feat:* dainty.   16 *bulks:* massive bodies.
                        NOTES: p. 216

Unto your patron I am here. This band
Shows not my neck enough – I trouble you, sir;
Let me request you bid one of my women
Come hither to me. In good faith, I am dressed
Most favourably to-day. It is no matter:
'Tis well enough.

[*Enter* 1 Lady's Maid.]

                  Look, see these petulant things,
How they have done this!
Volpone [*aside*].   I do feel the fever
Entering in at mine ears. O for a charm   40
To fright it hence!
Lady P. W.   Come nearer: is this curl
In his right place, or this? Why is this higher
Than all the rest? You have not washed your eyes yet?
Or do they not stand even in your head?
Where is your fellow? Call her. [*Exit* 1 Lady's Maid.]
Nano.   Now St Mark
Deliver us! Anon she'll beat her women
Because her nose is red.

[*Enter* 1 *and* 2 Lady's Maids.]

Lady P. W.   I pray you, view
This tire, forsooth: are all things apt, or no?
1 *Maid.* One hair a little here sticks out, forsooth.
Lady P. W. Does't so, forsooth? And where was your dear
     sight   50
When it did so, forsooth? What now, bird-eyed?
And you, too? Pray you both, approach and mend it.
Now, by that light I muse you're not ashamed.
I, that have preached these things so oft unto you,
Read you the principles, argued all the grounds,
Disputed every fitness, every grace,
Called you to counsel of so frequent dressings —

46 *anon:* any minute now.   48 *tire:* head-dress; *apt:* as they should be.
                 52 *mend it:* put it right.
NOTES: p. 217

Nano [*aside*]. More carefully than of your fame or honour.
Lady P. W. Made you acquainted what an ample dowry
    The knowledge of these things would be unto you,   60
    Able alone to get you noble husbands
    At your return: and you thus to neglect it!
    Besides, you seeing what a curious nation
    The Italians are, what will they say of me?
    'The English lady cannot dress herself' —
    Here's a fine imputation to our country!
    Well, go your ways, and stay in the next room.
    This fucus was too coarse too; it's no matter.
    Good sir, you'll give them entertainment?
                   [*Exeunt* NANO *and* Lady's Maids.]

Volpone. The storm comes toward me.
Lady P. W.   How does my Volp?   70
Volpone. Troubled with noise, I cannot sleep. I dreamt
    That a strange fury entered now my house,
    And with the dreadful tempest of her breath
    Did cleave my roof asunder.
Lady P. W.   Believe me, and I
    Had the most fearful dream, could I remember it —
Volpone [*aside*]. Out on my fate! I have given her the occa-
    sion
    How to torment me: she will tell me hers.
Lady P. W. Methought the golden mediocrity,
    Polite, and delicate —
Volpone.   O, if you do love me,
    No more: I sweat and suffer at the mention   80
    Of any dream. Feel how I tremble yet.
Lady P. W. Alas, good soul! the passion of the heart.
    Seed-pearl were good now, boiled with syrup of apples,
    Tincture of gold, and coral, citron-pills,
    Your elecampane root, myrobalanes —
Volpone [*aside*]. Ah me, I have taken a grasshopper by the
    wing.

        63 *curious:* precise, particular.
        82 *passion of the heart:* heartburn.
           NOTES: pp. 217–18

Lady P. W. Burnt silk and amber. You have muscadel
    Good in the house —
Volpone.   You will not drink, and part?
Lady P. W. No, fear not that. I doubt we shall not get
    Some English saffron – half a dram would serve;   90
    Your sixteen cloves, a little musk, dried mints;
    Bugloss, and barley-meal —
Volpone [*aside*].   She's in again.
    Before I feigned diseases, now I have one.
Lady P. W. And these applied with a right scarlet cloth —
Volpone [*aside*]. Another flood of words! a very torrent!
Lady P. W. Shall I, sir, make you a poultice?
Volpone.   No, no, no:
    I'm very well; you need prescribe no more.
Lady P. W. I have a little studied physic; but now
    I'm all for music, save, in the forenoons,
    An hour or two for painting. I would have   100
    A lady, indeed, to have all letters and arts,
    Be able to discourse, to write, to paint,
    But principal, as Plato holds, your music
    (And so does wise Pythagoras), I take it,
    Is your true rapture: when there is consent
    In face, in voice, and clothes; and is, indeed,
    Our sex's chiefest ornament.
Volpone.   The poet
    As old in time as Plato, and as knowing,
    Says that your highest female grace is silence.
Lady P. W. Which of your poets? Petrarch, or Tasso, or
    Dante?   110
    Guarini? Ariosto? Aretine?
    Cieco di Hadria? I have read them all.
Volpone [*aside*]. Is everything a cause to my destruction?
Lady P. W. I think I have two or three of them about me.
Volpone [*aside*]. The sun, the sea, will sooner both stand still
    Than her eternal tongue. Nothing can scape it.

92 *She's in:* she's off.   99 *forenoons:* mornings.
105 *consent:* harmony.   116 *scape:* escape.
NOTES: pp. 218–19

Lady P. W. Here's Pastor Fido —
Volpone [*aside*].   Profess obstinate silence,
    That's now my safest.
Lady P. W.   All our English writers,
    I mean such as are happy in the Italian,
    Will deign to steal out of this author mainly,   120
    Almost as much as from Montagnié:
    He has so modern and facile a vein,
    Fitting the time, and catching the court-ear.
    Your Petrarch is more passionate, yet he,
    In days of sonneting, trusted them with much.
    Dante is hard, and few can understand him.
    But, for a desperate wit, there's Aretine;
    Only his pictures are a little obscene —
    You mark me not.
Volpone.   Alas, my mind's perturbed.
Lady P. W. Why, in such cases we must cure ourselves,   130
    Make use of our philosophy —
Volpone.   Oh me!
Lady P. W. And as we find our passions do rebel,
    Encounter them with reason, or divert them
    By giving scope unto some other humour
    Of lesser danger; as in politic bodies
    There's nothing more doth overwhelm the judgment
    And cloud the understanding, than too much
    Settling and fixing, and, as 'twere, subsiding
    Upon one object. For the incorporating
    Of these same outward things into that part   140
    Which we call mental, leaves some certain fæces
    That stop the organs, and, as Plato says,
    Assassinates our knowledge.
Volpone [*aside*].   Now the spirit
    Of patience help me!

118 *mainly:* a great deal.   122 *facile:* straightforward.
127 *desperate:* reckless.   133 *encounter:* oppose.
134 *humour:* emotion, mood, passion.
135 *politic bodies:* public councils.

NOTES: pp. 219–20

H

Lady P. W. Come, in faith, I must
Visit you more a days, and make you well.
Laugh and be lusty.
Volpone [*aside*]. My good angel save me!
Lady P. W. There was but one sole man in all the world
With whom I e'er could sympathise; and he
Would lie you often three, four hours together
To hear me speak; and be sometime so rapt, 150
As he would answer me quite from the purpose,
Like you – and you are like him, just. I'll discourse,
And it be but only, sir, to bring you asleep,
How we did spend our time and loves together
For some six years.
Volpone. Oh, oh, oh, oh, oh, oh!
Lady P. W. For we were coætanei, and brought up —
Volpone [*aside*]. Some power, some fate, some fortune rescue
me!

Enter MOSCA.

Mosca. God save you, madam!
Lady P. W. Good sir.
Volpone. Mosca, welcome,
Welcome to my redemption!
Mosca. Why, sir?
Volpone. Oh,
Rid me of this my torture, quickly, there; 160
My madam with the everlasting voice:
The bells, in time of pestilence, ne'er made
Like noise, or were in that perpetual motion.
The cock-pit comes not near it. All my house
But now steamed like a bath with her thick breath.
A lawyer could not have been heard; nor scarce
Another woman, such a hail of words
She has let fall. For hell's sake, rid her hence.
Mosca. Has she presented?

146 *lusty:* merry. 153 *And:* if.
165 *But now:* a moment ago.
NOTES: pp. 220–1

Volpone. Oh, I do not care.
I'll take her absence upon any price, 170
With any loss.
Mosca. Madam —
Lady P. W. I have brought your patron
A toy, a cap here, of mine own work —
Mosca. 'Tis well.
I had forgot to tell you I saw your knight
Where you'd little think it —
Lady P. W. Where?
Mosca. Marry,
Where yet, if you make haste, you may apprehend him,
Rowing upon the water in a gondola
With the most cunning courtesan of Venice.
Lady P. W. Is't true?
Mosca. Pursue them, and believe your eyes.
Leave me to make your gift.
[*Exit* LADY POLITIC WOULD-BE.]
I knew 'twould take:
For lightly, they that use themselves most licence 180
Are still most jealous.
Volpone. Mosca, hearty thanks
For thy quick fiction, and delivery of me.
Now to my hopes, what sayst thou?

[*Enter* LADY POLITIC WOULD-BE.]

Lady P. W. But, do you hear, sir? —
Volpone. Again! I fear a paroxysm.
Lady P. W. Which way
Rowed they together?
Mosca. Toward the Rialto.
Lady P. W. I pray you lend me your dwarf.
Mosca. I pray you take
him. [*Exit* LADY POLITIC WOULD-BE.]
Your hopes, sir, are like happy blossoms, fair,

180 *lightly:* very often, commonly.   181 *still:* always.
NOTES: p. 221

And promise timely fruit, if you will stay
But the maturing. Keep you at your couch.
Corbaccio will arrive straight with the will;   190
When he is gone, I'll tell you more.   [*Exit.*]

Volpone.   My blood,
My spirits are returned; I am alive;
And like your wanton gamester at primero,
Whose thought had whispered to him, 'Not go less',
Methinks I lie and draw – for an encounter.

MOSCA *leads in* BONARIO *at one side.*

Mosca. Sir, here concealed, you may hear all. But pray you
Have patience, sir. (*Knocking.*) The same's your father
knocks.
I am compelled to leave you.

Bonario.   Do so. Yet
Cannot my thought imagine this a truth.

[*He conceals himself.*]

Enter CORVINO *and* CELIA *from the opposite side.* MOSCA
approaches them.

Mosca. Death on me, you are come too soon! What meant
you?   200
Did not I say I would send?

Corvino.   Yes, but I feared
You might forget it, and then they prevent us.

Mosca. Prevent? Did ere man haste so for his horns?
A courtier would not ply it so for a place.
Well, now there's no helping it, stay here.
I'll presently return.   [*He leaves them.*]

Corvino.   Where are you, Celia?
You know not wherefore I have brought you hither?

Celia. Not well, except you told me.

Corvino.   Now I will:
Hark hither.   [*They converse apart.*]

188 *timely:* seasonal.   190 *straight:* forthwith.
206 *presently:* straight away.

NOTES: pp. 221–2

MOSCA *returns to* BONARIO.

Mosca.   Sir, your father has sent word
    It will be half an hour ere he come;   210
    And therefore, if you please go walk the while
    Into that gallery – at the upper end
    There are some books to entertain the time;
    And I'll take care no man shall come unto you, sir.
Bonario. Yes, I will stay there. [*Aside*] I do doubt this fellow.
                    [*He walks aside alone, and reads.*]
Mosca. There he is far enough. He can hear nothing.
    And, for his father, I can keep him off.
Corvino [*to* CELIA]. Nay, now, there is no starting back; and
            therefore
    Resolve upon it: I have so decreed.
    It must be done. Nor would I move it afore,   220
    Because I would avoid all shifts and tricks
    That might deny me.
Celia.   Sir, let me beseech you,
    Affect not these strange trials. If you doubt
    My chastity, why, lock me up for ever;
    Make me the heir of darkness; let me live
    Where I may please your fears, if not your trust.
Corvino. Believe it, I have no such humour, I.
    All that I speak I mean; yet I am not mad,
    Not horn-mad, see you? Go to, show yourself
    Obedient, and a wife.
Celia.   O heaven!
Corvino.   I say it: 230
    Do so.
Celia.   Was this the train? *Was this where everything*
                                was leading?
Corvino.   I've told you reasons;
    What the physicians have set down; how much
    It may concern me; what my engagements are;

218 *starting back:* crying off.   221 *shifts:* stratagems.
229 *horn-mad:* impatient to be cuckolded.
233 *engagements:* business commitments.
                    NOTES: p. 222

My means; and the necessity of those means
For my recovery: wherefore, if you be
Loyal and mine, be won, respect my venture.
Celia. Before your honour?
Corvino.   Honour! tut, a breath:
There's no such thing in nature; a mere term
Invented to awe fools. What is my gold
The worse for touching, clothes for being looked on?   240
Why, this is no more. An old, decrepit wretch,
That has no sense, no sinew; takes his meat
With others' fingers; only knows to gape
When you do scald his gums; a voice; a shadow;
And what can this man hurt you?
Celia.   Lord! what spirit
Is this hath entered him?
Corvino.   And for your fame,
That's such a jig; as if I would go tell it,
Cry it on the Piazza. Who shall know it
But he that cannot speak it, and this fellow
Whose lips are in my pocket? – save yourself: 250
If you'll proclaim it, you may; I know no other
Should come to know it.
Celia.   Are heaven and saints then
    nothing?
Will they be blind or stupid?
Corvino.   How?
Celia.   Good sir,
Be jealous still, emulate them; and think
What hate they burn with toward every sin.
Corvino. I grant you. If I thought it were a sin
I would not urge you. Should I offer this
To some young Frenchman, or hot Tuscan blood
That had read Aretine, conned all his prints,
Knew every quirk within lust's labyrinth   260
And were professed critic in lechery;

<hr>

245 *spirit:* evil spirit.   246 *fame:* reputation.
247 *jig:* to-do, fuss about nothing.

NOTES: p. 222

And I would look upon him, and applaud him.
This were a sin: but here 'tis contrary,
A pious work, mere charity for physic,
And honest polity to assure mine own.
Celia. O heaven! canst thou suffer such a change?
Volpone. Thou art mine honour, Mosca, and my pride,
 My joy, my tickling, my delight. Go bring them.
Mosca [*advancing*]. Please you draw near, sir.
Corvino.   Come on, what —
 You will not be rebellious? By that light —   270
Mosca. Sir, Signor Corvino, here, is come to see you.
Volpone. Oh!
Mosca.   And hearing of the consultation had,
 So lately, for your health, is come to offer,
 Or rather, sir, to prostitute —
Corvino.   Thanks, sweet Mosca.
Mosca. Freely, unasked, or unentreated —
Corvino.   Well.
Mosca. As the true fervent instance of his love,
 His own most fair and proper wife; the beauty
 Only of price in Venice —
Corvino.   'Tis well urged.
Mosca. To be your comfortress, and to preserve you.
Volpone. Alas, I am past already. Pray you, thank him   280
 For his good care and promptness; but for that,
 'Tis a vain labour e'en to fight against heaven;
 Applying fire to a stone; – [*coughing*] Uh! uh! uh! uh! –
 Making a dead leaf grow again. I take
 His wishes gently, though; and you may tell him
 What I have done for him. Marry, my state is hopeless.
 Will him to pray for me; and to use his fortune
 With reverence when he comes to it.
Mosca.   Do you hear, sir?
 Go to him with your wife.

---

263 *contrary:* just the opposite.   265 *polity:* diplomacy.
268 *tickling:* gratification.   276 *instance:* demonstration.
    277 *proper:* comely.
    NOTES: pp. 222–3

Corvino.   Heart of my father!
   Wilt thou persist thus? Come, I pray thee, come.   290
   Thou seest 'tis nothing. Celia! By this hand
   I shall grow violent. Come, do it, I say.
Celia. Sir, kill me rather. I will take down poison,
   Eat burning coals, do anything —
Corvino.   Be damned!
   Heart, I will drag thee hence, home by the hair;
   Cry thee a strumpet through the streets; rip up
   Thy mouth unto thine ears; and slit thy nose
   Like a raw rochet. Do not tempt me: come,
   Yield. I am loath —. Death, I will buy some slave
   Whom I will kill, and bind thee to him alive,   300
   And at my window hang you forth, devising
   Some monstrous crime, which I, in capital letters,
   Will eat into thy flesh with aquafortis
   And burning corsives, on this stubborn breast.
   Now, by the blood thou hast incensed, I'll do it.
Celia. Sir, what you please, you may. I am your martyr.
Corvino. Be not thus obstinate; I have not deserved it:
   Think who it is entreats you. Pray thee, sweet –
   Good faith, thou shalt have jewels, gowns, attires,
   What thou wilt think and ask. Do but go kiss him;   310
   Or touch him but. For my sake. At my suit –
   This once. No? Not? I shall remember this.
   Will you disgrace me thus? Do you thirst my undoing?
Mosca. Nay, gentle lady, be advised.
Corvino.   No, no.
   She has watched her time. God's precious, this is scurvy,
   'Tis very scurvy; and you are —
Mosca.   Nay, good sir.
Corvino. An arrant locust – by heaven, a locust! Whore,
   Crocodile, that hast thy tears prepared,
   Expecting how thou'lt bid them flow.

     293 *take down:* swallow.   304 *corsives:* corrosives.
     311 *but:* only.   317 *locust:* plague.
          319 *expecting:* waiting to see.

NOTES: p. 223

Mosca.   Nay, pray you, sir,
　　She will consider.
Celia.   Would my life would serve   320
　　To satisfy.
Corvino.   'Sdeath! if she would but speak to him,
　　And save my reputation, it were somewhat.
　　But spitefully to affect my utter ruin —
Mosca. Aye, now you have put your fortune in her hands.
　　Why, i'faith, it is her modesty. I must quit her.
　　If you were absent, she would be more coming;
　　I know it, and dare undertake for her.
　　What woman can, before her husband? Pray you,
　　Let us depart and leave her here.
Corvino.   Sweet Celia,
　　Thou mayst redeem all yet; I'll say no more: 330
　　If not, esteem yourself as lost. Nay, stay there.
　　　　　　　　　[*Exeunt* CORVINO *and* MOSCA.]
Celia. O God, and his good angels! whither, whither
　　Is shame fled human breasts, that with such ease
　　Men dare put off your honours, and their own?
　　Is that, which ever was a cause of life,
　　Now placed beneath the basest circumstance,
　　And modesty an exile made, for money?
Volpone (*leaping from his couch*). Aye, in Corvino and such
　　　　earth-fed minds,
　　That never tasted the true heaven of love.
　　Assure thee, Celia, he that would sell thee   340
　　Only for hope of gain, and that uncertain,
　　He would have sold his part of Paradise
　　For ready money, had he met a copeman.
　　Why art thou mazed to see me thus revived?
　　Rather applaud thy beauty's miracle –
　　'Tis thy great work – that hath, not now alone,

320 *consider:* think again.　　　　323 *affect:* seek.
325 *quit:* excuse, acquit.　　　　　326 *coming:* forward.
333 *fled:* fled from.　　　　　　　　334 *put off:* set aside.
343 *copeman:* dealer, merchant.　344 *mazed:* amazed.
NOTES: p. 223

But sundry times, raised me in several shapes,
And, but this morning, like a mountebank
To see thee at thy window. Aye, before
I would have left my practice for thy love,   350
In varying figures I would have contended
With the blue Proteus, or the horned flood.
Now art thou welcome.

Celia.   Sir!

Volpone.   Nay, fly me not.
Nor let thy false imagination
That I was bed-rid, make thee think I am so:
Thou shalt not find it. I am now as fresh,
As hot, as high, and in as jovial plight
As when, in that so celebrated scene,
At recitation of our comedy
For entertainment of the great Valois,   360
I acted young Antinous, and attracted
The eyes and ears of all the ladies present,
To admire each graceful gesture, note, and footing.
(*He sings:*)

> *Come, my Celia, let us prove,*
> *While we can, the sports of love.*
> *Time will not be ours for ever;*
> *He, at length, our good will sever:*
> *Spend not then his gifts in vain.*
> *Suns that set may rise again;*
> *But if once we lose this light,*   370
> *'Tis with us perpetual night.*
> *Why should we defer our joys?*
> *Fame and rumour are but toys.*
> *Cannot we delude the eyes*
> *Of a few poor household spies?*
> *Or his easier ears beguile,*
> *Thus removed, by our wile?*

347 *sundry:* various.   347 *several shapes:* different disguises.
351 *contended With:* vied with, outdone.   357 *plight:* condition.
363 *footing:* step.   364 *prove:* try, taste.

NOTES: pp. 223–4

> 'Tis no sin love's fruits to steal,
> But the sweet thefts to reveal:— *the only crime is to tell*
> To be taken, to be seen, 380
> These have crimes accounted been.

Celia. Some serene blast me, or dire lightning strike
    This my offending face!
Volpone.   Why droops my Celia?
    Thou hast, in place of a base husband, found
    A worthy lover: use thy fortune well,
    With secrecy and pleasure. See, behold,
    What thou art queen of – not in expectation,
    As I feed others, but possessed and crowned.
    See, here, a rope of pearl; and each more orient
    Than the brave Egyptian queen caroused:— *Cleopatra* 390
    Dissolve and drink them. See, a carbuncle
    May put out both the eyes of our St Mark;
    A diamond would have bought Lollia Paulina
    When she came in like star-light, hid with jewels
    That were the spoils of provinces. Take these
    And wear, and lose them; yet remains an earring
    To purchase them again, and this whole state.
    A gem but worth a private patrimony,
    Is nothing: we will eat such at a meal.
    The heads of parrots, tongues of nightingales, 400
    The brains of peacocks, and of ostriches
    Shall be our food, and, could we get the phœnix,
    Though nature lost her kind, she were our dish.
Celia. Good sir, these things might move a mind affected
    With such delights; but I, whose innocence
    Is all I can think wealthy, or worth the enjoying,
    And which, once lost, I have nought to lose beyond it,
    Cannot be taken with these sensual baits.
    If you have conscience —
Volpone.   'Tis the beggar's virtue.
    If thou hast wisdom, hear me, Celia. 410
    Thy baths shall be the juice of July-flowers,

398 *patrimony:* inheritance.   406 *wealthy:* valuable.
NOTES: pp. 224–5

Spirit of roses, and of violets,
The milk of unicorns, and panthers' breath
Gathered in bags, and mixed with Cretan wines.
Our drink shall be prepared gold and amber;
Which we will take until my roof whirl round
With the vertigo; and my dwarf shall dance,
My eunuch sing, my fool make up the antic,
Whilst we, in changed shapes, act Ovid's tales:
Thou like Europa now and I like Jove,   420
Then I like Mars and thou like Erycine;
So of the rest, till we have quite run through
And wearied all the fables of the gods.
Then will I have thee in more modern forms,
Attired like some spritely dame of France,
Brave Tuscan lady, or proud Spanish beauty;
Sometimes unto the Persian Sophy's wife;
Or the Grand Signor's mistress; and for change,
To one of our most artful courtesans,
Or some quick Negro, or cold Russian;   430
And I will meet thee in as many shapes,
Where we may, so, transfuse our wandering souls
Out at our lips, and score up sums of pleasures,
[*He sings:*]

> *That the curious shall not know*
> *How to tell them as they flow;*
> *And the envious, when they find*
> *What their number is, be pined.*

Celia. If you have ears that will be pierced, or eyes
That can be opened, a heart may be touched,
Or any part that yet sounds man about you;   440
If you have touch of holy saints, or heaven,
Do me the grace to let me scape. If not,
Be bountiful and kill me. You do know,
I am a creature hither ill betrayed
By one whose shame I would forget it were.

418 *antic:* fantastic performance.   437 *pined:* tormented.
442 *scape:* escape.
NOTES: pp. 225–6

If you will deign me neither of these graces,
Yet feed your wrath, sir, rather than your lust,
(It is a vice comes nearer manliness)
And punish that unhappy crime of nature
Which you miscall my beauty: flay my face,   450
Or poison it with ointments, for seducing
Your blood to this rebellion; rub these hands
With what may cause an eating leprosy,
E'en to my bones and marrow; anything
That may disfavour me, save in my honour;
And I will kneel to you, pray for you, pay down
A thousand hourly vows, sir, for your health,
Report and think you virtuous —

Volpone.   Think me cold,
Frozen, and impotent, and so report me?
That I had Nestor's hernia, thou wouldst think.   460
I do degenerate and abuse my nation
To play with opportunity thus long.
I should have done the act, and then have parleyed.
Yield, or I'll force thee.

Celia.   O! just God!

Volpone.   In vain —

BONARIO *leaps out from where* MOSCA *has placed him.*

Bonario. Forbear, foul ravisher! libidinous swine!
Free the forced lady, or thou diest, impostor.
But that I am loath to snatch thy punishment
Out of the hand of justice, thou shouldst yet
Be made the timely sacrifice of vengeance
Before this altar and this dross, thy idol.   470
Lady, let's quit the place: it is the den
Of villainy. Fear nought, you have a guard;
And he ere long shall meet his just reward.
                              [*Exeunt* BONARIO *and* CELIA.]
Volpone. Fall on me, roof, and bury me in ruin:
Become my grave, that wert my shelter. O!

455 *save:* except.
NOTES: p. 226

I am unmasked, unspirited, undone,
Betrayed to beggary, to infamy —

Enter MOSCA, *wounded and bleeding*.

Mosca. Where shall I run, most wretched shame of men,
    To beat out my unlucky brains?
Volpone.   Here, here.
    What! dost thou bleed?
Mosca.   O, that his well-driven sword   480
    Had been so courteous to have cleft me down
    Unto the navel ere I lived to see
    My life, my hopes, my spirits, my patron, all
    Thus desperately engaged by my error.
Volpone. Woe on thy fortune!
Mosca.   And my follies, sir.
Volpone. Thou hast made me miserable.
Mosca.   And myself, sir.
    Who would have thought he would have hearkened so?
Volpone. Whall shall we do?
Mosca.   I know not. If my heart
    Could expiate the mischance, I'd pluck it out.
    Will you be pleased to hang me, or cut my throat?   490
    And I'll requite you, sir. Let's die like Romans,
    Since we have lived like Grecians.   (*Knocking.*)
Volpone.   Hark! who's there?
    I hear some footing: officers, the saffi,
    Come to apprehend us! I do feel the brand
    Hissing already at my forehead. Now
    Mine ears are boring.
Mosca.   To your couch, sir. You
    Make that place good, however. [VOLPONE *lies down.*]
        Guilty men
    Suspect what they deserve still.

Enter CORBACCIO. VOLTORE *follows at a distance, unseen.*

                              Signor Corbaccio!

476 *unspirited:* cast down, dejected.   484 *engaged:* entangled, betrayed.
493 *footing:* footsteps.   498 *still:* always.

                    NOTES: pp. 226–7

Corbac. Why, how now, Mosca?

Mosca.   O, undone, amazed, sir.
    Your son, I know not by what accident,   500
    Acquainted with your purpose to my patron
    Touching your will and making him your heir,
    Entered our house with violence, his sword drawn,
    Sought for you, called you wretch, unnatural,
    Vowed he would kill you.

Corbac.   Me?

Mosca.   Yes, and my patron.

Corbac. This act shall disinherit him indeed: *Renounces his intension to re-establish Bonario later.*
    Here is the will

Mosca.   'Tis well, sir.

Corbac.   Right and well.
    Be you as careful now for me.

Mosca.   My life, sir,
    Is not more tendered; I am only yours.

Corbac. How does he? Will he die shortly, think'st thou?

Mosca.   I fear   510
    He'll outlast May.

Corbac.   Today?

Mosca.   No, last out May, sir.

Corbac. Couldst thou not give him a dram? *fatal dose*

Mosca.   O, by no means, sir.

Corbac. Nay, I'll not bid you.

Voltore [*aside*].   This is a knave, I see.

Mosca [*seeing* VOLTORE, *aside*]. How! Signor Voltore! Did
    he hear me?

Voltore. Parasite!

Mosca [*affecting surprise*]. Who's that? O, sir, most timely
                 welcome —

Voltore.   Scarce,
    To the discovery of your tricks, I fear.
    You are his only? and mine also, are you not? *You tell him the same as you told me.*

Mosca. Who? I, sir?

508 *careful:* solicitous, painstaking.   513 *bid:* command.
509 *tendered:* cared for, safeguarded.   515 *timely:* opportunely.

NOTES: p. 227

Voltore.   You, sir. What device is this
    About a will?
Mosca.   A plot for you, sir.
Voltore.   Come,
    Put not your foists upon me: I shall scent them.   520
Mosca. Did you not hear it?
Voltore.   Yes, I hear Corbaccio
    Hath made your patron, there, his heir.
Mosca.   'Tis true,
    By my device, drawn to it by my plot,
    With hope —
Voltore.   Your patron should reciprocate?
    And you have promised?
Mosca.   For your good, I did, sir.
    Nay, more, I told his son, brought, hid him here,
    Where he might hear his father pass the deed;
    Being persuaded to it by this thought, sir,
    That the unnaturalness, first, of the act,
    And then his father's oft disclaiming in him   530
    (Which I did mean to help on) would sure enrage him
    To do some violence upon his parent,
    On which the law should take sufficient hold,
    And you be stated in a double hope.
    Truth be my comfort, and my conscience,
    My only aim was to dig you a fortune
    Out of these two old, rotten supulchres —
Voltore. I cry thee mercy, Mosca.
Mosca.   — worth your patience
    And your great merit, sir. And see the change!
Voltore. Why, what success?
Mosca.   Most hapless! You must help, sir. 540
    Whilst we expected the old raven, in comes
    Corvino's wife, sent hither by her husband.
Voltore. What, with a present?
Mosca.   No, sir, on visitation

539 *change:* reversal (of my hopes).
540 *hapless:* luckless, unfortunate.
NOTES: pp. 227–8

(I'll tell you how anon) and, staying long,
The youth he grows impatient, rushes forth,
Seizeth the lady, wounds me, makes her swear
(Or he would murder her, that was his vow)
To affirm my patron to have done her rape,
Which how unlike it is, you see; and hence,
With that pretext, he's gone to accuse his father,   550
Defame my patron, defeat you —

Voltore.   Where's her husband?
Let him be sent for straight.

Mosca.   Sir, I'll go fetch him.

Voltore. Bring him to the Scrutineo.

Mosca.   Sir, I will.

Voltore. This must be stopped.

Mosca.   O, you do nobly, sir.
Alas, 'twas laboured all, sir, for your good;
Nor was there want of counsel in the plot;
But fortune can, at any time, o'erthrow
The projects of a hundred learned clerks, sir.

Corbac. [*overhearing*] What's that?

Voltore.   Wilt please you, sir, to
go along?

                    [*Exit* CORBACCIO *and* VOLTORE.]

Mosca. Patron, go in, and pray for our success.   560

Volpone [*rising*]. Need makes devotion. Heaven your labour
bless!   [*Exeunt.*]

553 *Scrutineo:* Venetian Senate House.   556 *counsel:* deliberation.
558 *clerks:* scholars.

NOTES: p. 228

I

Act IV

Scene I. [*A Street.*]

Enter SIR POLITIC WOULD-BE *and* PEREGRINE.

Sir P. W. I told you, sir, it was a plot. You see
What observation is. You mentioned me
For some instructions: I will tell you, sir,
(Since we are met here in this height of Venice)
Some few particulars I have set down
Only for this meridian, fit to be known
Of your crude traveller; and they are these –
I will not touch, sir, at your phrase, or clothes,
For they are old.
Peregr.   Sir, I have better.
Sir P. W.   Pardon;
I meant as they are themes.
Peregr.   O, sir, proceed.   10
I'll slander you no more of wit, good sir.
Sir P. W. First, for your garb, it must be grave and serious,
Very reserved and locked; not tell a secret
On any terms, not to your father: scarce
A fable but with caution. Make sure choice
Both of your company and discourse. Beware
You never speak a truth —
Peregr.   How?
Sir P. W.   Not to strangers,
For those be they you must converse with most;
Others I would not know, sir, but at distance,
So as I still might be a saver in them: 20

4 *height:* latitude.   7 *crude:* inexperienced.
8 *touch at:* touch upon.   9 *old:* familiar.
10 *themes:* general topics.   12 *garb:* bearing, manner.
13 *locked:* enigmatic; *not tell:* do not tell.   14 *terms:* pretext.
16 *discourse:* what you talk about.

NOTES: p. 228

You shall have tricks else passed upon you hourly.
And then, for your religion, profess none,
But wonder at the diversity of all;
And, for your part, protest, were there no other
But simply the laws of the land, you could content you.
Nick Machiavel and Monsieur Bodin, both
Were of this mind. Then must you learn the use
And handling of your silver fork at meals,
The metal of your glass – these are main matters
With your Italian; and to know the hour   30
When you must eat your melons and your figs.

Peregr. Is that a point of state too?

Sir P. W.   Here it is:
For your Venetian, if he see a man
Preposterous in the least, he has him straight;
He has: he strips him. I'll acquaint you, sir –
I now have lived here 'tis some fourteen months –
Within the first week of my landing here
All took me for a citizen of Venice,
I knew the forms so well.

Peregr. [*aside*].   And nothing else.

Sir P. W. I had read Contarene, took me a house,   40
Dealt with my Jews to furnish it with movables —
Well, if I could but find one man, one man
To mine own heart, whom I durst trust, I would —

Peregr. What, what, sir?

Sir P. W.   Make him rich; make him a fortune.
He should not think again; I would command it.

Peregr. As how?

Sir P. W.   With certain projects that I have
Which I may not discover.

Peregr. [*aside*].   If I had

---

29 *main:* important.   35 *strips him:* exposes him.
39 *forms:* conventions.   41 *movables:* chattels, movable possessions.
45 *command:* insist on.   47 *discover:* communicate, make known.
                               NOTES: pp. 228–9

But one to wager with, I would lay odds, now,
He tells me instantly.

Sir P. W.   One is – and that
I care not greatly who knows – to serve the state   50
Of Venice with red herrings for three years,
And at a certain rate, from Rotterdam,
Where I have correspondence. There's a letter,
Sent me from one of the States, and to that purpose;
He cannot write his name, but that's his mark.

Peregr. He is a chandler?

Sir P. W.   No, a cheesemonger.
There are some others too with whom I treat
About the same negotiation,
And I will undertake it; for, 'tis thus
I'll do't with ease; I have cast it all: your hoy   60
Carries but three men in her and a boy,
And she shall make me three returns a year.
So if there come but one of three, I save;
If two, I can defalk. But this is, now,
If my main project fail.

Peregr.   Then you have others?

Sir P. W. I should be loath to draw the subtle air
Of such a place without my thousand aims.
I'll not dissemble, sir: where'er I come,
I love to be considerative; and 'tis true,
I have at my free hours thought upon   70
Some certain goods unto the state of Venice,
Which I do call my cautions; and, sir, which
I mean, in hope of pension, to propound
To the Great Council, then unto the Forty,
So to the Ten. My means are made already —

Peregr. By whom?

Sir P. W.   Sir, one that, though his place be
obscure,

---

53 *correspondence:* agents.	57 *treat:* confer.
60 *cast:* calculated.	62 *returns:* round trips.
71 *goods:* benefits, good counsels.	72 *cautions:* precautions.

NOTES: p. 230

Yet he can sway, and they will hear him. He's
A commandator.
Peregr.   What a common sergeant?
Sir P. W. Sir, such as they are, put it in their mouths
What they should say, sometimes, as well as greater.   80
I think I have my notes to show you —
                              [*Searching his pockets.*]
Peregr.   Good, sir.
Sir P. W. But you shall swear unto me, on your gentry,
Not to anticipate —
Peregr.   I, sir?
Sir P. W.   Nor reveal
A circumstance — My paper is not with me.
Peregr. O, but you can remember, sir.
Sir P. W.   My first is
Concerning tinder-boxes. You must know,
No family is here without its box.
Now, sir, it being so portable a thing,
Put case that you or I were ill affected
Unto the state: sir, with it in our pockets,   90
Might not I go into the arsenal,
Or you? – come out again, and none the wiser?
Peregr. Except yourself, sir.
Sir P. W.   Go to, then. I therefore
Advertise to the state, how fit it were
That none but such as were known patriots,
Sound lovers of their country, should be suffered
To enjoy them in their houses; and even those
Sealed at some office, and at such a bigness
As might not lurk in pockets.
Peregr.   Admirable!
Sir P. W. My next is, how to inquire and be resolved,   100
By present demonstration, whether a ship,
Newly arrived from Soría, or from
Any suspected part of all the Levant,
Be guilty of the plague; and where they use

94 *Advertise:* make known.   104 *use:* are accustomed.

NOTES: pp. 230–1

To lie out forty, fifty days, sometimes,
About the Lazaretto, for their trial,
I'll save that charge and loss unto the merchant,
And, in an hour, clear the doubt.
Peregr.   Indeed, sir?
Sir P. W. Or I will lose my labour.
Peregr.   My faith, that's much.
Sir P. W. Nay, sir, conceive me. It will cost me in onions   110
Some thirty livres —
Peregr.   Which is one pound sterling.
Sir P. W. Beside my waterworks – for this I do, sir:
First, I bring in your ship 'twixt two brick walls,
But those the state shall venture; on the one
I strain me a fair tarpaulin, and in that
I stick my onions, cut in halves; the other
Is full of loopholes, out of which I thrust
The noses of my bellows; and those bellows
I keep, with waterworks, in perpetual motion,
Which is the easiest matter of a hundred.   120
Now, sir, your onion, which doth naturally
Attract the infection, and your bellows blowing
The air upon him, will show instantly
By his changed colour if there be contagion;
Or else remain as fair as at the first.
Now it is known, it is nothing.
Peregr.   You are right, sir.
Sir P. W. I would I had my note.
Peregr.   Faith, so would I.
But you have done well, for once, sir.
Sir P. W.   Were I false,
Or would be made so, I could show you reasons
How I could sell this state now to the Turk,   130
Spite of their galleys, or their —
                                   [*Examining his papers.*]

110 *conceive me:* understand me.   111 *livres:* French coins.
115 *strain:* stretch.   127 *note:* patent.
128 *false:* traitorous, disloyal.   131 *Spite of:* in spite of.

Peregr.   Pray you, Sir Poll.

Sir P. W. I have them not about me.

Peregr.   That I feared:
    They are there, sir?

Sir P. W.   No, this is my diary,
    Wherein I note my actions of the day.

Peregr. Pray you, let's see, sir. What is here? [*Reads:*] 'No-
        tandum,
    A rat had gnawn my spur-leathers; notwithstanding
    I put on new, and did go forth; but first
    I threw three beans over the threshold. Item,
    I went and bought two toothpicks, whereof one
    I burst immediately, in a discourse   140
    With a Dutch merchant about ragion del stato.
    From him I went and paid a moccenigo
    For piecing my silk stockings; by the way
    I cheapened sprats; and at St Mark's I urined.'
    Faith these are politic notes!

Sir P. W.   Sir, I do slip
    No action of my life, thus, but I quote it.

Peregr. Believe me, it is wise.

Sir P. W.   Nay, sir, read forth.

        Enter, at a distance, LADY POLITIC WOULD-BE,
              NANO, *and two Lady's Maids.*

Lady P W. Where should this loose knight be, trow? Sure,
        he's housed.

Nano. Why, then he's fast.

Lady P. W.   Aye, he plays both with me.
    I pray you stay. This heat will do more harm   150
    To my complexion than his heart is worth.
    (I do not care to hinder, but to take him.)
    How it comes off!   [*Rubbing her cheeks.*]

1 *Maid.*   My master's yonder.

---

143 *piecing:* repairing.   144 *cheapened:* haggled over.
145 *politic:* shrewd, handy; *slip:* pass over.
146 *quote it:* note it down.   147 *read forth:* read on.

NOTES: pp. 231–2

Lady P. W.   Where?

2 *Maid*. With a young gentleman.

Lady P. W.   That same's the party –
In man's apparel. Pray you, sir, jog my knight.
I will be tender to his reputation,
However he demerit.

Sir P. W. [*seeing her*].   My lady!

Peregr.   Where?

Sir P. W. 'Tis she indeed, sir; you shall know her. She is,
Were she not mine, a lady of that merit
For fashion and behaviour; and for beauty   160
I durst compare —

Peregr.   It seems you are not jealous,
That dare commend her.

Sir P. W.   Nay, and for discourse —

Peregr. Being your wife, she cannot miss that.

Sir P. W. [*introducing* PEREGRINE].   Madam,
Here is a gentleman; pray you, use him fairly.
He seems a youth, but he is —

Lady P. W.   None.

Sir P. W.   Yes, one
Has put his face as soon into the world —

Lady P. W. You mean as early? But today?

Sir P. W.   How's this?

Lady P. W. Why, in this habit, sir; you apprehend me.
Well, Master Would-be, this doth not become you;
I had thought the odour, sir, of your good name   170
Had been more precious to you; that you would not
Have done this dire massacre on your honour;
One of your gravity, and rank besides!
But knights, I see, care little for the oath
They make to ladies, chiefly their own ladies.

Sir P. W. Now, by my spurs, the symbol of my knighthood —

Peregr. [*aside*.] Lord, how his brain is humbled for an oath!

156 *be tender to:* avoid harming.
170 *odour:* reputation.

NOTES: p. 232

Sir P. W. I reach you not.

Lady P. W.   Right, sir, your polity
  May bear it through thus. [*To* PEREGRINE] Sir, a word
    with you.
  I would be loath to contest publicly   180
  With any gentlewoman, or to seem
  Froward, or violent, as the courtier says:
  It comes too near rusticity in a lady,
  Which I would shun by all means. And however
  I may deserve from Master Would-be, yet
  To have one fair gentlewoman thus be made
  The unkind instrument to wrong another,
  And one she knows not – aye, and to perséver –
  In my poor judgment, is not warranted
  From being a solecism in our sex,   190
  If not in manners.

Peregr.   How is this?

Sir P. W.   Sweet madam,
  Come nearer to your aim.

Lady P. W.   Marry, and will, sir.
  Since you provoke me with your impudence,
  And laughter of your light land-syren here,
  Your Sporus, your hermaphrodite —

Peregr.   What's here?
  Poetic fury and historic storms!

Sir P. W. The gentleman, believe it, is of worth,
  And of our nation.

Lady P. W.   Aye, your Whitefriars nation.
  Come, I blush for you, Master Would-be, I;
  And am ashamed you should have no more forehead 200
  Than thus to be the patron, or St George,
  To a lewd harlot, a base fricatrice,
  A female devil in a male outside.

178 *reach:* understand.   182 *Froward:* perverse, unseemly.
188 *perséver:* persevere.
200 *forehead:* modesty, capacity for blushing.
202 *fricatrice:* prostitute.   203 *outside:* disguise.

NOTES: pp. 232–3

Sir P. W. [*to* PEREGRINE].   Nay,
> And you be such a one, I must bid adieu
> To your delights. The case appears too liquid. [*Going.*]
Lady P. W. Aye, you may carry it clear with your state-face.
> But, for your carnival concupiscence,
> Who here is fled for liberty of conscience
> From furious persecution of the marshal,
> Her will I disple.

                    [*Exit* SIR POLITIC WOULD-BE.]
Peregr.   This is fine, i' faith!   210
> And do you use this often? Is this part
> Of your wit's exercise against you have occasion?
> Madam —
Lady P. W.   Go to, sir.
Peregr.   Do you hear me, lady?
> Why, if your knight have set you to beg shirts,
> Or to invite me home, you might have done it
> A nearer way by far.
Lady P. W.   This cannot work you
> Out of my snare.
Peregr.   Why, am I in it, then?
> Indeed your husband told me you were fair,
> And so you are; only your nose inclines,
> That side that's next the sun, to the queen-apple.   220
Lady P. W. This cannot be endured by any patience.

                    Enter MOSCA.

Mosca. What's the matter, madam?
Lady P. W.   If the Senate
> Right not my quest in this, I will protest them
> To all the world no aristocracy.
Mosca. What is the injury, lady?
Lady P. W.   Why, the callet
> You told me of, here I have taken disguised.
Mosca. Who, this? What means your ladyship? The creature

> 204 *And:* if.   205 *liquid:* manifest.
> 210 *disple:* discipline, whip.   225 *callet:* hussy.
>   NOTES: pp. 233–4

I mentioned to you is apprehended now,
Before the Senate; you shall see her —
Lady P. W.   Where?
Mosca. I'll bring you to her. This young gentleman,   230
I saw him land this morning at the port.
Lady P. W. Is it possible? How has my judgment wandered?
Sir, I must, blushing, say to you, I have erred,
And plead your pardon.
Peregr.   What, more changes yet?
Lady P. W. I hope you have not the malice to remember
A gentlewoman's passion. If you stay
In Venice here, please you to use me, sir —
Mosca. Will you go, madam?
Lady P. W.   Pray you, sir, use me. In
faith,
The more you see me, the more I shall conceive
You have forgot our quarrel.

   [*Exeunt* LADY WOULD-BE, MOSCA, NANO, *and*
                              Lady's Maids.]

Peregr.   This is rare!   240
Sir Politic Would-be? – no, Sir Politic Bawd,
To bring me thus acquainted with his wife!
Well, wise Sir Poll, since you have practised thus
Upon my freshmanship, I'll try your salt-head,
What proof it is against a counter-plot.   [*Exit.*]

   Scene II. [*The Scrutineo, or Senate House.*]

   Enter VOLTORE, CORBACCIO, CORVINO *and* MOSCA.

Voltore. Well, now you know the carriage of the business,
Your constancy is all that is required
Unto the safety of it.
Mosca.   Is the lie
Safely conveyed amongst us? Is that sure?
Knows every man his burden?

                    5 *burden:* tune.
                    NOTES: p. 234

Corvino.   Yes.

Mosca.   Then shrink not.

Corvino [*drawing* MOSCA *aside*]. But knows the advocate the
  truth?

Mosca.   O, sir,
  By no means. I devised a formal tale
  That salved your reputation. But be valiant, sir.

Corvino. I fear no one but him, that this his pleading
  Should make him stand for a co-heir —

Mosca.   Co-halter!   10
  Hang him; we will but use his tongue, his noise,
  As we do Croaker's here.

Corvino.   Aye, what shall he do?

Mosca. When we have done, you mean?

Corvino.   Yes.

Mosca.   Why, we'll
  think:
  Sell him for mummia – he's half dust already.
  (*To* VOLTORE) Do you not smile to see this buffalo,
  How he doth sport it with his head? [*To himself*] I
   should,
  If all were well and past. (*To* CORBACCIO) Sir, only
   you
  Are he that shall enjoy the crop of all;
  And these not know for whom they toil.

Corbac.   Aye, peace.

Mosca (*turning to* CORVINO). But you shall eat it. [*To him-*
  self] Much! (*To* VOLTORE) Worshipful sir,   20
  Mercury sit upon your thundering tongue,
  Or the French Hercules, and make your language
  As conquering as his club to beat along,
  As with a tempest; flat our adversaries –
  [*Aside*] But much more yours, sir.

Voltore.   Here they come:
  have done.

     7 *formal:* circumstantial.
    18 *crop:* end-product.
     NOTES: pp. 234–5

Mosca. I have another witness if you need, sir,
    I can produce.
Voltore.   Who is it?
Mosca.   Sir, I have her.

       Enter AVOCATORI, BONARIO, CELIA,
     NOTARIO, Commandatori, Saffi, *and other*
          Officers of Justice.

1 *Avoc.* The like of this the Senate never heard of.
2 *Avoc.* 'Twill come most strange to them when we report it.
4 *Avoc.* The gentlewoman has been ever held   30
    Of unreproved name.
3 *Avoc.*   So the young man.
4 *Avoc.* The more unnatural part that of his father.
2 *Avoc.* More of the husband.
1 *Avoc.*   I not know to give
    His act a name, it is so monstrous!
4 *Avoc.* But the impostor, he is a thing created
    To exceed example!
1 *Avoc.*   And all after-times!
2 *Avoc.* I never heard a true voluptuary
    Described but him.
3 *Avoc.*   Appear yet those were cited?
Notario. All but the old magnifico, Volpone.
1 *Avoc.* Why is not he here?
Mosca.   Please your fatherhoods,   40
    Here is his advocate. Himself's so weak,
    So feeble —
4 *Avoc.*   What are you?
Bonario.   His parasite,
    His knave, his pander. I beseech the court
    He may be forced to come, that your grave eyes
    May bear strong witness of his strange impostures.
Voltore. Upon my faith and credit with your virtues,
    He is not able to endure the air.

      31 *unreproved:* unimpugned.   36 *example:* precedent.
        39 *magnifico:* a Venetian title.
            NOTES: p. 235

2 *Avoc.* Bring him, however.
3 *Avoc.*   We will see him.
4 *Avoc.*   Fetch him.
Voltore. Your fatherhoods' fit pleasure be obeyed,

                                        [*Exeunt* Officers.]

  But sure, the sight will rather move your pities 50
  Than indignation. May it please the court,
  In the mean time, he may be heard in me.
  I know this place most void of prejudice,
  And therefore crave it, since we have no reason
  To fear our truth should hurt our cause.

3 *Avoc.*   Speak free.
Voltore. Then know, most honoured fathers, I must now
  Discover to your strangely abused ears
  The most prodigious and most frontless piece
  Of solid impudence and treachery
  That ever vicious nature yet brought forth 60
  To shame the state of Venice. This lewd woman,
  That wants no artificial looks or tears
  To help the visor she has now put on,
  Hath long been known a close adulteress
  To that lascivious youth there; not suspected,
  I say, but known, and taken in the act
  With him; and by this man, the easy husband,
  Pardoned; whose timeless bounty makes him now
  Stand here, the most unhappy, innocent person
  That ever man's own goodness made accused. 70
  For these, not knowing how to owe a gift
  Of that dear grace but with their shame, being placed
  So above all powers of their gratitude,
  Began to hate the benefit; and, in place
  Of thanks, devise to extirp the memory
  Of such an act. Wherein I pray your fatherhoods
  To observe the malice, yea, the rage of creatures
  Discovered in their evils; and what heart

58 *frontless:* shameless. 62 *wants:* lacks. 63 *visor:* mask.
68 *timeless:* untimely, misjudged.

NOTES: pp. 235–6

Such take, even from their crimes: but that anon
Will more appear. This gentleman, the father,   80
Hearing of this foul fact, with many others
Which daily struck at his too tender ears,
And grieved in nothing more than that he could not
Preserve himself a parent (his son's ills
Growing to that strange flood), at last decreed
To disinherit him.

1 *Avoc.*   These be strange turns!
2 *Avoc.* The young man's fame was ever fair and honest.
Voltore. So much more full of danger is his vice,
That can beguile so under shade of virtue.
But, as I said, my honoured sires, his father   90
Having this settled purpose (by what means
To him betrayed we know not) and this day
Appointed for the deed, that parricide –
I cannot style him better – by confederacy
Preparing this his paramour to be there,
Entered Volpone's house (who was the man,
Your fatherhoods must understand, designed
For the inheritance), there sought his father:
But with what purpose sought he him, my lords?
I tremble to pronounce it, that a son   100
Unto a father, and to such a father,
Should have so foul, felonious intent:
It was to murder him. When, being prevented
By his more happy absence, what then did he?
Not check his wicked thoughts; no, now new deeds.
(Mischief doth ever end where it begins.)
An act of horror, fathers! – he dragged forth
The aged gentleman, that had there lain bed-rid
Three years and more, out of his innocent couch,
Naked upon the floor, there left him; wounded   110
His servant in the face; and, with this strumpet,
The stale to his forged practice, who was glad
To be so active (I shall here desire
Your fatherhoods to note but my collections

NOTES: p. 236

As most remarkable) thought at once to stop
His father's ends, discredit his free choice
In the old gentleman, redeem themselves
By laying infamy upon this man,
To whom, with blushing they should owe their lives.

1 *Avoc.* What proofs have you of this?

Bonario.   Most honoured
    fathers,   120
I humbly crave there be no credit given
To this man's mercenary tongue.

2 *Avoc.*   Forbear.

Bonario. His soul moves in his fee.

3 *Avoc.*   O sir!

Bonario.   This fellow,
For six sols more, would plead against his Maker.

1 *Avoc.* You do forget yourself.

Voltore.   Nay, nay, grave fathers,
Let him have scope: can any man imagine
That he will spare his accuser, that would not
Have spared his parent?

1 *Avoc.*   Well, produce your proofs.

Celia. I would I could forget I were a creature.

Voltore. Signor Corbaccio!

                              [CORBACCIO *comes forward.*]

4 *Avoc.*   What is he?

Voltore.   The father.   130

2 *Avoc.* Has he had an oath?

Notario.   Yes.

Corbac.   What must I do now?

Notario. Your testimony's craved.

Corbac.   Speak to the knave?
I'll have my mouth first stopped with earth; my heart
Abhors his knowledge: I disclaim in him.

1 *Avoc.* But for what cause?

Corbac.   The mere portent of nature!
He is an utter stranger to my loins.

        124 *sols:* small coins; *plead:* present a court case.
                    NOTES: p. 236

Bonario. Have they made you to this?
Corbac.   I will not hear thee,
 Monster of men, swine, goat, wolf, parricide!
 Speak not, thou viper.
Bonario.   Sir, I will sit down,
 And rather wish my innocence should suffer 140
 Than I resist the authority of a father.
Voltore. Signor Corvino! [CORVINO *comes forward.*]
2 *Avoc.*   This is strange.
1 *Avoc.*   Who's this?
Notario. The husband.
4 *Avoc.*   Is he sworn?
Notario.   He is.
3 *Avoc.*   Speak then.
Corvino. This woman, please your fatherhoods, is a whore
 Of most hot exercise, more than a partridge.
 Upon record —
1 *Avoc.*   No more.
Corvino.   Neighs like a jennet.
Notario. Preserve the honour of the court.
Corvino.   I shall,
 And modesty of your most reverend ears.
 And yet I hope that I may say, these eyes
 Have seen her glued unto that piece of cedar, 150
 That fine well-timbered gallant; and that, here
 The letters may be read, thorough the horn,
 That make the story perfect.
Mosca [*to* VOLTORE]. Excellent, sir!
Corvino [*to* MOSCA]. There is no shame in this, now, is
 there?
Mosca. None.
Corvino. Or if I said, I hoped that she were onward
 To her damnation, if there be a hell
 Greater than whore and woman – a good Catholic
 May make the doubt.
3 *Avoc.*   His grief hath made him frantic.

151 *well-timbered:* well-built. 153 *perfect:* complete.
NOTES: pp. 236–7

K

1 *Avoc.* Remove him hence.

(CELIA swoons.)

2 *Avoc.*   Look to the woman.
Corvino.   Rare!
    Prettily feigned, again!
4 *Avoc.*   Stand from about her.   160
1 *Avoc.* Give her the air.
3 *Avoc.* [*to* MOSCA].   What can you say?
Mosca.   My wound,
    May it please your wisdoms, speaks for me, received
    In aid of my good patron, when he missed
    His sought-for father, when that well-taught dame
    Had her cue given her to cry out a rape.
Bonario. O, most laid impudence! Fathers —
3 *Avoc.*   Sir, be silent.
    You had your hearing free, so must they theirs.
2 *Avoc.* I do begin to doubt the imposture here.
4 *Avoc.* This woman has too many moods.
Voltore.   Grave fathers,
    She is a creature of a most professed   170
    And prostituted lewdness.
Corvino.   Most impetuous,
    Unsatisfied, grave fathers.
Voltore.   May her feignings
    Not take your wisdoms. But this day she baited
    A stranger, a grave knight, with her loose eyes
    And more lascivious kisses. This man saw them
    Together on the water in a gondola.
Mosca. Here is the lady herself that saw them too,
    Without; who then had in the open streets
    Pursued them, but for saving her knight's honour.
1 *Avoc.* Produce that lady.
2 *Avoc.*   Let her come.   [*Exit* MOSCA.]
4 *Avoc.*   These things,   180
    They strike with wonder.

166 laid: plotted.   167 free: free from interruptions.
173 take: take in, deceive; baited: ensnared.
NOTES: p. 237

3 *Avoc.*   I am turned a stone.

Enter MOSCA *with* LADY WOULD-BE.

Mosca. Be resolute, madam.
Lady P. W. [*pointing to* CELIA]. Aye, this same is she.
    Out, thou chameleon harlot! now thine eyes
    Vie tears with the hyæna. Dar'st thou look
    Upon my wrongèd face? I cry your pardons:
    I fear I have forgettingly transgressed
    Against the dignity of the court —
2 *Avoc.*   No, madam.
Lady P. W. And been exorbitant —
4 *Avoc.*   You have not, lady.
1 *Avoc.* These proofs are strong.
Lady P. W.   Surely, I had no purpose
    To scandalize your honours, or my sex's.   190
3 *Avoc.* We do believe it
Lady P. W.   Surely you may believe it.
2 *Avoc.* Madam, we do.
Lady P. W.   Indeed you may: my breeding
    Is not so coarse —
4 *Avoc.*   We know it.
Lady P. W.   To offend
    With pertinency —
3 *Avoc.*   Lady —
Lady P. W.   Such a presence;
    No surely.
1 *Avoc.*   We well think it.
Lady P. W.   You may think it.
1 *Avoc.* Let her o'ercome. What witnesses have you
    To make good your report?
Bonario.   Our consciences.
Celia. And heaven, that never fails the innocent.
4 *Avoc.* These are no testimonies.
Bonario.   Not in your courts,
    Where multitude and clamour overcomes.   200

188 *exorbitant:* exceeding proper limits.
NOTES: pp. 237–8

1 *Avoc.* Nay, then you do wax insolent.

VOLPONE *is brought in, as an invalid.* [LADY WOULD-BE
embraces him.]

Voltore.   Here, here
  The testimony comes that will convince
  And put to utter dumbness their bold tongues.
  See here, grave fathers, here's the ravisher,
  The rider on men's wives, the great impostor,
  The grand voluptuary! Do you not think
  These limbs should affect venery? or these eyes
  Covet a concubine? Pray you, mark these hands:
  Are they not fit to stroke a lady's breasts?
  Perhaps he doth dissemble?
Bonario.   So he does.   210
Voltore. Would you have him tortured?
Bonario.   I would have him
  proved.
Voltore. Best try him, then, with goads or burning irons;
  Put him to the strappado. I have heard
  The rack hath cured the gout: faith, give it him,
  And help him of a malady; be courteous.
  I'll undertake, before these honoured fathers,
  He shall have yet as many left diseases
  As she has known adulterers, or thou strumpets.
  O, my most equal hearers, if these deeds,
  Acts of this bold and most exorbitant strain,   220
  May pass with sufferance, what one citizen
  But owes the forfeit of his life, yea, fame,
  To him that dares traduce him? Which of you
  Are safe, my honoured fathers? I would ask,
  With leave of your grave fatherhoods, if their plot
  Have any face or colour like to truth.
  Or if, unto the dullest nostril here,
  It smell not rank, and most abhorred slander.

201 *wax:* grow.   207 *venery:* sexual indulgence.
211 *proved:* tested.   219 *equal:* just.
220 *strain:* nature, kind.   225 *leave:* permission.

NOTES: p. 238

I crave your care of this good gentleman,
Whose life is much endangered by their fable;   230
And as for them, I will conclude with this,
That vicious persons, when they are hot and fleshed
In impious acts, their constancy abounds:
Damned deeds are done with greatest confidence.

1 *Avoc.* Take them to custody, and sever them.
2 *Avoc.* 'Tis pity two such prodigies should live.
1 *Avoc.* Let the old gentleman be returned with care.
                              [*Exeunt* Officers *with* VOLPONE.]
I'm sorry our credulity wronged him.
4 *Avoc.* These are two creatures!
3 *Avoc.*   I have an earthquake in me.
2 *Avoc.* Their shame, even in their cradles, fled their faces.   240
4 *Avoc.* [*to* VOLTORE]. You have done a worthy service to
    the state, sir,
In their discovery.
1 *Avoc.*   You shall hear, ere night,
What punishment the court decrees upon them.
Voltore. We thank your fatherhoods.
        [*Exeunt* AVOCATORI, NOTARIO, *and* Officers *with*
                BONARIO *and* CELIA.]

                        How like you it?
Mosca.   Rare.
I'd have your tongue, sir, tipped with gold for this;
I'd have you be the heir to the whole city;
The earth I'd have want men ere you want living:
They're bound to erect your statue in St Mark's.
Signor Corvino, I would have you go
And show yourself, that you have conquered.
Corvino.   Yes.   250
Mosca. It was much better that you should profess
Yourself a cuckold thus, than that the other
Should have been proved.

---

230 *fable:* invention, slander.   233 *constancy:* resolution.
235 *sever them:* keep them apart.   247 *living:* means, income.
                    NOTES: p. 238

Corvino.   Nay, I considered that:
    Now it is her fault.
Mosca.   Then it had been yours.
Corvino. True. I do doubt this advocate still.
Mosca.   I' faith,
    You need not; I dare ease you of that care.
Corvino. I trust thee, Mosca.
Mosca.   As your own soul, sir.

                                        [*Exit* CORVINO.]

Corbac.   Mosca!
Mosca. Now for your business, sir.
Corbac.   How? Have you busi-
        ness?
Mosca. Yes, yours, sir.
Corbac.   O, none else?
Mosca.   None else, not I.
Corbac. Be careful then.
Mosca.   Rest you with both your eyes, sir.   260
Corbac. Dispatch it.
Mosca.   Instantly.
Corbac.   And look that all,
    Whatever, be put in: jewels, plate, moneys,
    Household stuff, bedding, curtains.
Mosca.   Curtain-rings, sir.
    Only the advocate's fee must be deducted.
Corbac. I'll pay him now: you'll be too prodigal.
Mosca. Sir, I must tender it.
Corbac.   Two chequeens is well?
Mosca. No, six, sir.
Corbac.   'Tis too much.
Mosca.   He talked a great while:
    You must consider that, sir.
Corbac.   Well, there's three —
Mosca. I'll give it him.
Corbac.   Do so, and there's for thee.   [*Exit.*]
Mosca. Bountiful bones! What horrid, strange offence   270
        Did he commit 'gainst nature in his youth,

small *tip brought*   NOTES: pp. 238–9
this caustic remark,

Worthy this age? [*To* VOLTORE] You see, sir, how I
   work
Unto your ends. Take you no notice.
Voltore.   No,
   I'll leave you.   [*Exit.*]
Mosca.   All is yours, the devil and all,
   Good advocate. [*To* LADY POLITIC WOULD-BE]
   Madam, I'll bring you home.
Lady P. W. No, I'll go see your patron.
Mosca.   That you shall not:
   I'll tell you why. My purpose is to urge
   My patron to reform his will; and, for
   The zeal you have shown today, whereas before
   You were but third or fourth, you shall be now   280
   Put in the first; which would appear as begged
   If you were present. Therefore —
Lady P. W.   You shall sway me.
                                     [*Exeunt.*]

278 *reform:* change.   282 *sway me:* persuade me.

NOTES: p. 239

Act V

Scene I. [*In* VOLPONE'S *house.*]

Enter VOLPONE.

Volpone. Well, I am here, and all this brunt is past.
I ne'er was in dislike with my disguise
Till this fled moment: here 'twas good, in private;
But in your public – *cave* whilst I breathe.
'Fore God, my left leg 'gan to have the cramp,
And I apprehended straight some power had struck me
With a dead palsy. Well, I must be merry
And shake it off. A many of these fears
Would put me into some villainous disease,
Should they come thick upon me: I'll prevent them.   10
Give me a bowl of lusty wine to fright
This humour from my heart. (*He drinks.*) Hum, hum,
        hum!
'Tis almost gone already: I shall conquer.
Any device, now, of rare, ingenious knavery,
That would possess me with a violent laughter,
Would make me up again. (*He drinks again.*) So, so, so,
        so.
This heat is life; 'tis blood by this time. Mosca!

Enter MOSCA.

Mosca. How now, sir? Does the day look clear again?
Are we recovered, and wrought out of error
Into our way, to see our path before us?   20
Is our trade free once more?
Volpone.   Exquisite Mosca!
Mosca. Was it not carried learnedly?

---

  1 *brunt:* crisis.   6 *straight:* immediately.
  12 *humour:* mood, feeling.   15 *possess:* fill, overcome.
                  22 *carried:* handled.

NOTES: pp. 239–40

Volpone.   And stoutly.
    Good wits are greatest in extremities.
Mosca. It were a folly beyond thought, to trust
    Any grand act unto a cowardly spirit.
    You are not taken with it enough, methinks.
Volpone. O, more than if I had enjoyed the wench:
    The pleasure of all woman-kind's not like it.
Mosca. Why, now you speak, sir. We must here be fixed;
    Here we must rest; this is our masterpiece: 30
    We cannot think to go beyond this.
Volpone.   True,
    Thou hast played thy prize, my precious Mosca.
Mosca.   Nay, sir,
    To gull the court —
Volpone.   And quite divert the torrent
    Upon the innocent.
Mosca.   Yes, and to make
    So rare a music out of discords —
Volpone.   Right.
    That yet to me's the strangest, how thou hast borne it:
    That these, being so divided amongst themselves,
    Should not scent somewhat, or in me or thee,
    Or doubt their own side.
Mosca.   True, they will not see it.
    Too much light blinds them, I think. Each of them   40
    Is so possessed and stuffed with his own hopes,
    That anything unto the contrary,
    Never so true, or never so apparent,
    Never so palpable, they will resist it —
Volpone. Like a temptation of the devil.
Mosca.   Right, sir.
    Merchants may talk of trade, and your great signors
    Of land that yields well; but if Italy
    Have any glebe more fruitful than these fellows,
    I am deceived. Did not your advocate rare?

---

29 *be fixed:* remain.   36 *borne it:* managed it.
41 *possessed:* taken up with.   48 *glebe:* soil.

NOTES: p. 240

Volpone. O – 'My most honoured fathers, my grave fathers,   50
    Under correction of your fatherhoods,
    What face of truth is here? If these strange deeds
    May pass, most honoured fathers —': I had much ado
    To forbear laughing.
Mosca.   It seemed to me, you sweat, sir.
Volpone. In troth, I did a little.
Mosca.   But confess, sir,
    Were you not daunted?
Volpone.   In good faith, I was
    A little in a mist, but not dejected;
    Never but still myself.
Mosca.   I think it, sir.
    Now, so truth help me, I must needs say this, sir,
    And out of conscience, for your advocate: 60
    He has taken pains, in faith, sir, and deserved,
    In my poor judgment (I speak it under favour,
    Not to contrary you, sir) very richly –
    Well – to be cozened.
Volpone.   Troth, and I think so too,
    By that I heard him in the latter end.
Mosca. O, but before, sir: had you heard him first
    Draw it to certain heads, then aggravate,
    Then use his vehement figures – I looked still
    When he would shift a shirt; and doing this
    Out of pure love, no hope of gain —
Volpone.   'Tis right.   70
    I cannot answer him, Mosca, as I would,
    Not yet; but for thy sake, at thy entreaty,
    I will begin even now – to vex them all,
    This very instant.
Mosca.   Good, sir.
Volpone.   Call the dwarf
    And eunuch forth.

---

54 *sweat:* sweated.   62 *under favour:* diffidently, deferentially.
64 *cozened:* cheated.   67 *aggravate:* dilate.
68 *figures:* figures of speech. 71 *answer:* recompense.

NOTES: pp. 240–1

Mosca.   Castrone, Nano!

Enter CASTRONE *and* NANO.

Nano.   Here.

Volpone. Shall we have a jig now?

Mosca.   What you please, sir.

Volpone.   Go,
 Straight give out about the streets, you two,
 That I am dead; do it with constancy,
 Sadly, do you hear? Impute it to the grief
 Of this late slander. [*Exeunt* CASTRONE *and* NANO.]

Mosca.   What do you mean, sir?

Volpone.   O,   80
 I shall have instantly my vulture, crow,
 Raven come flying hither, on the news,
 To peck for carrion, my she-wolf and all,
 Greedy and full of expectation —

Mosca. And then to have it ravished from their mouths?

Volpone. 'Tis true. I will have thee put on a gown,
 And take upon thee as thou wert mine heir;
 Show them a will. Open that chest, and reach
 Forth one of those that has the blanks; I'll straight
 Put in thy name.

Mosca.   It will be rare, sir.

Volpone.   Aye,   90
 When they e'en gape, and find themselves deluded —

Mosca. Yes.

Volpone.   And thou use them scurvily. Dispatch,
 Get on thy gown.

Mosca [*putting on a gown*]. But what, sir, if they ask
 After the body?

Volpone.   Say it was corrupted.

Mosca. I'll say it stunk, sir; and was fain to have it
 Coffined up instantly, and sent away.

Volpone. Anything; what thou wilt. Hold, here's my will.

76 *jig:* joke, 'lark'. 78 *with constancy:* consistently.
79 *sadly:* seriously. 91 *e'en gape:* just gape.

NOTES: p. 241

Get thee a cap, a count-book, pen and ink,
Papers afore thee; sit as thou wert taking
An inventory of parcels. I'll get up   100
Behind the curtain on a stool, and hearken;
Sometime peep over, see how they do look,
With what degrees their blood doth leave their faces!
O, 'twill afford me a rare meal of laughter.
Mosca. Your advocate will turn stark dull upon it.
Volpone. It will take off his oratory's edge.
Mosca. But your clarissimo, old round-back, he
    Will crump you like a hog-louse with the touch.
Volpone. And what Corvino?
Mosca.   O, sir, look for him
    Tomorrow morning with a rope and a dagger   110
    To visit all the streets: he must run mad.
    My lady too, that came into the court
    To bear false witness for your worship —
Volpone.   Yes,
    And kissed me 'fore the fathers, when my face
    Flowed all with oils.
Mosca.   And sweat, sir. Why, your gold
    Is such another medicine: it dries up
    All those offensive savours; it transforms
    The most deformed, and restores them lovely,
    As 'twere the strange poetical girdle. Jove
    Could not invent to himself a shroud more subtle   120
    To pass Acrisius' guards. It is the thing
    Makes all the world her grace, her youth, her beauty.
Volpone. I think she loves me.
Mosca.   Who? the lady, sir?
    She's jealous of you.
Volpone.   Dost thou say so?   [*Knocking.*]
Mosca.   Hark,
    There's some already.
Volpone.   Look.

98 *count-book:* account-book.
100 *parcels:* items.
NOTES: pp. 241–2

Mosca.   It is the vulture: *(Valtore)*
    He has the quickest scent.
Volpone.   I'll to my place,
    Thou to thy posture.   [*He conceals himself.*]
Mosca.   I am set.
Volpone.   But Mosca,
    Play the artificer now: torture them rarely.

Enter VOLTORE.

Voltore. How now, my Mosca?
Mosca [*writing*].   *Turkey carpets, nine* —
Voltore. Taking an inventory? That is well.   130
Mosca. Two suits of bedding, tissue —
Voltore.   Where's the will?
    Let me read that the while.

Enter CORBACCIO *in a sedan-chair.*

Corbac.   So, set me down,
    And get you home.   [*Exeunt* Chair-men.]
Voltore.   Is he come now to trouble us?
Mosca. Of cloth of gold, two more —
Corbac.   Is it done, Mosca?
Mosca. Of several velvets, eight —
Voltore.   I like his care.
Corbac. Dost thou not hear?

Enter CORVINO.

Corvino.   Ha! is the hour come, Mosca?
Volpone (*peeping from his hiding place*). Aye, now they
    muster.
Corvino.   What does the advocate here,
    Or this Corbaccio?
Corbac.   What do these here?

Enter LADY POLITIC WOULD-BE.

Lady P. W.   Mosca!
    Is his thread spun?

131 *suits:* sets.
NOTES: p. 242

Mosca.   *Eight chests of linen —*
Volpone.   O,
    My fine Dame Would-be too!
Corvino.   Mosca, the will,   140
    That I may show it these, and rid them hence.
Mosca. Six chests of diaper, four of damask. There.
Corbac. Is that the will?

> [VOLTORE, CORVINO *and* LADY WOULD-BE
> *cluster round to read the will.*]

Mosca.   *Down-beds, and bolsters —*
Volpone.   Rare!
    Be busy still. Now they begin to flutter:
    They never think of me. Look, see, see see!
    How their swift eyes run over the long deed
    Unto the name, and to the legacies,
    What is bequeathed them there —
Mosca.   *Ten suits of hangings —*
Volpone. Aye, in their garters, Mosca. Now their hopes
    Are at the gasp.
Voltore.   Mosca the heir!
Corbac.   What's that?   150
Volpone. My advocate is dumb. Look to my merchant:
    He has heard of some strange storm; a ship is lost;
    He faints. My lady will swoon. Old glazen-eyes,
    He hath not reached his despair yet.
Corbac.   All these
    Are out of hope; I am sure the man.
Corvino.   But Mosca —
Mosca. Two cabinets —
Corvino.   Is this in earnest?
Mosca.   One
    Of ebony —
Corvino.   Or do you but delude me?
Mosca. The other, mother of pearl – I am very busy.
    Good faith, it is a fortune thrown upon me —

NOTES: p. 243

Item, one salt of agate – not my seeking.   160
Lady P. W. Do you hear, sir?
Mosca.   *A perfumed box* – Pray you
     forbear:
     You see I am troubled – *made of an onyx* —
Lady P. W.   How!
Mosca. Tomorrow or next day I shall be at leisure
     To talk with you all.
Corvino.   Is this my large hope's issue?
Lady P. W. Sir, I must have a fairer answer.
Mosca.   Madam!
     Marry, and shall: pray you, fairly quit my house.
     Nay, raise no tempest with your looks; but hark you:
     Remember what your ladyship offered me
     To put you in an heir; go to, think on it;
     And what you said e'en your best madams did   170
     For maintenance, and why not you? Enough;
     Go home, and use the poor Sir Poll, your knight, well,
     For fear I tell some riddles; go, be melancholic.
                         [*Exit* LADY WOULD-BE.]
Volpone. O, my fine devil!
Corvino.   Mosca, pray you a word.
Mosca. Lord! will not you take your dispatch hence yet?
     Methinks, of all, you should have been the example.
     Why should you stay here? with what thought, what
        promise?
     Hear you: do not you know, I know you an ass?
     And that you would most fain have been a wittol
     If fortune would have let you? that you are   180
     A declared cuckold, on good terms? This pearl,
     You'll say, was yours? – right; this diamond? –
     I'll not deny it, but thank you. Much here else? –
     It may be so. Why, think that these good works
     May help to hide your bad. I'll not betray you;
     Although you be but extraordinary,

160 *salt:* salt-cellar.   162 *troubled:* over-worked.
166 *fairly:* in seemly manner.   173 *riddles:* secrets.
                         NOTES: p. 243

And have it only in title, it sufficeth.

Go home, be melancholic too, or mad. [*Exit* CORVINO.]

Volpone. Rare Mosca! How his villainy becomes him!

Voltore. Certain he doth delude all these for me.   190

Corbac. [*still perusing the will*]. Mosca the heir!

Volpone.   O, his four
eyes have found it.

Corbac. I am cozened, cheated by a parasite slave.
Harlot, thou hast gulled me.

Mosca.   Yes, sir. Stop your mouth,
Or shall I draw the only tooth is left.
Are not you he, that filthy covetous wretch
With the three legs, that here, in hope of prey,
Have, any time this three years, snuffed about
With your most grovelling nose, and would have hired
Me to the poisoning of my patron, sir?
Are not you he that have today in court   200
Professed the disinheriting of your son?
Perjured yourself? Go home, and die, and stink:
If you but croak a syllable, all comes out.
Away, and call your porters! Go, go, stink.

                                        [*Exit* CORBACCIO.]

Volpone. Excellent varlet!

Voltore.   Now, my faithful Mosca,
I find thy constancy —

Mosca.   Sir?

Voltore.   Sincere.

Mosca [*writing*].   *A table*
Of porphyry – I marvel you'll be thus troublesome.

Voltore. Nay, leave off now; they are gone.

Mosca.   Why, who are
you?
What, who did send for you? O, cry you mercy,
Reverend sir! Good faith, I am grieved for you,   210
That any chance of mine should thus defeat
Your (I must needs say) most deserving travails:

192 *cozened:* beguiled.   211 *chance:* good luck.

NOTES: pp. 243-4

　　But I protest, sir, it was cast upon me,
　　And I could almost wish to be without it,
　　But that the will of the dead must be observed.
　　Marry, my joy is that you need it not:
　　You have a gift, sir (thank your education),
　　Will never let you want while there are men,
　　And malice to breed causes. Would I had
　　But half the like, for all my fortune, sir.　　　　　　220
　　If I have any suits (as I do hope,
　　Things being so easy and direct, I shall not)
　　I will make bold with your obstreperous aid –
　　Conceive me, for your fee, sir. In mean time,
　　You that have so much law, I know have the conscience
　　Not to be covetous of what is mine.
　　Good sir, I thank you for my plate; 'twill help
　　To set up a young man. Good faith, you look
　　As you were costive: best go home and purge, sir.

　　　　　　　　　　　　　　　[*Exit* VOLTORE.]

Volpone [*coming from behind the curtain*]. Bid him eat lettuce
　　well. My witty mischief,　　　　　　　　　　　　230
　　Let me embrace thee. O, that I could now
　　Transform thee to a Venus! Mosca, go,
　　Straight take my habit of clarissimo,
　　And walk the streets: be seen, torment them more.
　　We must pursue, as well as plot. Who would
　　Have lost this feast?
Mosca.　　　　　　　　I doubt it will lose them.
Volpone. O, my recovery shall recover all.
　　That I could now but think on some disguise
　　To meet them in, and ask them questions.
　　How I would vex them still at every turn!　　　　　240
Mosca. Sir, I can fit you.
Volpone.　　　　　　Canst thou?
Mosca.　　　　　　　　　　Yes, I know
　　One of the commandatori, sir, so like you,

218 *want:* be in need.　　219 *causes:* law-suits.　　227 *plate:* gold-plate.
　　　　229 *costive:* constipated; *purge:* take a laxative.
　　　　　　　　NOTES: p. 244

L

Him will I straight make drunk, and bring you his habit.
Volpone. A rare disguise, and answering thy brain!
  O, I will be a sharp disease unto them.
Mosca. Sir, you must look for curses —
Volpone.   Till they burst;
  The Fox fares ever best when he is cursed.   [*Exeunt.*]

The Fox is cursed, of course, when he escapes, not when he is caught.

Scene II. [*In* SIR POLITIC WOULD-BE'S *house.*]

Enter PEREGRINE *disguised, and three* Merchants.

Peregr. Am I enough disguised?
1 *Merch.*   I warrant you.
Peregr. All my ambition is to fright him only.
2 *Merch.* If you could ship him away, 'twere excellent.
3 *Merch.* To Zant, or to Aleppo.
Peregr.   Yes, and have his
  Adventures put in the Book of Voyages,
  And his gulled story registered for truth.
  Well, gentlemen, when I am in a while,
  And that you think us warm in our discourse,
  Know your approaches.
1 *Merch.*   Trust it to our care.
                                   [*Exeunt* Merchants.]

Enter Waiting-woman.

Peregr. Save you, fair lady! Is Sir Poll within?   10
Woman. I do not know, sir.
Peregr.   Pray you, say unto him
  Here is a merchant, upon earnest business
  Desires to speak with him.
Woman.   I will see, sir.
Peregr.   Pray you.
                                   [*Exit* Woman.]
  I see the family is all female here.

244 *answering:* worthy of.   2 *ambition:* hope, intention.
  12 *earnest:* urgent.   14 *Pray you:* please do so.

Enter Waiting-woman.

Woman. He says, sir, he has weighty affairs of state
    That now require him whole; some other time
    You may possess him.
Peregr.   Pray you, say again,
    If those require him whole, these will exact him
    Whereof I bring him tidings. [*Exit* Woman.] What might
      be
    His grave affair of state, now? How to make   20
    Bolognian sausages here in Venice, sparing
    One of the ingredients?

Enter Waiting-woman.

Woman.   Sir, he says he knows
    By your word 'tidings' that you are no statesman,
    And therefore wills you stay.
Peregr.   Sweet, pray you return him:
    I have not read so many proclamations,
    And studied them for words, as he has done,
    But —— Here he deigns to come.   [*Exit* Woman.]

Enter SIR POLITIC WOULD-BE.

Sir P. W.   Sir, I must crave
    Your courteous pardon. There hath chanced today
    Unkind disaster 'twixt my lady and me;
    And I was penning my apology,   30
    To give her satisfaction, as you came now.
Peregr. Sir, I am grieved I bring you worse disaster:
    The gentleman you met at the port today,
    That told you he was newly arrived —
Sir P. W.   Aye, was
    A fugitive punk?
Peregr.   No, sir, a spy set on you;
    And he has made relation to the Senate
    That you professed to him to have a plot
    To sell the state of Venice to the Turk.

     28 *chanced:* befallen.   35 *punk:* prostitute.
NOTES: p. 245

Sir P. W. O me!

Peregr.   For which warrants are signed by this time
     To apprehend you, and to search your study   40
     For papers —

Sir P. W.   Alas, sir, I have none but notes
     Drawn out of play-books —

Peregr.   All the better, sir.

Sir P. W. And some essays. What shall I do?

Peregr.   Sir, best
     Convey yourself into a sugar-chest
     (Or, if you could lie round, a frail were rare)
     And I could send you aboard.

Sir P. W.   Sir, I but talked so,
     For discourse sake merely.   (*Knocking.*)

Peregr.   Hark, they are there.

Sir P. W. I am a wretch, a wretch.

Peregr.   What will you do, sir?
     Have you ne'er a currant-butt to leap into?
     They'll put you to the rack; you must be sudden.   50

Sir P. W. Sir, I have an engine —

3 Merch. [*within*].   Sir Politic Would-be!

2 Merch. [*within*]. Where is he?

Sir P. W.   — that I have thought upon
     before time.

Peregr. What is it?

Sir P. W.   — I shall ne'er endure the torture. —
     Marry, it is, sir, of a tortoise-shell,
     Fitted for these extremities. Pray you, sir, help me.
     Here I've a place, sir, to put back my legs –
     Please you to lay it on, sir – with this cap,
     And my black gloves. I'll lie, sir, like a tortoise
     Till they are gone.

          [PEREGRINE *helps him into the tortoise
                    disguise.*]

Peregr.   And call you this an engine?

50 *sudden:* quick.   51 *engine:* device.

NOTES: pp. 245–6

Sir P. W. Mine own device – Good sir, bid my wife's women   60
    To burn my papers.

                    The three Merchants *rush in.*

1 *Merch.*   Where's he hid?
3 *Merch.*   We must,
    And will sure, find him.
2 *Merch.*   Which is his study?
1 *Merch.*   What
    Are you, sir?
Peregr.   I'm a merchant that came here
    To look upon this tortoise.
3 *Merch.*   How?
1 *Merch.*   St Mark!
    What beast is this?
Peregr.   It is a fish.
2 *Merch.*   Come out here!
Pergr. Nay, you may strike him, sir, and tread upon him:
    He'll bear a cart.
1 *Merch.*   What, to run over him?
Peregr.   Yes.
3 *Merch.* Let's jump upon him.
2 *Merch.*   Can he not go?
Peregr.   He creeps, sir.
1 *Merch.* Let's see him creep.
Peregr.   No, good sir, you will hurt him.
2 *Merch.* Heart, I'll see him creep, or prick his guts.   70
3 *Merch.* Come out here!
Peregr.   Pray you, sir. [*Aside to* SIR POLI-
    TIC] Creep a little.
1 *Merch.*   Forth.
2 *Merch.* Yet further.
Peregr.   Good sir!
    [*Aside to* SIR POLITIC] Creep!
2 *Merch.*   We'll see his legs.

            60 *device:* invention.   70 *prick:* stab.
                71 *Forth:* Get on with it!
                    NOTES: p. 246

They pull off the shell and discover him.

3 *Merch.* Godso, he has garters!

1 *Merch.*   Aye, and gloves!

2 *Merch.*   Is this
Your fearful tortoise?

Peregr.   Now, Sir Poll, we are even.
For your next project I shall be prepared.
I am sorry for the funeral of your notes, sir.

1 *Merch.* 'Twere a rare motion to be seen in Fleet Street.

2 *Merch.* Aye, in the term.

1 *Merch.*   Or Smithfield, in the fair.

3 *Merch.* Methinks 'tis but a melancholic sight.

Peregr. Farewell, most politic tortoise.

                    [*Exeunt* PEREGRINE *and* Merchants.]

Enter Waiting-woman.

Sir P. W.   Where's my lady?   80
Knows she of this?

Woman.   I know not, sir.

Sir P. W.   Enquire.
O, I shall be the fable of all feasts;
The freight of the gazetti; ship-boys' tale;
And, which is worst, even talk for ordinaries.

Woman. My lady's come most melancholic home,
And says, sir, she will straight to sea, for physic.

Sir P. W. And I, to shun this place and clime for ever,
Creeping with house on back, and think it well
To shrink my poor head in my politic shell.   [*Exeunt.*]

77 *motion:* puppet play.

NOTES: p. 246

Scene III. [*In* VOLPONE'S *house.*]

Enter VOLPONE *dressed as a commandator,*
and MOSCA *as a clarissimo.*

Volpone. Am I then like him?
Mosca.   O, sir, you are he:
    No man can sever you.
Volpone.   Good.
Mosca.   But what am I?
Volpone. 'Fore heaven, a brave clarissimo; thou becom'st it!
    Pity thou wert not born one.
Mosca.   If I hold
    My made one, 'twill be well.
Volpone.   I'll go and see
    What news, first, at the court.   [*Exit.*]
Mosca.   Do so. My Fox
    Is out of his hole, and ere he shall re-enter
    I'll make him languish in his borrowed case,
    Except he come to composition with me.
    Androgyno, Castrone, Nano!

Enter ANDROGYNO, CASTRONE, *and* NANO.

All.   Here.   10
Mosca. Go, recreate yourselves abroad: go, sport.
                                [*Exeunt.*]
    So, now I have the keys, and am possessed.
    Since he will needs be dead afore his time,
    I'll bury him, or gain by him. I'm his heir,
    And so will keep me till he share at least,
    To cozen him of all were but a cheat
    Well placed: no man would construe it a sin:
    Let his sport pay for 't. This is called the Fox-trap.
                                [*Exit.*]

8 *borrowed case:* disguise.   11 *abroad:* out of the house.
12 *possessed:* in possession.   17 *well placed:* well deserved.

NOTES: p. 247

Scene IV. [*A Street.*]

Enter CORBACCIO *and* CORVINO.

Corbac. They say the court is set.
Corvino.   We must maintain
    Our first tale good, for both our reputations.
Corbac. Why, mine's no tale: my son would there have killed
    me.
Corvino. That's true, I had forgot. [*Aside.*] Mine is, I'm sure.
    But for your will, sir.
Corbac.   Aye, I'll come upon him
    For that hereafter, now his patron's dead.

Enter VOLPONE *as a commandator.*

Volpone. Signor Corvino! and Corbaccio! sir,
    Much joy unto you.
Corvino.   Of what?
Volpone.   The sudden good
    Dropped down upon you.
Corbac.   Where?
Volpone.   And none knows how,
    From old Volpone, sir.
Corbac.   Out, arrant knave!   10
Volpone. Let not your too much wealth, sir, make you furious.
Corbac. Away, thou varlet.
Volpone.   Why, sir?
Corbac.   Dost thou mock me?
Volpone. You mock the world, sir: did you not change wills?
Corbac. Out, harlot!
Volpone.   O! belike you are the man,
    Signor Corvino? Faith, you carry it well;
    You grow not mad withal; I love your spirit;
    You are not over-leavened with your fortune.
    You should have some would swell, now, like a wine-vat,
    With such an autumn — Did he give you all, sir?

1 *set:* ready, in session.   13 *change:* exchange.
NOTES: pp. 247–8

Corvino. Avoid, you rascal!

Volpone.   Troth, your wife has shown   20
Herself a very woman; but you are well;
You need not care; you have a good estate
To bear it out, sir, better by this chance –
Except Corbaccio have a share.

Corbac.   Hence, varlet.

Volpone. You will not be aknown, sir; why, 'tis wise.
Thus do all gamesters, at all games, dissemble:
No man will seem to win.

                    [*Exeunt* CORVINO *and* CORBACCIO.]
                          Here comes my vulture,
Heaving his beak up in the air and snuffing.

                    Enter VOLTORE.

Voltore. Outstripped thus, by a parasite, a slave
Would run on errands, and make legs for crumbs!   30
Well, what I'll do —

Volpone.   The court stays for your worship.
I e'en rejoice, sir, at your worship's happiness,
And that it fell into so learned hands
That understand the fingering —

Voltore.   What do you mean?

Volpone. I mean to be a suitor to your worship
For the small tenement out of reparations,
That at the end of your long row of houses
By the Piscaria; it was in Volpone's time
(Your predecessor), ere he grew diseased,
A handsome, pretty, customed bawdy-house   40
As any was in Venice, none dispraised;
But fell with him: his body and that house
Decayed together.

Voltore.   Come, sir, leave your prating.

Volpone. Why, if your worship give me but your hand

----

20 *Avoid:* Be gone.   24 *Except:* unless.
26 *gamesters:* gamblers.   31 *stays:* is waiting.
38 *Piscaria:* the fish market.   43 *prating:* chattering.
                    NOTES: p. 248

That I may have the refusal, I have done.
'Tis a mere toy to you, sir, candle-rents;
As your learned worship knows —

Voltore.   What do I know?

Volpone. Marry, no end of your wealth, sir, God decrease it!

Voltore. Mistaking knave! what, mock'st thou my misfortune?

Volpone. His blessing on your heart, sir; would 'twere
more! —   [*Exit* VOLTORE.]   50
Now to my first again, at the next corner.

> *Enter* CORBACCIO *and* CORVINO, *following*
> MOSCA, *who crosses the scene and goes out.*

Corbac. See, in our habit! see the impudent varlet!

Corvino. That I could shoot mine eyes at him like gun-stones!

Volpone. But is this true, sir, of the parasite?

Corbac. Again to afflict us, monster!

Volpone.   In good faith, sir,
I'm heartily grieved a beard of your grave length
Should be so over-reached. I never brooked
That parasite's hair; methought his nose should cozen:
There still was somewhat in his look did promise
The bane of a clarissimo.

Corbac.   Knave —

Volpone.   Methinks   60
Yet you, that are so traded in the world,
A witty merchant, the fine bird, Corvino,
That have such moral emblems on your name,
Should not have sung your shame and dropped your
cheese,
To let the Fox laugh at your emptiness.

Corvino. Sirrah, you think the privilege of the place,

46 *toy:* trifle.   51 *corner:* street-corner.
53 *gun-stones:* stone cannon-balls.
57 *never brooked:* could never abide.
60 *bane:* destruction, distress.   61 *traded:* experienced.
NOTES: pp. 248–9

And your red saucy cap, that seems to me
Nailed to your jolt-head with those two chequeens,
Can warrant your abuses. Come you hither:
You shall perceive, sir, I dare beat you. Approach.   70
Volpone. No haste, sir; I do know your valour well,
Since you durst publish what you are, sir.
Corvino.   Tarry,
I'd speak with you.
Volpone.   Sir, sir, another time —
Corvino. Nay, now.
Volpone.   O God, sir! I were a wise man
Would stand the fury of a distracted cuckold.

Enter MOSCA.

Corbac. What, come again!
Volpone [*aside*].   Upon them, Mosca; save me.
Corbac. The air's infected where he breathes.
Corvino.   Let's fly him.
            [*Exeunt* CORVINO *and* CORBACCIO.]
Volpone. Excellent basilisk! Turn upon the vulture.

Enter VOLTORE.

Voltore. Well, flesh-fly, it is summer with you now;
Your winter will come on.
Mosca.   Good advocate,   80
Pray thee not rail, nor threaten out of place thus;
Thou'lt make a solecism, as madam says.
Get you a biggin more: your brain breaks loose.
                                             [*Exit.*]
Voltore. Well, sir.
Volpone.   Would you have me beat the insolent
      slave,
Throw dirt upon his first good clothes?
Voltore.   This same
Is doubtless some familiar.

            68 *jolt-head:* block-head.
            82 *madam:* Lady Would-be.
                NOTES: p. 249

Volpone.   Sir, the court,
      In troth, stays for you. I am mad, a mule
      That never read Justinian should get up
      And ride an advocate. Had you no quirk
      To avoid gullage, sir, by such a creature?   90
      I hope you do but jest; he has not done it:
      This is but confederacy to blind the rest.
      You are the heir.
Voltore.   A strange, officious,
      Troublesome knave! Thou dost torment me.
Volpone.   I know —
      It cannot be, sir, that you should be cozened;
      'Tis not within the wit of man to do it:
      You are so wise, so prudent; and 'tis fit
      That wealth and wisdom still should go together.
                                        [*Exeunt.*]

Scene V. [*The Scrutineo or Senate House.*]

Enter 4 Avocatori, NOTARIO, BONARIO, CELIA,
      CORBACCIO, CORVINO, Commandatori.

1 *Avoc.* Are all the parties here?
Notario.   All but the advocate.
2 *Avoc.* And here he comes.

      Enter VOLTORE, *and* VOLPONE *as a commandator.*

1 *Avoc.*   Then bring them forth to sentence.
Voltore. O, my most honoured fathers, let your mercy
      Once win upon your justice, to forgive –
      I am distracted —
Volpone [*aside*].   What will he do now?
Voltore.   O,
      I know not which to address myself to first;

          90 *gullage:* being fooled.   95 *cozened:* tricked.
                  4 *win upon:* override.
                      NOTES: p. 250

Whether your fatherhoods, or these innocents —
Corvino [*aside*]. Will he betray himself?
Voltore.   Whom equally
    I have abused, out of most covetous ends —
Corvino. The man is mad!
Corbac.   What's that?
Corvino.   He is possessed.   10
Voltore. For which, now struck in conscience, here I prostrate
    Myself at your offended feet for pardon.
1, 2 *Avoc.* Arise.
Celia.   O heaven, how just thou art!
Volpone [*aside*].   I'm caught
    In mine own noose.
Corvino [*to* CORBACCIO]. Be constant, sir; nought now
    Can help but impudence.
1 *Avoc.*   Speak forward.
Commandatori.   Silence!
Voltore. It is not passion in me, reverend fathers,
    But only conscience, conscience, my good sires,
    That makes me now tell truth. That parasite,
    That knave, hath been the instrument of all.
1 *Avoc.* Where is that knave? Fetch him.
Volpone.   I go.   [*Exit.*]
Corvino.   Grave fathers   20
    This man's distracted – he confessed it now –
    For, hoping to be old Volpone's heir,
    Who now is dead —
3 *Avoc.*   How?
2 *Avoc.*   Is Volpone dead?
Corvino. Dead since, grave fathers.
Bonario.   O, sure vengeance!
1 *Avoc.*   Stay,
    Then he was no deceiver.
Voltore.   O no, none:
    The parasite, grave fathers.

14 *Be constant:* Stand firm.   15 *Speak forward:* Carry on.
16 *passion:* frenzy, madness.   21 *now:* just now.

NOTES: p. 250

Corvino.   He does speak
    Out of mere envy, 'cause the servant's made
    The thing he gaped for. Please your fatherhoods,
    This is the truth, though I'll not justify
    The other, but he may be some-deal faulty.   30
Voltore. Aye, to your hopes, as well as mine, Corvino –
    But I'll use modesty. Pleaseth your wisdoms
    To view these certain notes, and but confer them;
    As I hope favour, they shall speak clear truth.
                    [*He passes the papers to the Avocatori.*]
Corvino. The devil has entered him!
Bonario.   Or bides in you.
4 Avoc. We have done ill, by a public officer
    To send for him, if he be heir.
2 Avoc.   For whom?
4 Avoc. Him that they call the parasite.
3 Avoc.   'Tis true;
    He is a man of great estate, now left.
4 Avoc. Go you and learn his name, and say the court   40
    Entreats his presence here, but to the clearing
    Of some few doubts.   [*Exit* NOTARIO.]
2 Avoc.   This same's a labyrinth!
1 Avoc. Stand you unto your first report?
Corvino.   My state,
    My life, my fame —
Bonario [*aside*].   Where is it?
Corvino.   — are at the stake.
1 Avoc. [*to* CORBACCIO]. Is yours so too?
Corbac.   The advocate's a
        knave,
    And has a forked tongue —
2 Avoc.   Speak to the point.
Corbac. So is the parasite too.
1 Avoc.   This is confusion.
Voltore. I do beseech your fatherhoods, read but those —

32 *modesty:* moderation.   33 *confer:* study.
        35 *bides:* dwells.   43 *state:* estate.
                NOTES: pp. 250–1

Corvino. And credit nothing the false spirit hath writ:
    It cannot be but he is possessed, grave fathers.   50
                           [*The scene closes.*]

Scene VI. [*A Street.*]

Enter VOLPONE.

Volpone. To make a snare for mine own neck, and run
    My head into it, wilfully, with laughter,
    When I had newly scaped, was free and clear!
    Out of mere wantonness! O, the dull devil
    Was in this brain of mine when I devised it,
    And Mosca gave it second: he must now
    Help to sear up this vein, or we bleed dead.

Enter NANO, ANDROGYNO *and* CASTRONE.

    How now! Who let you loose? Whither go you now?
    What, to buy gingerbread, or to drown kitlings?
Nano. Sir, Master Mosca called us out of doors,   10
    And bid us all go play, and took the keys.
Androg.   Yes.
Volpone. Did Master Mosca take the keys? Why, so!
    I am farther in. These are my fine conceits!
    I must be merry, with a mischief to me!
    What a vile wretch was I that could not bear
    My fortune soberly! I must have my crochets,
    And my conundrums! Well, go you and seek him.
    His meaning may be truer than my fear.
    Bid him he straight come to me to the court.
    Thither will I, and, if it be possible,   20
    Unscrew my advocate upon new hopes:
    When I provoked him, then I lost myself.   [*Exeunt.*]

---

3 *scaped:* escaped.   10 *called us:* sent us.
16 *fortune:* good luck; *crotchets:* fancies.   17 *conundrums:* whims.
                    19 *straight:* immediately.
                    NOTES: pp. 251–2

Scene VII. [*The Scrutineo.*]

The Court scene reopens as before with
4 Avocatori, BONARIO, CELIA, CORBACCIO,
CORVINO, VOLTORE, Commandatori.

1 *Avoc.* [*referring to* VOLTORE'S *written statement*]. These
    things can ne'er be reconciled. He here
    Professeth that the gentleman was wronged,
    And that the gentlewoman was brought thither,
    Forced by her husband, and there left.
Voltore.   Most true.
Celia. How ready is heaven to those that pray!
1 *Avoc.*   But that
    Volpone would have ravished her he holds
    Utterly false, knowing his impotence.
Corvino. Grave fathers, he is possessed; again, I say,
    Possessed: nay, if there be possession and
    Obsession, he has both.
3 *Avoc.*   Here comes our officer.   10

Enter VOLPONE *as commandator.*

Volpone. The parasite will straight be here, grave fathers.
4 *Avoc.* You might invent some other name, sir varlet.
3 *Avoc.* Did not the notary meet him?
Volpone.   Not that I know.
4 *Avoc.* His coming will clear all.
2 *Avoc.*   Yet it is misty.
Voltore. May't please your fatherhoods —
Volpone (*aside to* VOLTORE).   Sir, the parasite
    Willed me to tell you that his master lives;
    That you are still the man; your hopes the same;
    And this was only a jest —
Voltore.   How?

8 *possessed:* i.e. with a devil.   11 *straight:* immediately.
14 *clear all:* clear everything up.
NOTES: p. 252

Volpone.   Sir, to try
   If you were firm, and how you stood affected.
Voltore. Art sure he lives?
Volpone.   Do I live, sir?
Voltore.   O me!   20
   I was too violent.
Volpone.   Sir, you may redeem it.
   They said you were possessed: fall down, and seem so.
   I'll help to make it good. (VOLTORE *falls.*) God bless the
      man!
   [*Aside*] Stop your wind hard, and swell. [*Aloud*] See,
      see, see, see!
   He vomits crooked pins! His eyes are set
   Like a dead hare's hung in a poulterer's shop!
   His mouth's running away! Do you see, signor?
   Now 'tis in his belly.
Corvino.   Aye, the devil!
Volpone. Now in his throat.
Corvino.   Aye, I perceive it plain.
Voltore. 'Twill out, 'twill out: stand clear. See where it flies,   30
   In shape of a blue toad with a bat's wings!
   Do not you see it, sir?
Corbac.   What? I think I do.
Corvino. 'Tis too manifest.
Volpone.   Look! he comes to himself!
Voltore. Where am I?
Volpone.   Take good heart, the worst is past, sir.
   You are dispossessed.
1 *Avoc.*   What accident is this?
2 *Avoc.* Sudden and full of wonder!
3 *Avoc.*   If he were
   Possessed, as it appears, all this is nothing.
                        [*Indicating* VOLTORE'S *statement.*]
Corvino. He has been often subject to these fits.
1 *Avoc.* Show him that writing. Do you know it, sir?

                    19 *affected:* disposed.
                    35 *accident:* unforeseen event.
                       NOTES: pp. 252–3

M

Volpone [*aside to* VOLTORE]. Deny it, sir; forswear it; know
    it not.   40
Voltore. Yes, I do know it well, it is my hand;
    But all that it contains is false.
Bonario.   O practice!
2 *Avoc*. What maze is this?
1 *Avoc*.   Is he not guilty, then,
    Whom you there name the parasite?
Voltore.   Grave fathers,
    No more than his good patron, old Volpone.
4 *Avoc*. Why, he is dead.
Voltore.   O no, my honoured fathers,
    He lives —
1 *Avoc*.   How? Lives?
Voltore.   Lives.
2 *Avoc*.   This is subtler yet.
3 *Avoc*. You said he was dead.
Voltore.   Never.
3 *Avoc*.   You said so.
Corvino.   I heard so.
4 *Avoc*. Here comes the gentleman; make him way.

Enter MOSCA.

3 *Avoc*.   A stool.
4 *Avoc*. A proper man, and, were Volpone dead,   50
    A fit match for my daughter.
3 *Avoc*.   Give him way.
Volpone [*aside*]. Mosca, I was almost lost: the advocate
    Had betrayed all; but now it is recovered.
    All's on the hinge again. Say I am living.
Mosca. What busy knave is this? Most reverend fathers,
    I sooner had attended your grave pleasures,
    But that my order for the funeral
    Of my dear patron did require me —

41 *hand:* handwriting.   42 *practice:* false practice.
43 *maze:* confusion, labyrinth.   47 *subtler:* more perplexing.
50 *proper:* handsome.   54 *on the hinge:* running smoothly.

NOTES: p. 253

Volpone [aside].   Mosca!
Mosca. Whom I intend to bury like a gentleman.
Volpone [aside]. Aye, quick, and cozen me of all.
2 Avoc.   Still stranger!   60
    More intricate!
1 Avoc.   And come about again!
4 Avoc. It is a match: my daughter is bestowed.
Mosca [aside]. Will you give me half?
Volpone [aside].   First I'll be hanged.
Mosca [aside].   I know
    Your voice is good, cry not so loud.
1 Avoc.   Demand
    The advocate – Sir, did you not affirm
    Volpone was alive?
Volpone [breaking in].   Yes, and he is;
    This gentleman [*indicating* MOSCA] told me so.
        [*Aside*] Thou shalt have half.
Mosca. Whose drunkard is this same? Speak, some that know
        him:
    I never saw his face. [*Aside*] I cannot now
    Afford it you so cheap.
Volpone [aside].   No?
1 Avoc.   What say you?   70
Voltore. The officer told me.
Volpone.   I did, grave fathers,
    And will maintain he lives with mine own life,
    And that this creature told me. [*To himself*] I was born
    With all good stars my enemies.
Mosca.   Most grave fathers,
    If such an insolence as this must pass
    Upon me, I am silent. 'Twas not this
    For which you sent, I hope.
2 Avoc.   Take him away.
Volpone [aside]. Mosca!

61 *intricate:* involved.
64 *Demand:* ask.
73 *this creature:* Mosca.
    NOTES: pp. 253–4

3 *Avoc.*   Let him be whipped—
Volpone [aside].   Wilt thou
     betray me?
     Cozen me?
3 *Avoc.*   And taught to bear himself
     Toward a person of his rank.
4 *Avoc.*   Away.
                    [VOLPONE *is seized*.]   80
Mosca. I humbly thank your fatherhoods.
Volpone.   Soft, soft: whipped?
     And lose all that I have? If I confess,
     It cannot be much more.
4 *Avoc.* [*to* MOSCA].   Sir, are you married?
Volpone. They'll be allied anon: I must be resolute.
     The Fox shall here uncase. (*He throws off his disguise.*)
Mosca [aside].   Patron!
Volpone.   Nay, now
     My ruins shall not come alone. Your match
     I'll hinder sure: my substance shall not glue you,
     Nor screw you into a family.
Mosca [aside].   Why, patron!
Volpone. I am Volpone, and this [*to* MOSCA] is my knave;
     This [*to* VOLTORE], his own knave; this [*to* CORBAC.],
       avarice's fool: 90
     This [*to* CORVINO], a chimera of wittol, fool, and knave;
     And, reverend fathers, since we all can hope
     Nought but a sentence, let's not now despair it.
     You hear me brief.
Corvino.   May it please your fatherhoods —
Commandatori.   Silence!
1 *Avoc.* The knot is now undone by miracle.
2 *Avoc.* Nothing can be more clear.
3 *Avoc.*   Or can more prove
     These innocent.

84 *allied:* related by marriage.
85 *uncase:* remove his disguise.
89 *knave:* henchman.

NOTES: p. 254

1 *Avoc.*   Give them their liberty.

Bonario. Heaven could not long let such gross crimes be hid.

2 *Avoc.* If this be held the highway to get riches,
    May I be poor.

3 *Avoc.*   This is not the gain, but torment.   100

1 *Avoc.* These possess wealth as sick men possess fevers,
    Which trulier may be said to possess them.

2 *Avoc.* Disrobe that parasite.

Corvino and Mosca.   Most honoured fathers —

1 *Avoc.* Can you plead aught to stay the course of justice?
    If you can, speak.

Corvino and Voltore.   We beg favour.

Celia.   And mercy.

1 *Avoc.* You hurt your innocence suing for the guilty.
    Stand forth; and first the parasite. You appear
    To have been the chiefest minister, if not plotter,
    In all these lewd impostures, and now, lastly,
    Have with your impudence abused the court,   110
    And habit of a gentleman of Venice,
    Being a fellow of no birth or blood:
    For which our sentence is, first thou be whipped;
    Then live perpetual prisoner in our galleys.

Volpone. I thank you for him.

Mosca.   Bane to thy wolfish nature!

1 *Avoc.* Deliver him to the saffi.   [MOSCA *is led off.*]
                        Thou, Volpone,
    By blood and rank a gentleman, canst not fall
    Under like censure; but our judgment on thee
    Is, that thy substance all be straight confiscate
    To the hospital of the Incurabili;   120
    And since the most was gotten by imposture,
    By feigning lame, gout, palsy, and such diseases,
    Thou art to lie in prison, cramped with irons,
    Till thou be'st sick and lame indeed. Remove him.

---

104 *stay:* detain, stop.   108 *minister:* agent.
109 *lewd:* base.   118 *censure:* judgement.
119 *substance:* property; *confiscate:* forfeited.

NOTES: pp. 254–5

Volpone. This is called mortifying of a Fox.

[He is led away.]

1 *Avoc.* Thou, Voltore, to take away the scandal
    Thou hast given all worthy men of thy profession,
    Art banished from their fellowship, and our state.
    Corbaccio! – Bring him near. We here possess
    Thy son of all thy state, and confine thee   130
    To the monastery of San Spirito;
    Where, since thou knewest not how to live well here,
    Thou shalt be learned to die well.

Corbac.   Ha! what said he?

1 *Commandator.* You shall know anon, sir.

1 *Avoc.*   Thou, Corvino, shalt
    Be straight embarked from thine own house, and rowed
    Round about Venice, through the Grand Canal,
    Wearing a cap with fair, long ass's ears
    Instead of horns; and so to mount, a paper
    Pinned on thy breast, to the berlino.

Corvino.   Yes,
    And have mine eyes beat out with stinking fish,   140
    Bruised fruit, and rotten eggs. 'Tis well: I am glad
    I shall not see my shame yet.

1 *Avoc.*   And to expiate
    Thy wrongs done to thy wife, thou art to send her
    Home to her father with her dowry trebled.
    And these are all your judgments —

All.   Honoured fathers —

1 *Avoc.* Which may not be revoked. Now you begin,
    When crimes are done and past and to be punished,
    To think what your crimes are. Away with them.
    Let all that see these vices thus rewarded
    Take heart, and love to study them. Mischiefs feed   150
    Like beasts till they be fat, and then they bleed.

139 berlino: pillory.

NOTES: pp. 255–6

VOLPONE *comes forward to speak the Epilogue.*

Volpone. The seasoning of a play is the applause.
    Now, though the Fox be punished by the laws,
    He yet doth hope there is no suffering due
    For any fact which he hath done 'gainst you.
    If there be, censure him: here he doubtful stands;
    If not, fare jovially, and clap your hands.

THE END

Notes

PERSONS OF THE PLAY

VOLPONE: Italian for 'fox'; it is glossed by John Florio in *A Worlde of Wordes* (1598) as 'an old fox, an old reinard, an old craftie, slie, subtle companion, sneaking lurking wily deceiuer'.

magnifico: a Venetian noble.

MOSCA: Italian for 'fly'. Voltore refers to him as 'flesh-fly'.

parasite: part of the definition in *Chambers's Twentieth Century Dictionary* (1952) is apt here: 'a hanger-on or sycophant who frequents another's table: one who lives at the expense of society or of others and contributes nothing.'

VOLTORE: 'vulture'; defined by Florio as 'a rauenous bird called a vultur, a geyre or grap. Also a greedy cormorant'.

advocate: a barrister.

CORBACCIO: 'a filthie great rauen' (Florio) – his spelling is 'Corbacchio'.

CORVINO: 'crow'. The *O.E.D.* has under 'Crow', 'A bird of the genus *Corvus*; in England commonly applied to the Carrion Crow . . .'

merchant: a significant profession for Corvino, since he barters with his wife's honour.

SIR POLITIC: spelt by Jonson 'Sir Politique'. The Politiques were originally members of a moderate party during the French Huguenot wars; the word came to mean a temporiser, a worldly-wise man, and in this sense merged in usage with 'politic'.

PEREGRINE: 'Peregrine, peregrin . . . upon one's travels' (*O.E.D.*), hence Peregrine Pickle, the hero of Smollett's novel. The Bastard in Shakespeare's *King John* describes such a man as 'My picked man of countries' (I, i, 193).

NANO: his name means 'dwarf'.

ANDROGYNO: from Greek *anēr*, *andros*, man; and *gynē*, *-aikos*, woman.

Commandatori: officers. A word applied especially to members of certain Orders of Knighthood which had a combined military and monastic character. I have adopted throughout the commonest modern English spellings 'commandator, commandatori'.

DEDICATION

The exact relationships in time between the writing of *Volpone*, its first production by the King's Men, the performances at Oxford and Cambridge, and the composition of the dedication, are uncertain, because we are unsure which method of dating Jonson employed – our present system, which was already current, or the old system in which the year ended on 25 March so that the first three months of our 1606, for instance, would have been accounted part of 1605. The play was written just before or soon after Christmas 1605; the dedication is dated '11 of February. 1607', which might mean 1608. Meanwhile *Volpone* was acted at both universities where, as Jonson here says, 'it was seen, judged, and, to my crown, approved'. This enthusiastic reception was important; not only did it greatly help the reputation of the play, but it vindicated Jonson's claims to stand apart from all writings which were debasing the stage, to be to reinstating the true dignity and seriousness of dramatic art, and thus to be outside the scope of the current attacks on the theatre. So the first edition of *Volpone* was headed by this grateful acknowledgement to the 'learned arbitresses', wherein the author eloquently distinguishes between the abuses of the poetasters and what he himself is trying to do.

1   *most equal sisters*: there was a constant rivalry between Oxford and Cambridge. With this phrase Jonson gracefully rejects any imputation of partisanship, which would have been altogether foreign to his present purpose.

   wit: a word which once had a wide range of meaning, from 'genius' to its present sense. Here perhaps 'ability' catches the intention.

   so presently excellent: so universally effective, so much with everything at its finger-tips. Jonson is saying that no-one can be successful entirely on his own merit, without both proper opportunities, and people to encourage and help him.

5   *provide well toward these accidents*: to cultivate opportunities
    and well-wishers; 'accidents' (that is, contributory effects)
    being essential accessories to success.

7   *the benefit of a friend is also defended*: the judgement and reputa-
    tion of one's supporters must also be safeguarded. Jonson
    goes on to say that his self-defence will also justify the
    universities' support of him.

12 *in the subject*: the universities' opinion should be enough, but
    in an age when poets hear criticism from all sides Jonson
    (the subject) will be expected to be able to justify himself.

14 *poetasters*: *O.E.D.*: 'A petty or paltry poet; a writer of poor or
    trashy verse; a rimester.'

24 *inform*: form into, shape, mould. The tone and the content are
    frequently reminiscent of Sidney's empassioned plea in *An
    Apologie for Poetrie*, which Jonson certainly knew well;
    though the more immediate sources here are Horace and
    Minturno.

44 *for my particular*: for my part.

50 *my youngest infant . . . all his teeth*: a reference to the outcry
    against *Sejanus*, his most recent or youngest creation, for
    which Jonson told Drummond he was 'called before the
    Council . . . and accused both of Popery and of Treason'.
    He is thinking, no doubt, of the myth concerning Richard
    III, referred to by Shakespeare in *3 Henry VI*, V, vi, 74–5:
    > The midwife wondered and the women cried
    > 'O Jesus bless us, he is born with teeth!'
    and indirectly in *Richard III*, II, iv, 27–32.

52 *politiques*: see note on 'Sir Politic', p. 184.

    what nation, society, or general order, or state: Jonson had been
    accused of ridiculing the Scots and the king in *Eastward Ho!*,
    the court in *Cynthia's Revels*, and the army, the law, and the
    stage in *Poetaster*.

56 *I speak of those that are entirely mine*: the two plays publicly
    denounced for sedition, which brought Jonson to gaol, *The
    Isle of Dogs* and *Eastward Ho!*, were joint compositions.

58 *a mimic*: an actor, especially a burlesque actor.

60 *so pointingly . . . ingenuously have confessed . . . wisely dissembled*:
    Jonson claims that even in attacking cheaters, bawds and so

forth, he has not been so personal as to deprive his victims either of the credit of confession or the opportunity for disavowal.

65   *made obnoxious to construction*: exposed to misconstruction.

67   *application*: explaining, or claiming to explain, the personal references and innuendos in other men's writings.

68   *key*: many unauthorised 'keys' were published to various works, purporting to uncover hidden meanings and applications.

72   *utter their own virulent malice under other men's simplest meanings*: authors of 'keys' issue their own slanders under cover of 'exposing' hidden meanings of innocent writings.

74   *raked up*: raked over. Jonson now lashes at those who, like columnists in certain less reputable newspapers of our own day, make capital out of reviving long-dead and forgotten scandals.

76   *whose living faces they entrench . . . petulant styles*: metaphorical: whose living faces they scar with their peevish pens.

82   *desire rather to see fools and devils*: would prefer to see a revival of more primitive rough-and-tumble plays than that more sophisticated forms should be used as a cloak for slander and sedition.

87   *Sibi quisque timet . . .*: Horace, *Satires*, II, i, 23. Jonson freely renders this satire as the last scene of the Folio version of *Poetaster*, Act III, where the present line is interpreted as follows:

In satires, each man, though untouched, complains
As he were hurt; and hates such biting strains.

90   *miscellane interludes*: miscellaneous entertainments; Q and F read "misc' line", from the Latin *ludi miscelli*.

98   *honest and learned*: substantives.

99   *a name*: that is, the name of 'poet'.

114   *turning back to my promise*: not living up to my claim to restore the ancient forms – because, contrary to the precepts of the purists, this comedy ends with disaster for the protagonists. The point is discussed in the Introduction, pp. 17–18.

116   *of industry*: deliberately. He goes on to say how easily he
       could have conformed on this point had his more serious
       purpose not dictated otherwise.

126   *to imitate justice*, etc.: the construction of the end of the sen-
       tence is strange, but the meaning is clear.

128   *elsewhere*: in his commentary on Horace's *Art of Poetry*, lost
       in the fire in Jonson's library in 1623.

145   *Cinnamus, the barber*: Traditionally the barber was also
       surgeon and dentist, though under Henry VIII surgery
       became a separate profession. The reference here is to
       Martial, VI, lxiv, 24–6, where he declares, in circumstances
       parallel to those imagined by Jonson, that even the art of
       Cinnamus will be ineffectual.

THE ARGUMENT

Plautus introduces all but one of his plays with an acrostic. Jonson
has another before *The Alchemist*.

5   *which ope themselves*: which unfold or develop.

PROLOGUE

1   *luck yet send us*: if we are lucky, a little ingenuity will make our
     play a success.

5   *bid to credit from our poet*: asked by our poet to believe.

12   '*He was a year about them*': In Dekker's *Satiromastix*, V, ii,
     Tucca says to Horace (who represents Jonson), 'you nasty
     tortoise, you and your itchy poetry break out like Christmas,
     but once a year'.

13   *this his creature*: i.e. the present play, *Volpone*.

17   *a coadjutor, Novice, journeyman, or tutor*: a summary of the
     various forms of dramatic collaboration. No doubt Jonson
     had been a novice (or apprentice) playwright at one time;
     and he certainly worked on an equal footing as coadjutor in,
     for instance, the first version of *Sejanus*. A tutor would
     simply have superintended and corrected. A journeyman
     was a literary hack.

21 *quaking custards*: John Marston's second satire opens with
these lines:

> It cannot hold, I cannot aye endure
> To view a big-wombed, foggy cloud immure
> The radiant tresses of the quickening sun.
> Let custards quake, my rage must freely run.

This was one of the passages Jonson mocked in *Poetaster*:
Crispinus, who stands for Marston, is made to spew up his
indigestible phrases, among them 'Snarling gusts – quaking
custards' (V, iii, 525). This still leaves the meaning of the
phrase in some doubt. Herford and Simpson note: 'An
allusion to the huge custard set on the Lord Mayor's table at
the city feasts for the fool to jump into. [Contemporary
allusions to this event are frequent.] It appears from
Jonson's reference to have been burlesqued on the stage.'
In Marston 'custard' seems to require the meaning 'coward'
– a sense current today in the children's chant 'Cowardy,
cowardy custard'. The preceding phrase in *Volpone* 'no eggs
are broken' might suggest a slap-stick stage skit of the
Mayoral joke (repudiated by Jonson, but comparable to a
Crazy Gang sketch) in which a clown was beaten up into a
'custard' and 'devoured'. Such a popular performance
might have originated a vernacular use of 'custard' in the
sense of 'a feeble or faint-hearted man'. In any case custards
and cowards are fairly obviously related by their trembling;
cp. Earle, *Microcosmographie* (1628), 'A Cook . . . ranging his
dishes in order military, and placing with great discretion in
the forefront meats more strong and hardy, and the more
cold and cowardly in the rear, as quaking tarts and quivering
custards, and such milksop dishes.'

23 *a gull, old ends reciting*: a foolish character repeating tags, pro-
verbs, and old jokes to pad out the play.

26 *make Bedlam a faction*: turn lunatics (the inmates of Bedlam)
into supporters.

28 *jests to fit his fable*: comedy not foisted in, but appropriate to the
plot, characters and action.

31 *time, place, persons*: Jonson's practice in *Volpone* with regard to
the so-called 'unities' is discussed in the Introduction,
pp. 18–20.

33 *gall and copperas*: ingredients of ink. Green copperas, or ferrous sulphate (also known as green vitriol), is intended. Jonson's metaphor, while clear, is imperfect, since salt was never a component of ink.

35 *laughter . . . after*: Cp. laughter . . . slaughter (I, i, 164–5). In modern English 'gh' is pronounced like 'f' in some words and is not pronounced at all in others. This distinction represents a dual development of one Old English consonant sound. In the early seventeenth century the 'f' sound was still optional in many of these words, and also in the word 'after'. Thus in each case here we have a perfect rhyme, the 'f' sound being consistently either introduced or omitted.

ACT I, SCENE i

2 *Open the shrine*: for comment on the elevation of gold to a deity in the imagery, see the Introduction, pp. 32–3.

5 *the celestial Ram*: the sun enters Aries, the Ram, at the vernal equinox (21 March in our Gregorian calendar); therefore the earth is teeming and longing for sunshine.

10 *Sol*: the sun personified. In alchemy 'sol' came to mean gold.

12 *relic*: O.E.D.: '. . . a memorial of a departed saint, martyr, or other holy person, and as such . . . carefully preserved and held in esteem or veneration.'

15 *that age*: the Golden Age, the imaginary age during which mankind was supposed, according to Greek and Roman poetry, to have lived untroubled, happy and free.

19 *to Venus*: Homer, Vergil and Ovid all describe Venus Aphrodite as 'golden'.

24 *to boot*: as part of the bargain.

28 *Riches are in fortune . . . wisdom is in nature*: The distinction between the innate gifts of Nature and the acquired gifts of Fortune is a mediaeval commonplace. It is discussed by Rosalind and Celia in *As You Like It*, I, ii: 'Fortune reigns in the gifts of the world, not in the lineaments of nature.'

37 *subtle glass*: Venice has long been famed for its glassware.

41   *swallow A melting heir*: cheat a young man out of the wealth he has just inherited.

42   *your Dutch Will pills of butter*: the Dutch were mocked by other nations for the amount of butter they ate. Alva called them 'men of butter'. In *Every Man In His Humour*, III, Cob says of fasting days, when meat was prohibited: 'They are of Flemish breed, I am sure on't, for they raven up more butter than all days of the week beside.' The use of the term 'pill' shows that the Dutch enthusiasm for butter was not universal.

47   *forth-coming*: coming forth. They will never get out of prison alive.

58   *Romagnia . . . Candian . . . Lombard's*: Romagnia, or Romney was a sweet wine of Greek origin, very popular in England. Candy, in Crete, was one of the sources of Malmsey. Lombard is Lombardy in northern Italy.

71   *cocker up my genius*: indulge my disposition.

82   *to engross me whole*: to monopolise me.

83   *counter-work the one unto the other*: undermine each other's schemes.

84   *Contend in gifts, as they would seem in love*: outbid each other in the value of their presents, so as to appear more loving.

88   *bearing them in hand*: leading them on, beguiling them.

89   *the cherry*: an allusion to the game of bob-cherry (or chop-cherry) in which one tries to bite a dangling cherry.

91   *The Doggerel*: This 'sport' is a skit on the Pythagorean tenet of metempsychosis, or transmigration of souls, which maintains that at death the soul of a living creature passes into a new body, not necessarily of the same species, and thus over a period of time inhabits a variety of forms. This belief is mentioned in *Twelfth Night*:

> *Clown.* What is the opinion of Pythagoras concerning wild fowl?
> *Malvolio.* That the soul of our grandam might haply inhabit a bird.
> *Clown.* What think thou of his opinion?
> *Malvolio.* I think nobly of the soul, and no way approve his opinion.

> *Clown.* Fare thee well. Remain thou still in darkness: thou
>   shalt hold the opinion of Pythagoras ere I will allow of
>   thy wits; and fear to kill a woodcock, lest thou dis-
>   possess the soul of thy grandam.

Jonson is not simply indulging in burlesque, however. The
passage provides the opportunity for Androgyno to claim
that it is as fool that he is happiest, 'The only one creature
that I can call blessed'. This is an ironic comment on the
world the play is about to reveal. Moreover, it implies the
special status of the comic writer who, like the fool, achieves
true understanding and insight through the medium of
humour.

   This grotesque interlude of warped bodies is an apt prelude to the drama of warped minds.

94 *the false pace of the verse*: irregular four-stressed verse was
    common in moralities and early drama. The deformity of
    the metre here matches the deformity of the speakers; the
    performance is rounded off with a song in dwarf couplets.

96 *here is enclosed*: Nano points to Androgyno.

98 *fast and loose*: a trick, often used to cheat fair-goers, depending
    on an optical illusion: the dupe is invited to put a stick
    through a false loop in a belt and stop it being drawn away;
    after he has wagered he can do so, he is shown to have been
    deceived by the folding of the belt.

   Apollo . . . Æthalides . . . Euphorbus, etc.: the earlier transmi-
    grations of Pythagoras's own soul, and the various forms he
    is said to have claimed to remember inhabiting, can be
    summarised as follows, from Lucian, *Gallus*, 708–727, and
    Diogenes Lartius, *De Philosophorum Vitis*, VIII, i, 4, 5: the
    derivation from Apollo is misty; later the soul entered
    Æthalides, son of Mercury (also known as Hermes), the
    herald of the Argonauts, who had from his father the gift of
    remembering everything in life and after death: hence the
    fact that Pythagoras's memory of his previous incarnations
    was unique. When Æthalides died, the soul entered in
    succession Euphorbus, who was killed by Menelaus at Troy,
    Hermotimus, Pyrrhus (the fisherman), and eventually
    Pythagoras.

103 *the cuckold of Sparta*: Menelaus, husband to Helen, whose
     abduction by Paris started the Trojan War.

107   *sophist of Greece*: Pythagoras, a native of Samos, though he
        settled in Crotona in Italy.

108   *From Pythagore . . .*: the later history of Pythagoras's soul is
        derived from Lucian, *Gallus*, 729–733: from Pythagoras to
        Aspasia of Miletus, then to Crates, the cynic philosopher,
        to a king, a pauper, a Satrap, a horse, a jackdaw, a frog, and
        thousands of other forms, including, more than once, a cock.

111   *the cynic*: one of a sect of philosophers, founded by a pupil of
        Socrates, who foreswore ease, wealth and all enjoyments.
        Diogenes was a cynic.

114   *In all which it hath spoke as in the cobbler's cock*: Lucian's
        Gallus is a dialogue between Micyllus, a cobbler, and the
        cock which is the latest embodiment of the soul.

116   *his great oath, 'By quater!'*: the Pythagoreans attempted to
        combine mysticism and mathematics. They regarded num-
        bers as the essence of all substances, and established an
        intricate numerical symbolism – odd and even correspond-
        ing with form and matter, the number 1 with reason, 2 with
        the soul, and so on. The harmony of the universe was
        thought to depend on number. 'Triangular' numbers were of

        special significance: ⦂, the triangle of two, ⦙, the

        triangle of three, ⦙⦙, the triangle of four, or 'trigon'. As
        Pythagoras is made to say in Lucian's *Vitarum Auctio*, 543:
        'What you think is four is really ten, the perfect triangle and
        the oath we swear by.'

117   *musics*: Pythagoras supposed the heavenly bodies to be
        separated by distances or intervals according to the law of
        harmony, whence arose the idea of the harmony and music
        of the spheres.

        trigon: see the note on line 116.

        golden thigh: There is a story that Pythagoras once exposed
        his thigh, which was seen to be of gold.

122   *Counting all old doctrine heresy*: an ironic comment from
        Jonson, at this time a Catholic, to the effect that those who
        believe only in the 'new learning' of the Reformation are
        fools. Jonson made no alteration in the Folio edition.

123   *forbid meats*: forbidden foods. Among other things, Pytha-
        goreans were not supposed to eat fish or beans.

N

124   *Carthusian*: a member of a strict monastic order.

125   *dogmatical silence*: A five years' silence was enjoined on Pythagoreans.

130   *eating of beans*: forbidden to Pythagoreans.

133   *precise, pure, illuminate brother*: a Puritan.

136   *a Nativity pie*: the Puritans avoided the Popish implications of '-mas' by calling Christmas the Nativity, or Christ-tide; cp. *The Alchemist* III, ii, 43:

   Subtle. . . . at Christmas.
   Ananias.   Christ-tide, I pray you.

165   *free from slaughter*: with impunity. On the rhyme see the note to Prologue, 35.

169   *When wit waits upon the fool*: This can mean 'when wit (i.e. the master of the house) makes provision for the fool'; or 'wit' may be virtually personified so that the meaning would be, that he is the grace of every feast, etc., 'when the fool is served by Wit'.

175   *is changing*: is being changed. An excuse to keep them waiting while he prepares himself.

178. *Vulture, kite, Raven, and gorcrow*: the symbolism of the names is quite explicit. The 'kite' must be Lady Politic Would-be. A gorcrow is a carrion crow; Old English 'gor' is dirt or dung.

184   *a fox . . . Mocking a gaping crow*: refers to the fable of the fox flattering the raven for its singing so that it opens its beak and drops the cheese it is carrying; and also to Horace's application of this fable to a fortune-seeker in *Satires*, II, v, 55–57.

195   *foot-cloths*: richly ornamented cloths to go over horses' backs, reaching the ground on either side.

197   *mule*: judges and serjeants, as well as advocates, customarily rode mules.

202   *ambitious*: both 'soaring into the air' and 'aspiring' – a pun.

212   *harpies*: fabulous monsters, rapacious and filthy, each with a woman's face and body, and the wings and claws of a bird; hence beings who are grasping and ruthless.

214   *phthisic*: literally, pulmonary consumption; also used of a severe cough or asthma.

225 *What say you*: Volpone feigns feebleness and poor hearing.

228 *bought of St Mark*: The famous Byzantine basilica of St Mark
was built in Venice in 830 to receive the relics of the
evangelist, and was rebuilt in 976 and 1052. At the time of
Volpone it was surrounded by shops, especially goldsmiths,
which formed an important market.

239 *Your love Hath taste*: your love proves itself.

253 *To write me in your family*: that is, to enter me in your 'Household Book' in which the names of servants and retainers
were recorded.
All my hopes Depend upon your worship: Mosca shows feigned
obsequiousness to all of Volpone's would-be heirs.

258 *your keys*: anticipating Voltore's inheriting Volpone's property.

267 *Thy modesty Is loath to know it*: Voltore imagines Mosca to
have been instrumental in gaining him the inheritance.

269 *your course*: your procedure, in bending the law to suit the
client.

271 *large*: expansive, suggesting both facility in public speaking
and unstinting devotion to the interests in hand.

272 *things mere contraries . . . yet all be law*, etc.: Jonson spares no
opportunity in this play of satirising professions and institu-
tions, often, as here, by means of ironic praise.

276 *forked*: equivocal; of doubtful or double meaning.
take provoking gold On either hand, and put it up: to provoke is
to ask for one's case to be taken up: he would take fees or
bribes from both parties to an action, and simply pocket
them.

278 *with their humility*: with their fawning manner.

280 *suffering*: ironic: one who will not complain about abuses.

281 *perplexed*: bewildering; able to confound opponents in the
intricacies of the law.

284 *chequeen*: a sequin, a Venetian gold coin later current in other
parts of Italy: derived from *Zecca*, the mint at Venice.

288 *swim in golden lard*, etc.: C. H. Herford comments: 'Perhaps
this overwrought image is meant to emphasise Mosca's
insincerity. Lard, liquid gold, and honey are clotted fluids
for a swimmer.'

294   *Anon!*: addressed off-stage to whoever has knocked.

301   *multiply*: with each caller the day's booty will mount up.

306   *What! mends he?*: Corbaccio is hard of hearing, and time and
       again does not quite catch what Mosca says.

310   *slumbers*: sleeps lightly and fitfully, dozes.

317   *Aye, his last sleep*: the implication is, of course, that the drug is
       poisoned.

318   *Say you?*: What do you say? Corbaccio has again failed to
       catch Mosca's words.

320   *Most of your doctors*: slightly contemptuous: today we would
       use 'these' in place of 'your' (see E. A. Abbott, *A Shake-
       spearan Grammar*, §221). Jonson seizes the opportunity to
       satirise the medical profession.

328   *do it by experiment*: they try out new treatments on their
       patients which turn out to be fatal.

334   *kill him too*: i.e. the judge, when he becomes a patient.

340   *O, good!*: Corbaccio's gloating over Volpone's supposedly
       increasing infirmity is a powerful and savage satire on
       avarice.

351   *scotomy*: dizziness accompanied by dimness of sight.

352   *left to snort*: stopped snorting.

366   *By your own scale*: Mosca observes to himself that Corbaccio
       guesses Voltore's designs because they are identical with his
       own.

370   *your sacred medicine*: The idea of gold as a panacea is a con-
       stant thread of ironic imagery in the play.

371   *elixir*: a liquor once thought to have the power of prolonging
       life indefinitely, or, in alchemy, of transmuting other metals
       to gold.

372   *'Tis aurum palpabile, if not potabile*: aurum potabile is 'drink-
       able gold' – particles of gold in a volatile oil, formerly taken
       as a medicine believed to invigorate the heart and stimulate
       circulation. Corbaccio makes a play of this, saying that
       even if his gold is not drinkable, it is touchable. Mosca
       maintains this idea by adding that he will 'administer' the
       chequeens to Volpone in his feeding bowl, so that he may
       benefit from their curative touch.

374   *cordial*: a restorative draught for the heart.

379   *therefore forbear*: Mosca puts a foot wrong: to flatter Corbaccio he says that his chequeens will do Volpone good. The last thing that Corbaccio wants is for Volpone to be cured, so he demands his offering back ('I'll take my venture'). But Mosca soon restores the situation. This is the first faint tremor of the earthquake of confusion which will shake the tricksters later.

386   *This fit he shall recover*: he will get over this attack.

395   *colour . . . more taking*: that pretence will make it much more tempting.

402   *proper issue*: your own offspring.

408   *pronounce me his*: i.e. his heir.

409   *I do believe it*: ironic, of course.

418   *Still my invention*: Corbaccio claims each new point Mosca suggests as his own idea.

423   *Rook go with you*: may you be rooked, or fooled.

425   *no better than your ears*: Corbaccio is half deaf.

427   *to gull my brother*: if Corbaccio were Mosca's father, Bonario, who is to be cheated or gulled, would be his brother. The allusion is to Jacob and Esau.

433   *this hope*: the hope of the inheritance.

436   *I cannot hold*: I can't contain myself.

439   *give them words*: beguile them.

440   *pour oil into their ears*: in modern vernacular 'soft-soap them'; flatter them.

443   *so many cares . . .*: This speech is a satire on avaricious senility.

455   *Æson*: Jason's father, who had his youth restored by Medea's magic.

458   *all turns air*: turns to air, becomes light-hearted, care-free.

466   *How shall I do, then?*: again Mosca miscalculates slightly and has to mend matters quickly. There is no point in Corvino contributing his pearl if Volpone cannot take cognisance of it.

470   *orient*: pearls of particular brilliance and value are called orient, as coming originally from the East.

475   *carat*: a measure of weight used for precious stones. Corvino's pearl weighs twenty-four carats.

500   *No more than a blind harper*: proverbial.

508   *The dwarf, the fool, the eunuch, are all his*: Mosca may well be talking more or less at random in the whole of this speech; but the concept of Volpone fathering these warped and pathetic bodies is apt.

516   *Throughly and throughly*: through and through.

520   *Nay, help, sir*: Mosca urges Corvino to play his part in jeering at the 'dying' man. The situation is comparable to that in *The Alchemist* when Subtle and Face abuse Surly, believing him to be a Spaniard who cannot understand them. However, there the joke is against the tricksters, here against the dupe.

524   *culverin*: in Jonson's time, a kind of hand-gun.

535   *Nay, at your discretion*: Do as you see fit. Mosca calls Corvino's bluff: the latter is anxious enough for Volpone to be dispatched, but only hesitates to suggest it himself.

536   *to take my pearl*: from Volpone's grasp, which has closed upon it.

543   *Your gallant wife*: 'gallant' here means beautiful. How naturally the subject of Celia's beauty is introduced.

556   *the style . . . is directed*: Lady Would-be has given careful instructions how she is to be announced.

559   *some three hours hence*: Lady Would-be returns in Act III.

562   *let loose Their wives*: Italians, and Venetians in particular, were reported by English travellers to keep strict and jealous guard over their wives, as does Corvino.

566   *hath not yet the face to be dishonest*: is too ugly to be seduced. 'Yet' here is used in the sense of 'even'.

569   *a wench Of the first year*: a woman in her prime. Though the meaning is clear, it is not obvious from exactly what context Jonson has drawn his image. He uses the identical phrase in the last act of *Cynthia's Revels*.

574　*melteth in the touch to blood*: is flesh and blood as soon as you
　　　touch her. Mosca has pictured Celia's almost statuesque
　　　purity – 'whiter than a swan . . . silver, snow . . . lilies';
　　　but to bring warmth and colour to the portrait he hastens
　　　to add that she will be responsive to Volpone's embraces.
　　　Cp. *Much Ado About Nothing*, II, i, 166–7:

> for beauty is a witch
> Against whose charms faith melteth into blood.

575　*Bright as your gold, and lovely as your gold*: Even in his lyric
　　　description of womanly beauty Mosca employs gold as a
　　　criterion of desirability. At the same time as this tarnishes
　　　his romantic vision, it helps further to elevate gold itself
　　　into an ideal, though a false ideal.

582　*watched As near as they are*: as closely guarded as early crops
　　　of fruit.

585　*his whole household*: the husband's (Corvino's).

586　*have all their charge . . . examined*: Whenever he enters or
　　　leaves the house, Corvino demands a full report from every
　　　servant on the movements of Celia herself and on the other
　　　domestic spies. Thus each spy is himself being watched by
　　　his fellows.

589　*I must Maintain mine own shape still*: He must maintain his
　　　pose as a dying man, so he is forced to visit Celia in dis-
　　　guise.

ACT II, SCENE i

10　*with Ulysses*: as it was with Ulysses.

12　*Laid for this height of Venice*: directed towards the latitude of
　　　Venice.

14　*travel . . . with licence*: no English subject was permitted to
　　　travel overseas without a licence from the Privy Council.

15　*I dare the safelier converse*: I have less to fear in being seen
　　　talking to you.

17　*my lord ambassador*: the English ambassador in Venice from
　　　1604 to 1612 was Sir Henry Wotton, the poet and man of
　　　letters.

18　*vents our climate*: is given out by our country.

22 *raven*: a bird of ill omen. Swallows nesting 'in Cleopatra's
    sails' foreboded the outcome of Actium, according to
    Plutarch, followed by Shakespeare (*Antony and Cleopatra*,
    IV, xii, 3), so a raven in the shrouds would import even more
    to the superstitious.

    should build: is said to have built – an old construction, deriving
    from Anglo-Saxon usage.

23 *a ship royal of the king's*: one of the fleet provided and main-
    tained out of royal revenue, as opposed to those financed by
    subjects.

24 *trow*: equivalent to our modern 'do you think?'

25 *that speaks him*: his name describes his character.

28 *tires*: applied especially to head-dresses.

30 *the spider and the bee*: Peregrine caustically links Lady Would-be
    with the courtesans, the chief fashion-mongers; Sir Politic
    retorts with the proverb of the spider and the bee sharing the
    same nectar.

32 *I cry you mercy*: I beg your pardon. 'How silly of me' perhaps
    better conveys the modern vernacular equivalent.

34 *lion's whelping in the Tower*: James I showed interest in various
    wild and exotic animals; some of these he was shown, others
    were presented to him, among the latter being the lioness,
    Elizabeth. Stow in his *Annals* records that she whelped on
    5 August 1604, the cub dying next day; and again on 26
    February 1605. Gifford remarks: 'As the former had lived
    so short a time, James ordered this to be taken from the dam
    and brought up by hand; by which wise mode of management
    the animal was speedily dispatched after his brother.'

36 *the fires at Berwick*: Herford quotes a letter from Carleton to
    Chamberlain, among the State Papers, written on 15 January
    1605: 'We heare of a strange apparition on holydowne hilles
    neere Barwick of armies and fighting men, and such voiles of
    shott were thought to be heard, that it gaue the alarum to
    both yᵉ borders.' The traditional memory of the great
    border battle of Halidon Hill in the fourteenth century had
    never died, and there had been border disturbances on
    James I's departure for England. Perhaps with this back-
    ground a display of aurora borealis could have fired off these
    rumours, which had clearly spread widely if Jonson could

make such a glancing reference to them in *Volpone*. The aurora would at this time have been an alarming and totally mysterious phenomenon – it was not even named till 1632, by Gassendi; it can be a relatively local manifestation. Jean Jacques d'Ortons de Mairon records in his *Traité Physique de l'Aurore Boréale* (Paris, 1731), p. 172, that many hundreds of penitents came from certain villages in Brie to offer prayers in Paris in 1583 after being terrified by 'signes vûs au Ciel' over the Ardennes.

37   *the new star*: Kepler published in 1606 his *De stella nova in pede Serpentarii*, observations on a brilliant star which appeared suddenly on 30 September 1604 and remained visible for seventeen months.

40 . . . 46: *porpoises . . . a whale*: It is necessary to quote Stow's own words in reporting the incidents on which Sir Politic's exaggerations depend, since these events are relevant to dating *Volpone*. Under 1606 (new style) Stow writes:

> The 19 of Jan. a great Porpus was taken aliue at Westham, in a smalle creeke a mile, & a half within the land, and presented to *Franc*^ses *Gofton* Esquire, cheefe auditor of ye Imprests, and within few dayes after, a very great Whale came vp within 8. mile of London whose bought was seene diuers times aboue water, and Judged to exceede the length of the longest ship in the riuer, and when she tasted the fresh water and sented the land she returned into the Sea.

Peregrine says he has been away from London for seven weeks, and left on the day the whale was 'discovered'. It is impossible to build definite conclusions on dramatic statements; but it may have been that Jonson was taking the realistic background to this scene a step further by identifying stage time with the actual date of the first performance, which would put it about the middle of March 1606. This is compatible with the '1605' of the title-page, since in old style the year ended on 25 March.

49   *the Stode fleet*: the ships of the English Merchant Adventurers who, after forced migrations to Elbing and Emden, made a prolonged settlement at Stade, on the Elbe estuary, till in 1611 they were permitted to return to Hamburg upon favourable terms.

50   *the Archdukes*: the joint title of the Infanta Isabella, daughter
     of Philip II of Spain, and her husband, Albert. They were
     granted the Netherlands while Philip was still alive.

51   *Spinola's whale*: Spinola took command of the Spanish army
     in the Netherlands in 1604. Herford and Simpson quote
     Charles Herle, *Worldly Policy and Moral Prudence* (1654),
     p. 27, on the popular rumour of 'Spinola's Whale that should
     have been hir'd to have drowned London, by snuffing up the
     Thames and spouting it upon the City'.

55   *Stone*: not a great deal is known of this popular figure; the two
     anecdotes recorded of him show him quipping at great men.
     That Peregrine calls him a 'tavern fool' while Sir Politic
     mourns for him indicates Jonson's reaction to the profes-
     sional witty clown. 'Mass' is simply a familiar shortening
     of 'Master'.

58   *should write But such a fellow*: should put a character like Sir
     Politic in a play.

60   *Stone dead!*: cp. Shallow's similar harping, *2 Henry IV*, III, ii:
     'And is old Double dead?'

63   *That I know of*: negative understood.

70   *cabbages*: at this time imported from the Low Countries.

72   *musk-melons*: now known simply as melons.

73   *pome-citrons*: citrons, or perhaps limes.

74   *Colchester oysters*: they were already renowned among the
     Romans.

     your: the familiar use of 'your', where we would say 'these', has
     already been remarked: see E. A. Abbott, *A Shakespearian
     Grammar*, §221. Sir Politic's over-use of this form is part of
     his assumption of hearty intimacy.

76   *ordinary*: an eating-house providing meals at a fixed price.

78   *statesman*: one concerned with affairs of state.

81   *the meat was cut So like his character*: the meat was cut in the
     form of a code message. It was fashionable to cut meat in
     elaborate shapes.

85   *In polity*: as a matter of policy, for diplomatic reasons.

87   *And to't, as sound a noddle*: And besides, as level a head . . .

90 *Mamaluchi*: Sir Politic here confuses a number of ideas. 'Mamlūk' (or 'mameluke') is Arabic for slave. A group of Circassian slaves rose to power by devious means in thirteenth-century Egypt and established themselves as the ruling class, founding a dynasty which held sway from 1254 till 1811. Within the Ottoman empire after 1517, the mamelukes became beys, or local governors for the Turks. The term was borrowed in the sixteenth century to describe the fighting slaves of the Pope. Sir Politic uses the Italian plural form – in Arabic this would be mamālīk.

95 *one of their own coat*: one of their party. Sir Politic is still talking of the baboons, which he identifies with the Mamaluchi: he is at his most absurd.

105 *I hold myself in no small tie unto my fortunes*: I thank my lucky stars.

112 *Empty of rules for travel*: Jonson satirises a number of times the current predeliction for making a mystique out of ordinary matters, with elaborate rules and instructions, certain men setting themselves up as virtuosos. Kastril learning the art of quarrelling in *The Alchemist* is a notable example.

114 *he that cried Italian to me*: both written grammars and tutors would use fashionable precepts as sentences for translation. Peregrine contemptuously uses 'cried' for 'taught', Italian being heavily intonated.

118 *of ingenuous race*: of noble or honourable birth.

120 *I have been consulted with*: Sir Politic is 'modestly' declaring himself a master of the mystique of travel, to whom great men have entrusted their sons for instruction.

124 *mount a bank*: the word does indeed derive from the Italian 'monta in banco' (mount on bench). A mountebank was 'An itinerant quack who from an elevated platform appealed to his audience by means of stories, tricks, juggling, and the like, in which he was often assisted by a professional clown' (*O.E.D.*). The mountebanks of Venice were particularly renowned. Jonson's depiction of their proceedings is very close to contemporary accounts.

The status of such quacks in general is described by Lynn Thomas, *A History of Magic and Experimental Science* (New York, 1941): 'Like the princes and nobles of the fourteenth and fifteenth centuries, their fellows in the sixteenth and also the town magistrates and municipal councils of that century, unless restrained and guided by a resident university and medical faculty or college, showed themselves singularly gullible with regard to wandering astrologers, transient alchemists, unlicensed medical practitioners, printers of pirated editions, and other similar quacks, charlatans and intellectual vagabonds. Some such pretentious fakir, rather than a sound and deserving scholar or the holder of an M.D. degree from a reputable university, was all too liable to be made court historian, local schoolmaster, or municipal physician. Some members of this questionable class, like Henry Cornelius Agrippa and Theophrastus Bombastus von Hohenheim, even made eventually a deep impression upon the thought and learning of the time' (V, 7–8). A representative of this tribe in modern fiction is O. Henry's Jeff Peters. Later Thomas brings the subject even nearer home (VI, 219): 'Quacks and empirics flourished in medical practice of the second half of the sixteenth century, albeit contrary to the wishes of the medical faculties. Queen Elizabeth of England was always taking up with superstitious charlatans, as was her secretary Walsingham.'

125   *dear*: principal – those of highest estimation.

127   *quacksalvers*: a word of Dutch origin, of which 'quack' is a shortened form.

135   *only languaged men*: the men most skilled in languages.

137   *terms and shreds*: shreds and patches. Cp. 'They have been at a great feast of languages, and stolen the scraps' (*Love's Labour's Lost*, V, i).

139   *utter*: sell. 'Upon' here means 'with' or 'with the aid of'.

144   *Scoto of Mantua*: Volpone impersonates this professional actor, leader of an Italian company, who was known in England particularly as a juggler.

146   *phant'sied*: phantasied, pictured, described. Sir Politic anticipates that 'Scoto' will alter Peregrine's low opinion of mountebanks.

148   *Here in this nook*: instead of a usual 'stand', Volpone chooses the space outside Corvino's house.

150   *zany*: 'a clown's or mountebank's assistant' (*O.E.D.*).

153   *I do use to observe*: I always watch.

154   *The state he keeps in getting up*: his ceremony in mounting the
      platform.

158   *Portico of the Procuratia*: 'the Procuratie Vecchie with an
      arcade of fifty arches running along the north side of the
      Piazza di San Marco' (Herford and Simpson).

164   *cold on my feet*: in so desperate condition that I have to sell my
      wares for whatever I can get.

167   *Buttone*: Nothing is known of such a man.

168   *sforzato*: from Italian *sforzare*, to force, thus here a galley-
      slave.

169   *the Cardinal Bembo's – cook*: Cardinal Bembo (1470–1547)
      was a great humanist. The pause before 'cook' suggests it
      to be a euphemism for a more scandalous relationship.

172   *ciarlitani*: mountebanks who address the crowd from ground
      level instead of from a platform.

175   *Tabarine*: 'a zany in a troop of Italian comedians, headed by
      Zan Ganassa, who visted France in 1572' (Herford and
      Simpson).

182   *facy*: impudent: or perhaps two compounds are being coined
      and joined to describe appearance – turdy-faced and nasty-
      pated. I have not otherwise traced 'paty'. The whole
      compound is Aristophanic.

183   *groatsworth*: a groat was fourpence.

184   *scartoccios*: 'scarto' is a useless scrap of paper. Scartoccios
      were, particularly, pieces of paper folded to hold spices or
      for use in priming firearms.

185   *and play*: and live well from it.

187   *earthy oppilations*: obstructions. Their minds, as it were, have
      become constipated by gross materialism.

200   *Terra-firma*: Venetian possessions on the mainland.

204   *moscadelli*: muscatel; rich, spicy wine.

207   *O, health!*: the corollary in the play to the significant dwelling
      on disease, is this mockery of health and medicine.

213   *humid flux*: mucus – the equivalent of 'a runny nose'.

215 *chequeen*: see the note to I, i, 284.

216 *see what good effect it can work*: it is ironic that moral truisms on the unrelatedness of gold and health are in *Volpone* uttered as part of the fabric of chicanery.

219 *hot, cold, moist*, etc.: see the section on 'Humours' in the Introduction.

226 *mal caduco*: 'falling sickness' or epilepsy.

227 *tremor-cordia*: palpitations of the heart.

      retired nerves: shrunken sinews or tendons.

229 *ventosa*: windy, flatulent: i.e. a hernia causing flatulence.
      iliaca passio: pains in the small intestines.

231 *melancholia hypocondriaca*: melancholy, thought to be seated in the hypochondria – the liver, gall-bladder and spleen.

236 *theoric and practic in the Æsculapian art*: theory and practice of medicine. Æsculapius was the Greek god of healing.

238 *Zan Fritada*: a well-known zany.

241 *Broughton's books*: Hugh Broughton (1549–1612) was a strong Puritan and a rabbinical scholar. In *The Alchemist* Face, in the process of gulling Mammon, introduces him to Doll thus:

> a most rare scholar;
> And she is gone mad with studying Broughton's works.
> If you but name a word touching the Hebrew
> She falls into her fit.

Mammon's failure in this respect, and Doll's mad scene in which she reels off screeds 'out of Broughton', are crucial to the plot.

242 *Hippocrates . . . Galen*: Greek physicians, born respectively in 460 B.C. and A.D. 130; the first originated and the second expounded the theory of humours.

249 *sassafras*: a stimulant derived from the root and bark of the tree so named.

250 *guacum*: guaiacum, the wood of a West Indian tree used in medicine, and a drug obtained from its resin.

251 *Raymond Lully*: Raymond Lull or Lully (1235–1315), Catalan author, scholar, astrologer and missionary, set out to expose infidel errors and evangelise Moslems. Though

his works abound in formulae, to which he believed every scientific principle could be reduced, the tradition that he was an alchemist is largely false, and the attribution to him of the discovery of the elixir (see I, i, 371 note) is of much later origin.

252 *Danish Gonswart*: not definitely identified. Herford and Simpson summarise the conjectures that have been made.

253 *Paracelsus*: a pseudonym adopted by Theophrastus Bombastus von Hohenheim (1493–1541), the German-Swiss natural philosopher and physician, controversial but influential, who in his travels carried a long sword with a hollow pommel to hold his drugs and medicaments; the sword became renowned in fact and fable. See the note to II, i, 124.

261 *the signory of the Sanita*: a body formed in 1485 with powers to issue licences to physicians and mountebanks.

274 *simples*: a simple is a medicament of one constituent, especially a single herb.

277 *decoction*: boiling to extract the soluble parts of a solution.

278 *in fumo*: like the sham experiments at the climax of *The Alchemist*.

289 *balloo*: or balloon, a game played by a group of men with a large inflated leather ball, which is hit high in the air with shaped wooden strikers fixed to the arm.

301 *Cardinals Montalto, Fernese*: both historical figures. The former became Pope Sixtus V in 1585.

302 *Duke of Tuscany*: a title created by Pope Pius V in 1569 for Cosimo de' Medici.

   gossip: originally god-parent; later familiar acquaintance or crony.

313 *threepence*: It is noteworthy that sums of money are quoted in both Italian and English coinage in this scene.

318 *Tart*: keen or sensitive, when applied to the taste.

320 *Moist of hand*: a sign of youth and health.

> With this she seizeth on his sweating palm,
> The precedent of pith and livelihood . . .
>   (Shakespeare, *Venus and Adonis*, stanza v).

321 *come nearer to't*: come to the point.

324 *aches*: pronounced as two syllables.

325 *for the nones*: for the nonce, that is, for the particular purpose.
I have kept the earlier spelling to preserve the rhyme.

331 *ducat . . . moccenigo*: there were both gold and silver ducats,
and thus the value varied considerably: they circulated in
most European countries. A moccenigo was of no great
worth. Any attempt to give modern monetary equivalents
would be fairly arbitrary, especially since money values
today still alter rapidly. Italian coinage is here again mentioned in the same breath as the crown and the sixpence.

333 *the banner of my front*: the banner hung out by the mountebank to advertise his prowess and his wares.

334 *I will not bate a bagatine*: I won't knock off a farthing.

336 *toss your handkerchiefs*: the handkerchief would have the sixpence for the oil knotted into one corner – this was the
normal way for a mountebank to do business.

341 *a double pistolet*: a valuable gold coin.

342 *spark*: a gallant, or man-about-town.

350 *if I should speak to the worth*: if I should try to value it.

355 *bank*: the modern term originates from the money-dealer's
table.

359 *derived to*: passed to the possession of.

362 *moiety*: literally a half, but more commonly a part.

368 *virginal jacks*: In a virginal, spinet or harpsichord, an upright
piece of wood or 'jack' is fixed to the back of each note, and
across the top of each jack is fixed a quill. When the note is
depressed, the jack rises, and the quill plucks the string to
produce the sound.

370 *Spite of the devil*: the Quarto has 'blood of the devil'. The
explosive 'spite' is more effective as an imprecation. The
general meaning is clear enough – that the devil's malice is
somehow behind the mountebank's presence: presumably
Corvino is, in fact, addressing the disguised Volpone as an
embodiment of Satan's ill-will.

372 *Flaminio*: Flaminio Scale was a well-known actor of the
Commedia dell'Arte.

373   *Franciscina*: the Commedia dell'Arte was built round certain stock characters who always bore the same names. Franciscina was the servant maid.

375   *To make your properties*: to appropriate; to use as stage trappings.

377   *Pantalone di Besogniosi*: often alluded to simply as Pantalone another stock character in the Commedia dell'Arte, a lean, slippered old man, dressed in red, with a black gown and cap; not only senile and jealous, but usually portrayed as a cuckold – which explains Corvino's allusion.

380   *It may be some design on you*: Peregrine is, of course, banteringly leading Sir Politic on.

ACT II, SCENE ii

7   *Whose vent is stopped*: the vent in a furnace is the outlet for smoke and fumes; if this is stopped up the fire will at first be turbulent.

9   *liver*: supposedly the seat of love and jealousy; a later poetic tradition has transferred these passions to the heart.

16   *to effect my best To your release of torment*: to do my best to relieve you from pain.

18   *Dear Mosca . . . Sir, more than dear*: Jonson takes every occasion to emphasise their close relationship to throw their eventual rupture into starker relief.

21   *My better angel*: my good angel. The concept of each man having a good and a bad angel is well illustrated by *Dr Faustus*.

23   *coin me too*: melt me down into coinage too: a particularly powerful idea in this play of values perverted by the pursuit of gold.

28   *if you can horn him*: if you can make Corvino a cuckold. The horns of the cuckold are frequently alluded to in drama of the period. On the sources of this tradition see R. B. Onians, *The Origins of European Thought About the Body etc.* (1951).

31   *To make me known*: to give me away.
       I did it well: the following passage shows Volpone's delight in his own skill as an actor, which Mosca tactfully flatters.

34   *your epilogue*: being beaten by Corvino.
       O

37 *I have not time to flatter you now*: a characteristically wry comment from Mosca, and double-pronged, since he takes his ironic cut at Volpone's conceit while dutifully implying that what he has already said is so patently true as not to amount to flattery.

ACT II, SCENE iii

2 *tooth-drawing*: a function which mountebanks and quacks shared with barbers.

4 *strained action*: his forced performance. The mountebank employed all the tricks of the ham actor.
dole of faces: his range of expressions.

6 *noted lechers*: those well known to be lechers.

8 *favours*: a lady's small gifts to her admirers, both in smiles and glances, and in tokens.

12 *toad-stone*: a stone or concretion supposed in mediaeval times to be found in the head of a toad, and worn, often set in a ring, as an amulet (a charm with occult powers). It was said to have the 'power to repulse poisons' (Fenton, *Secret Wonders of Nature* (1569)), the supposedly venomous toad thus bearing its own antidote.

> Sweet are the uses of adversity,
> Which, like a toad, ugly and venomous,
> Wears yet a precious jewel in his head.
> (*As You Like It*, II, i, 12–14).

13 *cope-stitch*: the stitch employed for the straight edges of copes.

14 *hearse-cloth*: black cloth used for the coverings of biers.
old tilt-feather: presumably Corvino is suggesting that the mountebank's finery is really the flotsam of the tilt-yard where noblemen jousted with lances from opposite sides of a 'barrier' for sport or exercise.

15 *starched beard*: a beard which has been waxed, or otherwise stiffened and fixed.

17 *fricace for the mother*: a massage for a 'fit of the mother' (hysteria), though, of course, Corvino is playing on the phrase with bitter irony.

18 *you'd rather mount*: you would prefer to mount his platform to be treated there; again with salacious innuendo. She may be

seen 'down to the foot' from the street when she mounts the 'bank'; and 'mount' has a still blunter second meaning.

21 *cittern*: the same as a cither, a metal-stringed musical instrument played with a plectrum, and appropriate for the role in which Corvino is now casting Celia.

Lady Vanity: the metaphor now turns to morality plays, in which Vanity is a stock character.

22 *be a dealer*: have dealings with, be a tradeswoman: 'the virtuous man' is heavy irony for the mountebank.

23 *Make one*: be at one; be as one.

24 *save your dowry*: if Celia is proved unfaithful, she will have forfeited her right to any part of Corvino's estate at his death, which would otherwise be her due by law and by the marriage agreement.

I'm a Dutchman: that is, phlegmatic. He suggests she would not have dared behave in this way if she had believed him to be a hot-blooded Italian.

27 *the murder of father, mother, brother*: there are even today certain Mediterranean communities in which a feud or vendetta might spring from adultery; but one would expect this to be directed against the seducer, not the wife's family, and in any case to involve one act of revenge in the first instance, not the massacre which Corvino hysterically suggests. It is relevant here to remember the dangers Romeo faced in wooing Juliet.

55 *conjuror that had heedless left His circle's safety*, etc.: a conjuror was one who conjured up supernatural powers, spirits or devils; he was held to be able to command them, while himself remaining immune from their power so long as he kept within the magic circle or pentagram he had previously drawn, where he must remain until he had 'laid' them, or sent them back to the spirit world.

58 *backwards*: at the back of the house. Corvino realises that his simplest course is to banish Celia from rooms overlooking the street.

67 *pain of thy life*: on pain of death.

70 *anatomy*: a body used for anatomical demonstration.

74 *His master's dead: there's yet Some good to help the bad*: a line which epitomises the inversion of values by the principal characters in the play.

79   *crosses*: afflictions. The associations, of course, imply trials
     sent by God to be borne with Christian patience, and thus
     provide deeply ironic overtones.

80   *with Scoto's oil*: a very neat piece of comic dovetailing of
     various elements in the plot.

86   *fiddling*: the fiddle was part of the equipment of all travelling
     entertainers.

87   *tumbling*: a play on the word. Tumbling was a part of the
     repertoire of troupes of entertainers.

93   *fasting spittle*: the spittle of one who is fasting.

100 *At extreme fees*: at greatest cost.

101 *Consulting on him*: consulting together about him.

102 *Where one would have . . . Another . . . A third*: Jonson takes
     the opportunity to satirise physicians.

107 *some young woman*, etc.: the remedy is Biblical in origin. Cp.
     the opening of *I Kings*, i: 'Now King David was old, and
     stricken in years; and they covered him with clothes, but he
     gat no heat. Wherefore his servants said unto him, "Let
     there be sought for my lord the king a young virgin: and let
     her cherish him, and let her lie in thy bosom, that my lord
     the king may get heat." So they sought for a fair damsel
     throughout all the coasts of Israel, and found Abishag a
     Shunammite, and brought her to the king. And the damsel
     was very fair, and cherished the king, and ministered to
     him: but the king knew her not.'

114 *my sole dependence*: Mosca fawns on all the vultures in the
     same manner.

115 *dilate*: make known, inform against someone.

120 *present him*: provide him with a virgin.

121 *briefly conclude somewhat*: come to a decision quickly.

128 *Light on a quean may cheat us all*: we may pick a prostitute who
     will have the wit to betray us by wheedling the whole in-
     heritance for herself.

130 *a creature made unto it*: a dependant who is cut out for the job.

132 *Think, think, think . . .*: a daring but effective line. Shake-
     speare has Lear repeat 'never' five times at the tragic
     climax.

141　*If any man But I had had this luck*: Think what anyone else would do in my position.

146　*The cases are all one of wife and daughter*: There's nothing to choose in this case between offering a wife and a daughter (and Mosca has already invented for him the story of a Signor Lupo offering his daughter).

148　*Slight!*: an exclamation; an abbreviation of 'God's light'.
　　who is not engaged Unless it be for counsel: who is concerned with Volpone's case only as an advisor.

150　*that am So deeply in*: that am so deeply involved.

152　*Covetous wretch!*: Corvino accuses the imaginary Lupo of having covetous designs on the inheritance in offering his daughter. The irony is superb.

153　*The party you wot of*: the person you know about – a euphemism for 'the bedfellow for Volpone'.

157　*you have cut all their throats*: you have done all your rivals in the eye.

159　*we may let him go*: once he has made Corvino heir, then in his next paroxysm Volpone can be allowed to die.

160　*'Tis but to pull the pillow from his head*: we have only to pull away his pillow and let his head drop. Corvino is made to face the macabre realities of his scheme, so there can be no suggestion that he acts thoughtlessly or in ignorance.

163　*wit*: here the meaning is 'common sense' or 'intelligence'.

168　*Mine own free motion*: Corvino wants the full credit for prostituting his wife!

172　*I have something else To ripen*: in fact, Mosca's plot to persuade Corbaccio to disinherit his son in favour of Volpone. Corvino proves too impatient to await Mosca's bidding, and arrives with Celia at Volpone's house before he is expected, to Mosca's confusion in Act III.

183　*They'll do't 'gainst all the watches of the world*: Corvino is claiming that his threats cannot have been serious, since even if he were jealous, he would not have any faith in prohibitions, since a woman's determination can outwit any guards in the world, and no spies are proof against bribery.

ACT III, SCENE i

6   *subtle*: the meanings 'slender' and 'of fine texture' mingle with
     the more modern senses of 'cunning' and 'finely discriminat-
     ing'.

9   *clotpoles*: or clodpolls, i.e. thick-heads.

10 *mystery*: a profession which partakes both of art and of craft.
     The trades regulated by guilds, for instance, were often
     referred to as mysteries.

     a science: a recognised department of learning: hence an occu-
     pation which demands a specific training.

11 *so liberally professed*: 'liberal' in the sense 'suitable for gentle-
     men'. Mosca is saying that the art of acting the parasite is
     so widely embraced by gentlemen that he is surprised the
     trade has not been adopted as a regular branch of study and
     culture.

14 *town-art*: the knack of getting a living by knowing the ins and
     outs of city life: Mosca goes on to define this occupation in
     greater detail.

15 *To know who's fit to feed them*: to know in whose house they can
     get themselves invited to a meal.

16 *mould Tales for men's ears, to bait that sense*: ensnare men
     through the sense of hearing by the fictions they whisper in
     their ears.

20 *court-dog*: the dog symbolises fawning. A dog or spaniel is
     constantly associated with flatterers in Shakespearian
     imagery.

21 *Make their revenue out of legs and faces*: make their living out of
     bows (legs) and smirks. Mosca despises these common-or-
     garden toadies.

22 *lick away a moth*: an extreme image to express the flatterer's
     fawning subservience, officious to anticipate the great man's
     slightest whim or discomfort.

23 *that can rise And stoop almost together*: who by demeaning him-
     self can insinuate himself into power at the same time.

28 *Present to any humour, all occasion*: who can take advantage of
     the mood of the moment, and of whatever may happen.

29   *change a visor*: change his mask: that is, switch from one role
        to another.

30   *the art*: the art of being a true parasite.

32   *sparks*: men-about-town. In the present context the modern
        vernacular expression might be 'live wires'.

33   *zanies*: Nano was accurately described as a zany in assisting
        Volpone as mountebank. Our stage equivalents today are
        known as 'stooges' or 'feeds'.

35   *I was bound to seek*: I was on my way to look for.

37   *know thy way*: go about your business.

44   *Thy means of feeding*: that is, being kept by a great man as a
        sycophant. Bonario is accusing Mosca of being the typical
        parasite Mosca himself has been despising in his preceding
        soliloquy.

45   *These imputations are too common*: such slanders are all too often
        heard.

47   *unequal to me*: above me in station.

48   *Your sentence may be righteous, yet you are not*, etc.: I may de-
        serve your strictures, but you have no right to make them,
        since you are judging me before you know the facts of my
        case.

50   *St Mark*: the saint to whom it would be natural for an innocent
        Venetian to appeal. See the note to I, i, 228.

56   *spin my own poor raiment*: a metaphor for 'make my own
        poor living'.

58   *done Base offices*: undertaken dishonourable tasks.

61   *mining men with praises*: 'mining' is undermining or undoing:
        Mosca denies that he has flattered men to persuade them to
        take him into their confidence so that he could then betray
        them – part of the parasite's duties in his patron's service.
        'Trained their credulity with perjuries' continues the same
        idea – 'gained their confidence by lying'.

66   *redeem my present estimation*: restore my good name.

68   *This cannot be a personated passion*: This display of grief cannot
        be assumed. Bonario's naivety prevents his stealing our
        sympathies.

72   *make a main offence in manners*: be guilty of a serious breach of
       good manners.

82   *for which mere respect*: for which reason alone.

86   *lend it any thought*: give any countenance to it.

98   *The common issue of the earth*: of obscure or unknown parentage.

100   *score your vengeance*: record your vengeance; apt since scoring
       is, in origin, marking by means of incisions.

ACT III, SCENE ii

1   *Mosca stays long*: Volpone is awaiting Mosca's return from his
       visit to Corvino's house. Impatiently Volpone complains of
       the length of time Mosca has been away on his errand.

4   *whether of us three*: which of us three.

8   *set you both to school*: teach you both a lesson.

13   *why a pretty ape but for pleasing imitation*: why else should a
       dwarf be called an ape other than for his amusing mimicry.
       We still use 'to ape' meaning 'to mimic'.
       imitation . . . fashion; . . . crave . . . have: Good rhymes in
       Jonson's time: the vowels were long.

17   *Admit*: let us admit, let us grant.

18   *come after*: be second in importance.

22   *Cupid Send it be Mosca, and with fair return*: Please Cupid, let
       it be Mosca bringing good news. Volpone calls on Cupid
       since he is waiting for news of stratagems to entrap Celia.

24   *Would-be*: at the end of Act I Lady Would-be had been told to
       return in three hours' time. She now comes to keep the
       appointment.

26   *or dwell here for ever*: 'dwell' is tarry or stay. The lady proves,
       indeed, to be very difficult to get rid of.

27   *That my fit were past!*: Would that the agony of her visit were
       over!

28   *a second hell too . . . my appetite to the other*: and I fear a second
       torment – that my loathing of Lady Would-be will quench
       my desire for Celia.

31   *how it threats me*: how her visit fills me with misgiving.

33   *This band*, etc.: Lady Would-be discovers that her neck-band is not set low enough to show her charms to full advantage.

36   *I am dressed Most favourably today*: Lady Would-be's irony is directed against the maids who appear a moment later.

38   *see these petulant things . . . done this*: just look how these sulky minxes have performed their duties.

42   *his*: its. 'Its' was just coming into common use. Spenser never, and Shakespeare seldom, employed this form.

45   *your fellow*: your fellow serving-maid.

51   *bird-eyed*: cp. pop-eyed. The meaning here is 'startled': a modern equivalent for the whole phrase might be, 'It's no good looking so surprised.' Herford and Simpson quote other passages using this word (IX, 522), but I do not find the text here demands, as they suggest, that the Lady's Maid has started back as if to avoid a blow from Lady Would-be.

53   *by that light*: a common oath: an appeal to divine truth or to the light of day.

54   *preached*: Jonson's satire is two-edged here, and in the following lines, in making Lady Would-be talk of her trivial vanities in terms proper to matters ecclesiastical and philosophical: preached . . . read you the principles, argued all the grounds, Disputed . . . grace . . . counsel: this comments both on Lady Would-be and on the preoccupations of churchmen.

62   *At your return*: return to England, that is.

68   *fucus*: a cosmetic for beautifying the skin, prepared according to the prescription of a physician or expert.

70   *Volp*: Lady Would-be's affectionate shortening of the name.

74   *Believe me, and I Had the most fearful dream*: Volpone's savage innuendo passes over Lady Would-be's head, and she takes him up literally.

76   *Out on my fate*: Curse my luck.

78   *the golden mediocrity*: presumably another term for the classical 'golden mean' which Lady Would-be has read of somewhere; but she is presumably talking at a venture for the pleasure of hearing her own voice, and so any meaningless 'dream' will serve her purpose.

83 *Seed-pearl*: regarded as a tonic for the heart when dissolved in liquid.

84 *Tincture of gold*: also employed as a stimulant.

    coral: Lady Would-be is generously indiscriminate in her remedies. Coral hung round the neck was held to keep away bad dreams (Herford and Simpson quote interesting passages from Burton here, and also on seed-pearls and myrobalanes).

85 *elecampane*: this aromatic plant was also thought to yield a stimulant.

    myrobalanes: astringent, plum-like fruit said to cure melancholia and agues.

86 *grasshopper*: apt for Lady Would-be, both for its noise and its flightiness.

87 *Burnt silk*: administered in water as a remedy against the small-pox.

    amber: ambergris was formerly used in cookery and perfumery as well as in medicine.

88 *You will not drink, and part?*: Would you like to have a drink before you go? Another broad hint from Volpone, which Lady Would-be does not grasp.

89 *I doubt we shall not get*: I don't suppose we can get.

90 *saffron*: a yellow spice, now mainly associated with the East, but once commonly grown in England for confectionery and medicine, as the name Saffron Walden in Essex still bears witness.

92 *Bugloss*: a herb once used as a cordial.

94 *scarlet cloth*: wrapping in a scarlet cloth was another remedy against small-pox.

103 *principal, as Plato holds, your music*: *The Republic* approves only of such music as will inspire courage and moderation – hardly ideals shared by Lady Would-be.

104 *Pythagoras*: Lady Would-be remembers only that Pythagoras had something or other to say about music. Reference is made to this in the note to I, i, 117.

107 *The poet*: Sophocles, *Ajax*, 293, where he makes Tecmessa report the words of her husband, Ajax: 'Women should be seen, not heard.'

110   *your poets*: Lady Would-be parades the names of a number of
       Italian poets.

       Petrarch: Francesco Petrarch or Petrarca (1304–74), poet of
       humanism, of patriotism, and of love.

       Tasso: Torquato Tasso (1544–95), epic, pastoral and tragic
       poet.

       Dante: Dante Alighieri (1265–1321), author of the great epic
       Divina Commedia, and love poet.

111   *Guarini*: Giovanni Guarini (1537–1612), author of the pastoral
       drama *Il Pastor Fido* (1590), produced by Lady Would-be
       a moment later, which had a considerable vogue in England,
       being first translated into English in 1602.

       Ariosto: Ludovico Ariosto (1474–1533), author of the romantic
       epic *Orlando Furioso*.

       Aretine: Pietro Aretine or Aretino (1492–1556), a licentious
       poet, author of comedies, a tragedy, and satires, of a more
       or less scandalous and witty nature.

112   *Cieco di Hadria*: Luigi Groto, 'the blind man of Adria' (1541–
       85), who wrote tragedies, comedies, pastorals and other
       poems.

       I have read them all: though not well enough to know that
       they were not contemporary with Plato.

117   *Pastor Fido*: see the note on Guarini, line 111 above.

118   *That's now my safest*: That's now my safest course (to avoid
       giving occasion for further effusions).

119   *happy in the Italian*: have good command of Italian.

121   *Montagnié*: the Quarto spelling, which indicates the pro-
       nunciation: the Folio drops the accent. The idea of a
       poet's writings being private property from which one
       should not borrow did not prevail at this time. Poets and
       dramatists freely repeated in their own works whatever had
       pleased or impressed them in Guarini, Montaigne and
       Petrarch. But mere copying on a larger scale, which was
       also common at a time when authors were not protected by
       copyright, would then, as now, have been regarded as
       unscrupulous plagiarism.

124   *yet he, In days of sonneting, trusted them with much*: yet
       Petrarch, when it was the fashion to write sonnets, gave
       poets plenty of material. It is interesting to observe the

vogue for sonneteering being emphatically spoken of as a thing of the past in the first decade of the seventeenth century. Shakespeare's sonnets were written in the 1590s. We must not, however, take Lady Would-be as a reliable authority.

126   *Dante is hard*: in contrast to the 'facile' Montaigne, an opinion echoed by not a few of Lady Would-be's contemporaries.

128   *his pictures*: sixteen obscene engravings from designs by Giulio Romano, for which Aretine wrote sixteen *Sonnetti lussurioso* (1523).

137   *too much Settling and fixing . . . Upon one object*: Lady Would-be is advising Volpone to 'snap out of' his state of mind; similarly a council cannot let itself become befogged by dwelling (settling and fixing) too long on one topic and so sinking into lethargy (subsiding).

139   *For the incorporating,* etc.: For drawing these passions into the mind. . . . Lady Would-be's description of mental constipation does not make very clear sense, let alone good medicine or physiology. Her random appeal to Plato adds further confusion.

145   *more a days*: on more or other days. Compare this construction with the still current 'nowadays'.

148   *he Would lie you*: the 'you' is an 'ethic dative' with no precise meaning; as in Bottom's 'I will roar you as gently as any sucking dove'.

152   *you are like him, just*: you are just like him.

156   *coœtanei*: beings enjoying eternal existence together. Another extravagant abuse of language by Lady Would-be.

162   *The bells, in time of pestilence*: the persistent ringing of the death-knells during visitations of the plague, a stark reality to Jonson's audiences.

164   *the cock-pit*: an enclosed area constructed for cock-fighting. Though the scene is Venice, this allusion would probably have brought to the audience's mind the roofed public enclosure in Drury Lane, though the cockpits at Whitehall and St James in the royal precincts must have been noisy enough. The building in Drury Lane was converted in the next decade into a theatre, known alternatively as The Phoenix or The Cockpit.

168 *rid her hence*: get her out of here.

169 *Has she presented?*: Has she presented you with her gift? Like the other legacy-hunters, she has an offering to make.

172 *A toy*: a trifle. She grotesquely underbids her rivals.

173 *I saw your knight*: Mosca invents a pretext to send Lady Would-be about her business.

175 *Marry*: an interjection derived from 'Mary'.

179 *I knew 'twould take*: I knew she'd fall for that.

185 *Rialto*: district of Venice where the Exchange is situated, and hence the Exchange itself.

193 *like your wanton gamester at primero*: like a reckless gambler playing primero – a game of chance which scholars have so far been unable to reconstruct completely, though some details have been gathered together. Each player had four cards; there was a hierarchy of values for different combinations of cards held – rather as in poker. Four cards of the same suit represented a 'prime', all of the same colour a 'flush'. There was a kitty. I suggest that the present passage shows that a player could improve his hand by returning a card and drawing another (lie and draw), and that he paid for this venture by raising the stake (not go less). Volpone would then be comparing himself to a gambler who is tempted to raise the odds and exchange a card in the hope of winning when the hands are shown (an encounter). Lie and draw also means lie on the bed and attract Celia as metal is drawn to a lodestone; an encounter, in this other sense, is a lovers' meeting.

199 *imagine this a truth*: what Mosca told him in the previous scene, that his father intends to disinherit him.

201 *Did not I say I would send?*: at parting with Corvino in II, iii Mosca insisted: 'But come not, sir, Until I send.' Corvino's impatience puts Mosca in a dilemma since he is expecting Corbaccio.

202 *they prevent us*: then the rival legacy-hunters would forestall us.

203 *for his horns*: the horns of a cuckold.

204 *A courtier would not ply it so for a place*: A courtier would not press his suit this hard for a sinecure.

208 *except you told me*: only what you told me before.

210 *half an hour*: Mosca must find an excuse to hold back his business with Corbaccio and Bonario till the matter with Corvino and Celia is dispatched.

220 *Nor would I move it afore*: Nor would I make this known to you before.

223 *Affect not these strange trials*: Don't pretend to make these extraordinary tests of my virtue. Celia cannot believe he is in earnest.

226 *please your fears*: set your jealous fears at rest.

227 *I have no such humour*: I am making no such pretence.

231 *Was this the train?*: Was this where everything was leading?

232 *how much It may concern me*: how much I may stand to gain.

234 *My means; and the necessity of those means For my recovery*: my capital, and how much more I need to put my affairs in order.

236 *respect my venture*: support my endeavours, make this deal good.

237 *Honour! tut, a breath*: savage irony on Jonson's part after all Corvino has said in II, iii.

242 *takes his meat With others' fingers*: who has to be fed.

248 *Cry it on the Piazza*: Announce publicly in the town square what you've done.

249 *he that cannot speak it*: Volpone, supposed incapable.

250 *Whose lips are in my pocket*: who says what I pay him to say.
save yourself: except for yourself – Celia herself is the only other person who will know what has happened.

254 *emulate them*: that is, the saints.

259 *Aretine . . . his prints*: see notes on lines 111 and 128.

261 *professed critic*: one who claims to be an expert.

265 *mine own*: Corvino talks as if Volpone's bequest should be his by right.

274 *Thanks, sweet Mosca*: Corvino is anxious to have full credit for his conduct.

277 *the beauty Only of price*: the beauty beyond compare.

286   *What I have done for him*: This is bait for Corvino, a hint of
        what Volpone intends to leave him in his will.

298   *rochet*: a red gurnard – he threatens to slit her nose as one
        slits open a fish.

300   *bind thee to him*, etc.: a variation of one of Tarquin's threats
        to Lucrece: see Shakespeare's *Rape of Lucrece*, stanzas 74
        and 96.

303   *aquafortis*: nitric acid, used for etching.

313   *Do you thirst my undoing?*: Do you want to ruin me?

315   *God's precious*: a shortened form of the oath 'By God's pre-
        cious blood'.

318   *Crocodile*: In fable, the crocodile was said to weep both to
        attract his victims and while devouring them. Richard
        Hakluyt (1552?–1616), the geographer, wrote in an account
        of one of Hawkins's voyages, 'In this river we saw many
        crocodiles . . . His nature is even when he would have his
        prey, to cry and sob like a Christian body, to provoke them
        to come to him, and then he snatcheth at them.'

321   *'Sdeath*: a contraction of the oath 'By God's death'.

335   *a cause of life*: a matter of life and death.

336   *Now placed beneath the basest circumstance*: Now valued less
        than the meanest matters.

345   *thy beauty's miracle*: the miracle effected by your beauty.

349   *before I would have left my practice for thy love*: before I would
        have abandoned my schemes (practice) to gain your love
        . . . Volpone is saying that he had intended to carry on
        adopting new disguises till he should find a way to Celia's
        presence, and her love. There is no reason why we should
        believe him when he says his performance as the mounte-
        bank was only one of many to win her: he is talking to
        sweep her off her feet, regardless of mere fact.

351   *In varying figures*: in various assumed roles.

352   *blue Proteus*: the shepherd of Poseidon's (Neptune's) aquatic
        flocks, who had the gift of prophecy but was difficult to
        consult because he was a shape-shifter who could change
        into whatever he liked. Vergil describes him as 'caeruleus',
        sea- or sky-coloured, hence 'blue'.

the horned flood: 'flood' is a poetic term for a river. The allusion is to the river-god, Achelous, son of Oceanus. He and Hercules were rival suitors for Dejanira. They fought; Achelous turned himself first into a serpent, then into a bull, in which shape Hercules overthrew him, wrenching off a horn in the process.

360 *the great Valois*: 'In 1574 the Doge and senators of Venice entertained Henry of Valois, Duke of Anjou, King of Poland, on his way back to France when the death of his brother Charles IX made him king as Henry III' (Herford and Simpson); a characteristically accurate piece of background detail.

361 *young Antinous*: favourite of the Emperor Hadrian, and renowned for his youthful beauty – hence Volpone's allusion to his having played the role.

373 *Fame and rumour are but toys*: Reputation and gossip are only trifles. Ironically, Volpone here echoes what Corvino was saying a few moments before.

375 *spies*: servants set to watch over their mistress's honour.

376 *Or his easier ears beguile, Thus removed, by our wile*: or make your husband later believe what we like, now that we have got him out of the way by our stratagem.

379 *But the sweet thefts to reveal*: the only crime is to tell . . .

380 *To be taken*: . . . or to be found out.

382 *serene*: 'A light fall of moisture or fine rain after sunset in hot countries, formerly regarded as a noxious dew or mist' (O.E.D.).

387 *not in expectation As I feed others*: a reference to the way he keeps the legacy-hunters in suspense.

389 *orient*: see the note to I, i, 470.

390 *Than the brave Egyptian queen caroused*: Cleopatra. She claimed she would spend '100 hundred thousand' sesterces on one meal (according to Pliny) and Antony challenged her accordingly. She won the wager simply by dissolving in vinegar one of the priceless pearls hanging at her ears and drinking the draught.

391 *a carbuncle May put out both the eyes of our St Mark*: an allusion now lost. Though it was usual to set valuable gems

in the eye-sockets of holy images, no record of such a statue has come down to us. Perhaps 'the eyes of St Mark' was a popular name for two carbuncles of great note in Venice, one in the Treasury of St Mark, the other in the Doge's coronation cap.

393 *Lollia Paulina*: wife and later widow of the Emperor Caligula, who also possessed fabulous wealth in her own right inherited from her father, an extortioner. Pliny pictures her attending a minor social function smothered in jewels so that she glittered like the sun.

396 *and lose them*: and don't worry about losing them – a way of suggesting that all he has already mentioned is but an insignificant part of the whole. We do not need to take literally these magnificent hyperboles, which extend Jonson's picture of limitless riches.

399 *we will eat such at a meal*: we will spend as much on a single meal.

402 *phoenix*: the mythical bird supposed by the Greeks to return every five hundred years to Heliopolis in Egypt to renew its youth, which it effected by enclosing itself in an egg of myrrh and setting this on fire; then rising from the ashes gifted with new life. There are a number of variants of the myth.

403 *Though nature lost her kind*: Even if it became extinct as a result, since there was only one phoenix.

411 *July-flowers*: a corrupted form of 'gilly flowers'.

413 *The milk of unicorns*: 'Imaginary, even in an age which believed in the unicorn and used its powdered horn as medicine' (Herford and Simpson). This legendary beast was pictured with a horse's body and a single, long, straight horn projecting from its forehead.
   panthers' breath: it was a common mediaeval belief that the panther enticed its prey by the sweetness of its breath.

414 *Cretan wines*: Herford and Simpson: 'The Earl of Shrewsbury, when keeper of Mary Queen of Scots, petitioned for a larger allowance on account of her habit of bathing in wine' (Lodge, *Illustrations of British History*, i, p. 490). Crete is known for sweet wines.

415 *gold and amber*: see notes on lines 84 and 87 above.

P

416 *until my roof whirl round . . .*: till even my house, dizzied by
the splendour, spins round.

420 *Europa . . . Jove*: Zeus, chief of the Greek gods (in Roman
mythology Jove or Jupiter), carried off Europa while he was
in the guise of a bull; he appeared while she was playing on
the shore and bore her off, swimming, to Crete.

421 *Mars . . . Erycine*: Mars is the god of war. Erycine is one of
many names for Venus, goddess of love, who had a temple
on Mount Eryx in Sicily.

427 *Persian Sophy*: the Shah of Persia.

428 *the Grand Signor*: the Sultan of Turkey.

432 *transfuse*: pour out into another vessel.

440 *any part that yet sounds man about you*: anything in you that
still proclaims you a man.

441 *If you have touch . . .*: If you have the least trace in you of the
saints or of heaven – the two sources of 'grace'.

455 *disfavour me*: make me unattractive, mar my beauty.

460 *Nestor's hernia*: Nestor, king of Pylos, accompanied the
Greeks to Troy in spite of his age. It is Juvenal who suggests his hernia: *Satires*, vi, 326.

461 *degenerate*: lose the qualities proper to one's race or kind.
abuse my nation: cast aspersions on Italian virility.

470 *dross*: literally 'scum'. Here contemptuously for lucre, money.
thy idol: Volpone's worship of gold, expressed in the opening
speech of the play, is thrown in his teeth.

487 *Who would have thought he would have hearkened so?*: Who
could have foreseen that Bonario would have eavesdropped
like that?

491 *Let's die like Romans*: stoically, by falling on one's sword to
avoid the dishonour of capture.

492 *Since we have lived like Grecians*: The Romans thought of the
Greeks as dissolute and unscrupulous; Juvenal has a long
passage on the Greeks in his third satire in which he calls
them 'a nation of play-actors' (line 100) and declares 'there
is nothing sacred to his (the Greek's) lusts' (109). The
tradition was passed on through the classics: 'the mad
Greeks' and 'the merry Greeks' had long been current

phrases in Jonson's time – Shakespeare has the latter twice
in *Troilus and Cressida*, II, i and IV, iv: 'A woeful Cressid
'mongst the merry Greeks.'

493   *saffi*: 'Saffo, a catchpole, a sergeant . . .' (Florio, 1598); 'the
       saffi are mere bailiffs' followers, and subordinate to the
       commandadori' (Gifford).

494   *the brand Hissing already*: branding, on the forehead or else-
       where, was not an uncommon punishment for certain
       infamous crimes (Jonson was branded on the thumb, see
       the Introduction, p. 8). In cases of treason, in particular,
       the culprit's ears might be cut off, but why Volpone should
       anticipate the 'boring' of his ears I do not know.

497   *Make that place good, however*: Maintain that pretence, at
       least.
       Guilty men Suspect, etc.: Mosca is rallying; he suggests that
       their guilty consciences may be exaggerating the disaster.

500   *Your son*, etc.: one of Mosca's masterpieces of ingenious deceit
       follows, and one of Jonson's most brilliant pieces of narra-
       tive dovetailing.

506   *This act shall disinherit him indeed*: This pious indignation is
       belated: Corbaccio has already plotted to make over his
       goods to Volpone; but he now renounces his intention of
       re-establishing Bonario as his heir later.

511   *Today?*: Corbaccio is still troubled with deafness.

512   *a dram*: a dose, here a dose that would be fatal.

515   *Scarce, To the discovery of your tricks*: sardonic. Voltore says
       he can hardly imagine he is welcome at the moment when
       he has just overheard Mosca's double-dealing. He shows,
       by repeating some of Mosca's words, that he has heard
       part of the conversation with Corbaccio. The whirligig is
       speeding up, but Mosca is still able to survive from crisis to
       crisis.

517   *You are his only? and mine also*: You tell him the same as you
       told me.

520   *Put not your foists upon me: I shall scent them*: Don't try your
       roguery on me: I shall see through you.

530   *disclaiming in him*: renouncing his son's legal claim on him.

534   *you be stated in a double hope*: with Corbaccio and Bonario both
       out of the way (the one killed, the other in prison) and

Volpone's bequest to Voltore swelled with Corbaccio's wealth.

537 *sepulchres*: tombs, a metaphor for the two old men, supposedly on their last legs, Volpone and Corbaccio.

560 *pray . . . devotion*: by now a familiar line of imagery.

ACT IV, SCENE i

1 *You see What observation is*: you see what keeping one's eyes open and one's wits about one can do.

2 *You mentioned me For some instructions*: You said something about my being able to give you some tips: Peregrine certainly said no such thing.

6 *Only for this meridian*: especially for this part of the world. It will be remembered that Sir Politic sets himself up as an expert in all matters relating to travel.

8 *your phrase*, etc.: On Sir Politic's use of 'your' see note to II, i, 75. Here Peregrine, in an unsuccessful attempt to embarrass him, pretends to mistake him and to take his words as a personal aspersion.

11 *slander you no more of wit*: Sir Politic has missed the point. Peregrine promises for the future never to do him the injustice of saying he is quick-witted.

12 *First*, etc.: advice to young travellers was a stock commodity. Polonius proffers it to Laertes, and the Countess to Helena in *All's Well that Ends Well*.

14 *scarce A fable but with caution*: and don't even tell a story without thinking twice.

19 *Others*: those whom one *can* avoid conversing with.

20 *So as I still might be a saver in them*: so that I can always save myself all the trouble and inconvenience they might cause me.

21 *tricks else passed upon you hourly*: Sir Politic imagines everyone has designs against him; but the one time a trick is played on him he is taken quite by surprise. 'Else' here is 'otherwise'.

23 *the diversity of all*: the contradictions that exist between sects.

26 *Nick Machiavel*: Niccolo Machiavelli (1469–1527), a Florentine statesman and political philosopher whose best-known

work, *The Prince*, was a shrewd and realistic analysis of the policies which could lead to the unification of Italy. He was often grossly misrepresented, especially by dramatists, as a monster of self-seeking unscrupulousness and ungodliness. By making Sir Politic falsely attribute the views here stated to Machiavelli Jonson is far from contributing to this myth, but is satirising those who ignorantly misquote this author.

Bodin: Jean Bodin (1530–96) was a founder of modern political science. He argued that since complete religious unity was impossible, it was wanton to wreck the state in attempting to achieve it.

28 *your silver fork at meals*: Herford and Simpson have the following note (I have modernised the text of the quotation): 'Knives for eating purposes began commonly to take the place of fingers in 1563, and forks were not in much use before 1611. Thus in 1616 Jonson makes a projector plan

> The laudable use of forks,
> Brought into custom here, as they are in Italy,
> To the sparing of napkins.
> (*The Devil Is An Ass*, V, iv, 18–20 [V, iii, 46–48
> in Gifford]).'

29 *metal*: 'the material used for making glass, in a molten state' (*O.E.D.*). Sir Politic is stating the need to understand the niceties of using glassware at table: Venetians have long been connoisseurs of glass.

32 *point of state*: matter of moment, a point of diplomacy.

34 *Preposterous*: literally, putting last what should be first, hence contrary to nature or reason (or, with Sir Politic, to convention).

he has him straight: he sums him up in a trice.

40 *Contrarene*: Cardinal Gasparo Contarine published a book about Venice in 1589, *De Magistratibus et Republica Venetorum*, which appeared in an English translation by Lewis Lewknor in 1599.

46 *As how?*: How, for instance?

projects: most projectors were clever frauds who persuaded people to invest money in fabulous schemes (like the South Sea Bubble, but on a smaller scale). Gulliver visited the Academy of Projectors in Lagado. Sir Politic is genuinely infatuated with his own ideas.

54 *one of the States*: a member of the Dutch States-General.
to that purpose: about this matter.

57 *some others*: both Quarto and Folio have 'some other'.

60 *hoy*: a large, one-decked boat, commonly rigged as a sloop.

63 *So if there come but one of three, I save*: So even if only one of these trips is completed, I shall cut my losses.

64 *If two, I can defalk*: If two come home, I can take my profit out of the turn-over; 'defalk' is to allow a deduction.

66 *the subtle air*: the refining air or atmosphere.

67 *my thousand aims*: a thousand tricks up my sleeve.

69 *considerative*: pensive, summing up the prospects.

73 *pension*: a common form of recognition for service to the state.

74 *Great Council . . . the Forty . . . the Ten*: the hierarchy of administrative bodies in Venice.

75 *My means are made already*: my contacts (with the administration) are already established.

77 *he can sway*: he has some influence.

78 *sergeant*: 'An officer . . . who is charged with the arrest of offenders or the summoning of persons to appear before the court' (*O.E.D.*).

79 *such as they are, put it in their mouths What they should say*, etc.: such men as this commendator may sometimes put into the senators' mouths the very words which they will deliver in council, just as easily as great men may.

83 *to anticipate*: to try and get in first.
Nor reveal A circumstance: nor give away any details.

89 *Put case*: put the case, let us suppose.

93 *Except yourself, sir*: A teasing reply.
Go to, then: Very well, then.

97 *To enjoy them*: To have the benefit of tinder-boxes.

98 *Sealed at some office*: registered – the modern equivalent would be to issue a licence.

101 *By present demonstration*: by a test on the spot.

102 *Soria*: Syria. With the pronunciation here marked, the 'arrived' earlier in the line must be given three syllables, as was common.

103   *suspected*: plague-ridden. Fear of the plague was an ever-present concern.

106   *Lazaretto*: there were two outer islands of Venice with Lazarettos or pest-houses, at this time. Suspected ships would be made to remain in quarantine off these islands for long periods.

      for their trial: to see whether they carry plague or not.

107   *I'll save that charge*: I'll avoid that expense.

108   *clear the doubt*: free everyone of uncertainty as to whether the ship is infected.

109   *Or I will lose my labour*: or I'm wasting my time.

110   *onions*: Regarded as 'the best fortification against the plague ... Three or four peeled onions left on the ground for ten days would gather all the infection in the neighbourhood' (F. P. Wilson, *The Plague in Shakespeare's London*, 9: quoted by Herford and Simpson).

114   *venture*: put up the money for.

119   *waterworks*: contrivances operated by water.

124   *By his changed colour*: Sir Politic's theory being that plague will change the surface hue of the onions.

126   *Now it is known, it is nothing*: Now I've told you, it seems obvious.

138   *I threw three beans over the threshold*: a hodge-podge of superstitious practices. Theophrastus in his portrait of a superstitious man makes him throw three stones across the way if a cat crosses in front of him. Beans play a part in many magic practices, perhaps because Pythagoras prohibited them.

139   *one I burst immediately, in a discourse*: modern visitors to the Continent will have noticed the many uses to which toothpicks can be put in an argument to emphasise a point. In Jonson's time the English had not lost the custom of using toothpicks.

141   *ragion del stato*: the pros and cons of state affairs.

142   *moccenigo*: a coin of negligible value.

148   *Sure, he's housed*: Doubtless he's indoors – the implication being that by now Sir Politic has accompanied the lady to her home.

149 *fast*: safe from detection. Also a play on the phrase 'fast and loose', as Lady Would-be notices in 'he plays both with me'.

150 *stay*: give up the chase, rest.

152 *I do not care to hinder, but to take him*: Lady Would-be is interested only in catching Sir Politic in the act, not in merely preventing the transgression.

153 *How it comes off*: Lady Wishfort in Congreve's *The Way of the World* (1700) describes herself when her make-up is cracked by violent annoyance as 'arrantly flayed – I look like an old peeled wall'.

154 *That same's the party – In man's apparel*: Lady Would-be, not to be fooled of her quarry, at once convinces herself that the courtesan invented by Mosca exists in the person of Peregrine, whom she supposes to be a harlot in disguise.

157 *However he demerit*: however little he deserves.

159 *Were she not mine*: Though it's not for me to say so.

161 *It seems you are not jealous*: Corvino and Sir Politic are equally cavalier with their wives' reputations, the one from viciousness, the other from mere folly.

163 *Being your wife . . .*: If she's your wife, I'm sure she knows how to talk.

165 *None*: Lady Would-be triumphantly seizes the opportunity to show that she 'knows' that Peregrine is really a woman in disguise.

166 *Has put his face as soon into the world –*: Knows his way about at so early an age . . .

167 *You mean as early? but today?*: She takes him up sarcastically, implying that Sir Politic's companion has assumed a man's appearance only for the occasion.

172 *massacre*: two pronunciations were current – with stress on the first syllable (as today) or on the second (as here).

177 *humbled*: Peregrine mocks the paltriness of the oath Sir Politic uses to express his knighthood. Jonson is glancing scornfully at James I's wholesale creation of knights.

178 *your polity May bear it through thus*: your brazenness may try to carry off the affair like this.

181 *With any gentlewoman*: Lady Would-be now addresses
     Peregrine directly, still taking him to be a woman in dis-
     guise.

182 *the courtier*: Castiglione's manual of behaviour entitled *The
     Courtier* (*Il Cortegiano*) (1528) discusses women's conduct
     in Lady Would-be's vein.

189 *is not warranted From being a solecism*: does not escape the
     imputation of impropriety. Lady Would-be, far from being
     ironic, is absurdly trying to avoid what she would regard as
     vulgar plain speaking or strong feeling.

192 *Come nearer to your aim*: Stop beating about the bush.

195 *Sporus*: Nero's favourite, a eunuch, whom he dressed as a
     woman and publicly 'married'.

195 *hermaphrodite*: Lady Would-be yet again expresses her belief
     that Sir Politic's companion is both man and woman, the
     one in appearance, the other in fact.

196 *historic storms*: in a text as well presented as Jonson's there
     seems no ground for suggesting 'historic' has been confused
     with 'hysteric'. Peregrine is, rather, ironically describing
     Lady Would-be's rage as comparable to the furies of the
     great, which shake dynasties and affect epochs.

198 *Whitefriars nation*: the modern equivalent of 'nation' would
     be 'set' or 'gang'. The precinct of the former priory of the
     Carmelites or White Friars lay between Fleet Street and the
     River Thames. Even after the disappearance of the monks
     it remained a 'liberty', outside the jurisdiction of the City
     of London, and therefore a refuge for the disreputable.

206 *you may carry it clear, with your state-face*: you can try to pass
     the matter off, with your pose of innocence: Sir Politic is
     pretending, as she thinks, that he did not know Peregrine
     to be a woman.

207 *carnival*: originally specifically applied to the revels before
     Lent in Catholic countries; these were often riotous and
     licentious.

208 *for liberty of conscience From furious persecution of the marshal*:
     Lady Would-be is playing on the term 'liberty of con-
     science', which means freedom from religious persecution.
     She suggests that this 'harlot' has fled to that part of the

city from the marshal (a prison officer) since he would per-
secute her for her faith, which is prostitution.

211 *do you use this often?*: do you often behave like this?

212 *against you have occasion*: whenever you find the opportunity.

216 *A nearer way*: without all this ado. Peregrine is at last getting
angry.

work you Out: release you, let you wriggle out.

220 *queen-apple*: O.E.D.: 'an early variety of apple'. *Chambers's
Twentieth Century Dictionary*: 'apparently a quince'.
Peregrine likens Lady Would-be's nose to a fruit which is
redder on one side than the other. Nano has already re-
marked on its redness (III, ii, 47).

223 *Right not my quest*: don't do me justice in this suit.

protest them . . . no aristocracy: deny they are a true aristo-
cractic government (that is, a council of state comprising
the best or noblest citizens).

237 *use me*: let me do whatever I can for you – though the
innuendo is strengthened by the equivocal use of 'conceive'
in 239.

241 *Sir Politic Bawd*: Peregrine now supposes the whole farcical
situation to have been calculated.

243 *practised thus Upon my freshmanship*: plotted against my
inexperience.

244 *salt-head*: another double meaning: salt = salacious and
salt = dried (as opposed to 'fresh').

ACT IV, SCENE ii

1 *the carriage of the business*: how the affair is to be managed.

4 *Safely conveyed*: consistently passed on. They want to be sure
that their accounts will tally.

6 *the advocate*: Voltore; he is being employed to present the dishonest case of the other parties whose reputations are
engaged.

10 *Should make him stand for co-heir*: that he will make such a
good case that Volpone will be moved to make him a legatee.

11　*use his tongue . . . As we do Croaker's here*: we'll just make use
　　of Voltore's tongue as we're doing with Corbaccio's here.
　　Mosca coins the nickname Croaker for The Raven.

12　*Aye, what shall he do*: Corvino is now tormented by Cor-
　　baccio's rivalry as legacy-hunter.

14　*mummia*: powdered flesh from Egyptian mummies was prized
　　for its supposed medicinal qualities. There was a brisk trade
　　in fake mummia produced by baking corpses. Corbaccio,
　　Mosca hints, will need no such preparation.

15　*buffalo . . . sport it with his head*: referring to Corvino's
　　cuckold's horns.

20　*But you shall eat it*: Never fear, it is you who will enjoy the
　　legacy – Mosca is going the rounds reassuring each of his
　　dupes in turn.
　　Worshipful sir: Mosca now addresses Voltore in the hearing of
　　all.

21　*Mercury*: not only messenger of the gods, but also patron of all
　　ready-tongued, quick-witted folk.

22　*French Hercules*: The tenth task of Hercules was to capture the
　　oxen of the monster Geryon, who dwelt in the distant west.
　　On his way home he fathered the founders of the Celtic race
　　– and so passed into Celtic mythology, wherein he is the
　　symbol of eloquence.

25　*But much more yours*: because Voltore hopes to gain most.

27　*I have her*: We know this is Lady Would-be.

31　*So the young man*: The Quarto reads 'So has the youth'.

36　*And all after-times*: and never will be equalled in future.

38　*Appear yet those were cited?*: Are those who have been called as
　　witnesses in court yet?

52　*he may be heard in me*: I can speak for him.

54　*crave it*: beg to be allowed to represent him.

71　*not knowing how to owe a gift Of that dear grace but with their
　　shame*: not knowing how to repay such gracious generosity
　　other than by admitting their shame, and being quite
　　beyond such gratitude, instead began to hate their indebted-
　　ness.

75　*to extirp*: how to root out.

78   *heart*: boldness. Voltore suggests they have become hardened and hence further emboldened by their own crimes.

86   *turns*: we still use the phrase 'a turn of events'.

91   *this settled purpose*: of disinheriting his son.

97   *designed For the inheritance*: chosen as heir in the son's place.

103   *It was to murder him*: This is the main drift of the ingenious misrepresentation of the facts the rogues have contrived.

106   *ever*: the reading of both Q and F. Whalley suggested 'never' in his 1756 edition, and has been followed by later editors.

112   *The stale to his forged practice*: the decoy in his deceitful plot.

114   *to note but my collections*: to take special note of my summing-up, my conclusions.

115   *stop His father's ends*: foil his father's intentions.

116   *discredit his free choice In the old gentleman*: show Corbaccio's unsolicited choice of Volpone as heir to be ill-judged.

129   *I would I could forget I were a creature*: 'creature' probably means a 'human being', so that the whole would be roughly equivalent to the modern 'I wish I were dead'; it implies 'God's creature' and hence 'His canon 'gainst self-slaughter' which restrains Celia. If, on the other hand, it is used in the sense of 'a creature dependant on another', Celia is regretting her close tie with Corvino, one of the instigators of the whole fraud.

132   *Speak to the knave?*: Corbaccio has simply been asked to give his evidence, but once again his hearing fails him.

133   *my heart Abhors his knowledge*: my very being draws back from acknowledging him. The cleavage between father and child is made very emphatic since it is an important element in the distorted world of the play.

135   *The mere portent of nature!*: He's simply a freak of nature.

137   *made you to this*: persuaded you into this.

139   *Sir, I will sit down*, etc.: Bonario's filial submissiveness underlines the heinousness of Corbaccio's conduct, without allowing the good character to become too forceful or dramatically dominant.

145   *partridge*: traditionally known as a lustful creature.

146　*jennet*: a small but high-mettled Spanish horse. Corvino's
　　　language is reaching a hysterical pitch.

151　*here*: 'Corvino touches his forehead, making with his fingers
　　　the letter V, the sign of the cuckold' (Herford and Simpson).
　　　'Thorough the horn' (between the horns) is yet another
　　　reference to the emblem of the deceived husband, but now,
　　　as the feverish tempo increases, in the mouth of the self-
　　　styled cuckold himself. There is a pun on horn-book, which
　　　was a primer.

154　*There is no shame* . . .: a savagely satirical line, far more telling
　　　than the Quarto version, which reads 'harm' for 'shame'.

155　*Or if I said, I hoped*, etc.: Let me add, I hope she is well on the
　　　way to being damned, since a good Catholic may well doubt
　　　whether there is a worse hell than whoredom and woman-
　　　hood. Needless to say, this is a complete perversion of
　　　theology. When the Quarto appeared Jonson was a Roman
　　　Catholic: the Quarto text reads 'Christian' instead of
　　　'Catholic'. The latter is more appropriate to Venice.

159　*Rare!*: Marvellous! Cp. the playwright's epitaph, 'O rare
　　　Ben Jonson'.

163　*when he missed*: referring to Bonario.

168　*doubt the imposture*: have real misgivings that Bonario's case
　　　may be an imposture.

178　*Without*: outside, attending on the court.

182　*Be resolute, madam*: This prompting makes it doubly clear
　　　that Mosca has rehearsed Lady Would-be in her part.

183　*chameleon*: the small lizard that can change its colour to blend
　　　with its background.

184　*Vie tears with the hyaena*: Compete with the hyaena in weep-
　　　ing 'crocodile tears'. The hyaena was symbolic of treachery.

185　*I cry your pardons*: I beg forgiveness.

190　*or my sex's*: or my sex's honour. One of Lady Would-be's less
　　　graceful constructions. Not even the court can control her
　　　tongue.

193　*To offend With pertinency*: Lady Would-be speaks truer than
　　　she knows. Her words actually mean that she is not one to

occupy the court with saying anything that might be relevant. Presumably the meaning she aims at is 'impertinency',
irrelevance.

196 *Let her o'ercome*: let her have her way, let her have the last
word.

201 Stage direction – LADY WOULD-BE *embraces him*: Volpone
recalls this embrace later (V, i, 114); this is the only opportunity for Lady Would-be to administer it.

213 *strappado*: a form of torture in which the victim is suspended
at a great height by a rope from his wrists, which are
strapped together behind his back: he is then jerked
violently downwards, so that enormous strain is put on all
his muscles, and excess of blood is forced to the extremities
of his body.

214 *The rack hath cured the gout*: a popular tradition. Herford and
Simpson quote two other dramatic references to this
notion.

215 *help him of*: cure him of – ironic, of course.

217 *as many left diseases*: (even supposing the rack *did* cure his
gout) Volpone would still have as many diseases left as . . .

223 *traduce*: slander. Voltore argues that if Bonario and Celia
escape unpunished, every citizen will be at the mercy of any
slanderer or blackmailer.

226 *face or colour*: appearance or semblance.

232 *hot and fleshed*: violent and hardened.

239 *These are two creatures!*: What monsters these two are!
I have an earthquake in me: the judges' indignation has now
been diverted from the guilty to the innocent.

242 *In their discovery*: in uncovering their actions.

248 *St Mark's*: the central square in front of the cathedral.

249 *I would have you go*: I think it would be a good idea if you
went.

252 *the other*: that he had prostituted his wife to Volpone.

255 *doubt this advocate*: Corvino is still concerned lest Voltore
should persuade Volpone to make him an heir.

256 *ease you of that care*: relieve you of that worry.

260   *Rest you with both your eyes*: leave everything to me, in other
      words.

262   *be put in*: is included in the inventory of what I am to inherit.

263   *Curtain-rings,   sir*:   Mosca's   heavy   sarcasm   passes   over
      Corbaccio's head.

265   *you'll be too prodigal*: Corbaccio's meanness towards Voltore,
      who has carried through their schemes, is the finishing touch
      to the picture of warped values in the first court scene.

266   *I must tender it*: I must give it to him. Mosca does not want to
      miss any chance of ingratiating himself with his prey.
      chequeens: gold coins: see the note to I, i, 284.

270   *Bountiful bones!*: the smallness of the tip accompanying
      'There's for thee' no doubt provokes this caustic comment.

272   *Worthy this age*: to make him deserve to be like this in his old
      age.

273   *Unto your ends*: to serve your interests.
      Take you no notice: a conspiratorial touch. 'Don't let people
      see us talking together,' says Mosca. This little perfor-
      mance keeps Voltore content, and gets rid of him.

274   *the devil and all*: 'the whole damned lot'. Mosca mutters these
      imprecations at Voltore's departing back.

ACT V, SCENE i

  2   *was in dislike with*: disliked.

  3   *this fled moment*: the time that has just passed.
      here: in his own house.

  4   *in your public*: in a public gathering.
      cave: Latin, literally 'Beware'; roughly equivalent to the
      modern 'Heaven forbid'.

  5   *'gan*: began. The apostrophe indicates that Jonson recognised
      this as an archaic form.

  8   *A many*: too many, a great number.

 12   *Hum, hum, hum*: simply a way of indicating the musing noises
      Volpone makes as he considers the effect the wine is having
      on his spirits.

 16   *make me up again*: make me my old self.

17 *This heat*: the warmth engendered by the wine.
'tis blood by this time: Volpone feels as if the wine has run straight into his bloodstream.

18 *Does the day*, etc.: Mosca's questions are rhetorical, a means of basking in their triumph.

19 *wrought out of error Into our way*: rescued from straying and set once more on our intended way.

21 *Is our trade free*: Are we to practise our profession?

23 *Good wits are greatest in extremities*: This comment goes straight to the heart of Mosca's genius; and also serves as an apt comment on Jonson's creation of climax, and indeed of plot.

26 *taken with it*: thrilled with it. Mosca is now revelling in his own virtuosity after Volpone's manner, and wants to see his master equally impressed with his skill.

27 *more than if I had enjoyed the wench*: a key line in presenting the protagonists' exultation in the exercise of the pure art of deceit, or, even more, of manipulating human beings.

29 *now you speak*: now you're talking.

30 *Here we must rest*: This is a major crux in the whole play, discussed in the Introduction.

32 *played your prize*: a prize is a contest or match. The modern equivalent is roughly 'You've had a good run for your money' or 'You've shot your bolt'.
Nay, sir: an interjection rather than a negative. The implication is: 'Maybe I'm played out, but just look what's been achieved.'

33 *To gull the court*: to make fools of the court of justice.

38 *Should not scent somewhat, or in me or thee*: should not smell a rat either in my conduct or yours.

45 *Like a temptation of the devil*: complex irony. It completes Mosca's analogy; but, in fact, we have seen all the characters concerned submitting on all sides to devilish temptations.

49 *Did not your advocate rare?*: Didn't Voltore give a brilliant performance?

50 *'My most honoured fathers*, etc.': Volpone, the born mimic and actor, seizes the chance to imitate Voltore.

54　*forbear laughing*: stop myself from laughing.

58　*Never but still myself*: Never anything but in full command of myself: as, indeed, one would expect of Volpone.

60　*And out of conscience*: my conscience prompts me.

63　*to contrary you*: to go against you. Mosca is mocking Voltore's oratory in these lines.

65　*By that I heard him in the latter end*: from what I heard of the end of his speech (after Volpone had been brought into the court).

67　*Draw it to certain heads*: summarise his arguments.

68　*I looked still When he would shift a shirt*: I was in constant expectation that he was going to change his shirt. Mosca compares Voltore's dramatic gestures with those one makes in dressing and undressing.

70　*no hope of gain*: ironic, of course.

80　*What do you mean, sir?*: What are you about?

85　*have it ravished*: Mosca naturally jumps to the conclusion that the legacy-hunters will arrive to find Volpone alive; till Volpone goes on to explain his real purpose.

89　*one of those that has the blanks*: wills completed but for spaces where the legatees are to be named.

95　*and was fain*: the pronoun 'I' is to be understood.

103　*With what degrees*: how quickly and completely.

105　*dull*: downcast. 'Will be completely put out of countenance' is the meaning of the whole line.

107　*clarissimo*: Venetian nobleman – Corbaccio.

108　*crump you like a hog-louse with the touch*: curl up like a wood-louse when it's touched. The 'you' is ethic dative.

110　*a rope and a dagger*: the characteristic weapons of those driven mad by despair (cp. the victims of Despair in the *Faerie Queene*, Book I, canto IX, stanzas 22 and 51). Mosca pictures Corvino running mad through the streets carrying them.

114　*kissed me*: This can only have been at his entry at IV, ii, 201, where I have added a stage direction accordingly.

115　*your gold Is such another medicine*: This important line of imagery is taken up again from Acts I and II.

Q

119   *the strange poetical girdle*: the Cestus, or girdle of Venus,
      which endowed even the ugly or deformed with grace and
      beauty, and kindled desire in the aged.

      Jove . . . To pass Acrisius' guards: An oracle declared that
      Danae, the daughter of Acrisius, would bear a son who
      would slay him. So Acrisius shut Danae in a tower of brass;
      but Jove came to her from above as a shower of gold (hence
      the aptness of the image here) and she bore Perseus, who
      did in fact kill his grandfather accidentally with a discus.
      'To himself' means 'for himself'.

122   *Makes all the world her grace . . .*: provides all the grace,
      youth and beauty in the world. Gold lends or casts over the
      world a pall of glamour.

123   *I think she loves me*: Volpone cannot believe that Celia could
      seriously reject him. When Mosca replies: 'She's jealous of
      you' his words are tinged with irony, but are still pandering
      to Volpone's hopes – 'of you' being 'concerning you':
      Mosca explains her conduct as feminine wiles, or pique.

127   *posture*: act. Mosca replies that he is quite ready (set).

128   *artificer*: craftsman. Mosca is to show himself a skilled tor-
      turer.

131   *tissue*: a rich cloth – originally interwoven with gold and silver.

132   *the while*: meanwhile. He lists the items for Voltore's benefit.

135   *his care*: the trouble he is taking.

137   Stage direction: *peeping from his hiding-place*: The Folio has
      the stage direction: *Volpone peeps from behind a traverse*. It
      is difficult to fix exactly the meaning of 'traverse'. It has
      sometimes been taken as a curtain dividing off the inner
      stage, but this interpretation presents difficulties (E. K.
      Chambers, *The Elizabethan Stage*, iii, 78). Chambers else-
      where (ibid., iii, 26) – partly in reference to *Volpone* – sum-
      marises his own view: 'Properly a "traverse" means, I
      think, not a curtain suspended from the roof, but a screen
      shutting off from view a compartment within a larger room,
      but leaving it open above. Such a screen might, of course,
      very well be formed by a curtain on a rod or cord.'
      What does the advocate: What is the advocate doing . . .?

139   *Is his thread spun?*: i.e. spun to the end. Lady Would-be can-
      not bring herself to say simply 'Is he dead?' The reference

is to the three Fates spinning the thread of man's destiny; death comes when the thread is cut.

141   *rid them hence*: get rid of them, pack them off.

142   *diaper*: an elaborately woven linen fabric.

148   *suits of hangings*: sets of tapestries – for hanging against walls or around four-poster beds.

149   *in their garters*: Volpone plays on the word 'Hangings', hoping the vultures will hang themselves with their garters (bands for keeping up their hose) when they learn the truth.

150   *at the gasp*: at their last gasp.

153   *glazen-eyes*: Corbaccio wears spectacles. He is always the last to grasp what is happening. His next speech shows that he believes the others are desperate on learning that he, Corbaccio, is heir.

156   *cabinets*: boxes or cases for keeping valuables or documents securely.

159   *thrown*: thrust. Mosca exasperates them by expressing a certain weariness with all the business of wealth that has been forced on him unexpectedly.

164   *Is this my large hope's issue?*: Is this all that is to come of my great expectations?

170   *e'en your best madams did For maintenance*: what even the greatest ladies do to get an income.

176   *been the example*: led the way.

179   *wittol*: one who connives at his wife's adultery.

181   *on good terms*: fair and square, without any doubt.

184   *good works*: charity, Mosca sardonically implies.

186   *extraordinary . . . in title*: Corvino is cuckold extraordinary, in title only, because Celia's publicly declared adultery is a pretence: Corvino has, so to speak, an honorary post. Mosca promises not to 'betray' the fact that he really tried to prostitute his wife himself (the secret which still gives Mosca a hold over him).

188   *melancholic*: in a state of nervous depression.

191   *his four eyes*: Corbaccio is spectacled: see line 153.

193   *Harlot*: used in the older sense, a person of low birth or vulgar (rather than immoral) behaviour. Chaucer's Summoner was 'a gentle harlot and a kind'.

196   *three legs*: The riddle of the Sphinx was: 'What has in the morning four legs, in the daytime two, and at night three?' Oedipus gave the correct answer – man, who crawls in childhood, walks in manhood, and hobbles with a stick in old age.

198   *would have hired Me to the poisoning of my patron*: see III, ii, 512.

211   *defeat . . . travails*: frustrate your efforts.

224   *Conceive me, for your fee*: Understand me, I shall expect to pay the usual fee. Under this show of good-will, Mosca is being bitingly patronising.

230   *lettuce*: recognised as a laxative, but no doubt specially mentioned here by Volpone since it was also regarded as a cure for choler and frenzies.

233   *habit of clarissimo*: nobleman's robes. Herford and Simpson quote Coryat, *Crudities*, 259, on the clarissimo's regalia: 'Most of their gownes are made of blacke cloth, and ouer their left shoulder they haue a flappe made of the same cloth, and edged with blacke Taffeta. And most of their gownes are faced before with blacke Taffeta.'

235   *We must pursue*: this 'must' means simply that Volpone cannot resist the idea, not that there is anything necessary for their schemes in this tormenting of the victims.

236   *I doubt it will lose them*: I'm afraid after this we've seen the last of them. Mosca realises they have killed the goose (or geese) which laid the golden eggs.

237   *My recovery shall recover all*: They'll get over it when they find I'm not dead after all. Volpone is blandly confident.

242   *commandatori*: officers: see the note under 'Persons of the Play'.

247   *The Fox fares ever best . . .*: 'The fox fares best when he is cursed', an apt proverb here. The fox is cursed, of course, when he escapes, not when he is caught.

ACT V, SCENE ii

1　*I warrant you*: I assure you of that.

4　*Zant*: Zante or Xanthe in Thrace.

5　*Book of Voyages*: quips at the expense of the fashion for travel books are common in literature of the period. Hackluyt's have remained the best known.

6　*his gulled story*: the story of how he has been gulled.

7　*when I am in a while*: when I have been in with him for a time.

8　*warm in our discourse*: busy talking.

9　*Know your approaches*: be ready to enter.

16　*require him whole*: require his whole attention.

17　*possess him*: enjoy his company.

18　*exact him*: demand immediate action from him.

21　*Bolognian sausages*: 'The *mortadella* of Bologna is still famous. Sir Thomas Gresham imported it to England from Rotterdam' (Herford and Simpson).
　　sparing One of the ingredients: doing without one of the constituents, in order to increase the profits.

23　*your word 'tidings'*: a homely word. 'You are no statesman' coming from Sir Politic might mean (implying relief) 'You are no spy' – he always fears himself under observation, in which case 'wills you stay' is 'asks you to remain as a welcome guest'; or the first phrase could mean 'you are a person of no consequence', in which case 'wills you stay' would be 'bids you to wait until he is ready'. Peregrine seems to assume the latter sense; but Sir Politic's immediate appearance the former.

36　*has made relation*: has given an account.

37　*a plot To sell the state of Venice to the Turk*: part of Sir Politic's chatter in IV, i – lines 128–131.

42　*Drawn out of play-books*: Sir Politic's fear betrays the source of his conversational material.

45　*if you could lie round, a frail were rare*: if you could curl up, a rush basket would be ideal. Frails were containers made of rushes for figs and raisins.

46   *I but talked so, For discourse sake merely*: Peregrine is achieving
      his aim of calling the bluff of Sir Politic's pretentious folly.

48   *a wretch*: one who is wretched or unfortunate.

52   – *that I have thought upon before time*: (a device) I have prepared
      for just such an emergency.

55   *Fitted for these extremities*: designed for such a crisis.

66   *you may strike him*: under pretence of substantiating Sir
      Politic's disguise, Peregrine urges the merchants to give him
      a beating.

68   *Can he not go?*: Can't it move?

74   *even*: quits: for the humiliation Peregrine underwent in being
      mistaken for a woman by Lady Would-be, which Peregrine
      laid to Sir Politic's door.   It is an added irony that Sir
      Poll is punished for the one bit of folly he did not originate.

76   *funeral of your notes*: Sir Politic's order 'Bid my wife's women
      to burn my papers' has been carried out: Peregrine likens the
      burning to a funeral pyre.

78   *in the term*: the law terms would be specially busy periods in
      the Fleet Street area, with the adjacent Inns of Court in full
      residence, and the lawyers' country clients being in town,
      many of them with their families.
      Smithfield: the site of Bartholomew Fair.   A puppet-play is a
      centre-piece in Jonson's play of *Bartholomew Fair*.

79   *melancholic*: Sir Politic is lent a touch of pathos at the last.

82   *the fable of all feasts*: Sir Politic fears that his 'gulled story' will
      be the chief gossip of every fashionable dinner party . . .

83   *The freight of the gazetti; ship-boys' tale*: . . . and the main item
      both in the news-sheets and the ship-boys' chatter . . .

84   *even talk for ordinaries*: . . . and, worst of all, the chief topic in
      common eating-houses.

86   *she will straight to sea, for physic*: she will set sail from Venice
      for the sake of her health.

88   *Creeping with house on back*: a hint that he will carry the lesson
      he has learnt in the tortoise-shell with him, supported again
      by the next line, his last in the play.

ACT V, SCENE iii

2　*sever you*: tell you apart. Volpone has asked if he now looks
　　like the commandator he is impersonating.

3　*thou becom'st it*: the part suits you.

4　*If I hold My made one, 'twill be well*: Even if I only act out the
　　part, I shall be doing quite well. Nominally a modest reply
　　to Volpone's compliment; we are about to learn that it has a
　　private double meaning for Mosca – he does not mean to
　　relinquish his role as Volpone's heir.

6　*My fox Is out of his hole*: a play on the name of the children's
　　game Fox-in-the-Hole. The original text has 'out on' for
　　'out of'; the former is found now only in dialects.

9　*Except he come to composition*: unless he strikes a bargain.

11　*go, sport*: go and enjoy yourselves.

16　*cozen him of all*: cheat him of everything. In the court scene
　　Mosca first asks Volpone to go halves; only when he refuses
　　does Mosca bid for the whole fortune.

18　*Let his sport pay for 't*: it's a proper price for him to pay for his
　　amusement.
　　the Fox-trap: direct allusions to Volpone as the Fox multiply
　　in the last act – instance his own concluding quip to V, i,
　　Mosca's 'My Fox is out of his hole' in the present scene, and,
　　of course, Volpone's final, sardonic 'This is called mortifying
　　of a Fox'.

ACT V, SCENE iv

3　*Why, mine's no tale*: Corvino has nearly given himself away.
　　Corbaccio, however, is also maintaining a false front, since
　　his claim that he intended to disinherit his son because of his
　　improper conduct is untrue: at the time Bonario's behaviour
　　had not been called in question.

5　*your will*: the will Corbaccio has made in Volpone's favour,
　　which is now in Mosca's hands.

13　*You mock the world*: you are one up on all the rest of us.

17　*over-leavened with your fortune*: puffed up (as with yeast) by
　　your good fortune.

18   *You should have some would*: Some people would . . .

19   *With such an autumn*: an allusion to Corvino's supposed harvest.

21   *a very woman*: a thorough woman – in (supposedly) being un-
      faithful.
      you are well: you've got nothing to worry about.

22   *you have a good estate To bear it out, sir, better by this chance*:
      this course of events has made you better off by an estate, so
      you can put up with it (bear it out).

25   *You will not be aknown*: You will not disclose your good fortune.
      To be aknown is to be recognised, or self-confessed.

30   *make legs for crumbs*: bow and scrape for what he could get.

35   *a suitor . . . For the small tenement*: Pretending to believe
      Voltore has the inheritance, he begs him to be his patron and
      grant him a piece of his newly-acquired property.

36   *the small tenement out of reparations*: the small house which is
      out of repair.

40   *customed bawdy-house*: a well patronised brothel.

41   *none dispraised*: and this is doing no injustice to any of the
      others.

42   *But fell with him*: As Volpone (supposedly) declined, so did the
      brothel.

44   *if your worship give me but your hand That I may have the
      refusal, I have done*: if your honour will simply put it in
      writing that I shall be allowed the first refusal, I shall have no
      more to say.

46   *candle-rents*: income from property which is deteriorating (like
      the light from a candle, which consumes its own substance).

48   *God decrease it*: Voltore takes this ('Mistaking knave') as an
      ignorant misplacing of a word, after the manner of Dog-
      berry in *Much Ado About Nothing*, and Volpone means him
      to do so; but the magnifico is enjoying his own sly joke in
      thus taking the opportunity to curse Voltore to his face with
      impunity. The device is repeated a moment later when
      Voltore speaks of his 'misfortune' and Volpone replies
      'would 'twere more!'

51   *to my first again*: to return to my first victim.

52   *in our habit*: Mosca is robed like a magnifico.

53   *That I could*: exclamatory – 'I wish I could'.

54   *of the parasite*: about Mosca (being the heir).

58   *methought his nose should cozen*: even his nose had an air of
      deceit. Volpone rubs salt in their wounds by saying how
      obvious it had always been that Mosca would cheat them.

63   *such moral emblems on your name*: such admonitory fables
      relating to your name; Corvino means 'crow'.

64   *sung . . . cheese . . . Fox*: see the note on I, i, 184–6. The
      parallel is closer than Corvino can know, since the Fox is
      there in person laughing at his 'emptiness', that is his losing
      out all round. 'Sung your shame' refers to Corvino's public
      declarations in court.

66   *privilege of the place*: the legal protections for those on the public
      highway.

67   *red saucy cap . . . with those two chequeens*: 'The dress of a com-
      mandadore (officer of justice), in which Volpone was now
      disguised, consisted of a black stiff gown and a red cap with
      two *gilt buttons* in front' (Gifford): Corvino likens these
      buttons to gold pieces or chequeens.

69   *Can warrant your abuses*: can protect you while you hurl abuse.

74   *I were a wise man Would stand the fury*: What a wise fellow I
      would be if I were to try and withstand the fury . . .

77   *Let's fly him*: Let's fly from him. Corvino is speaking of Mosca.
      The disguised Volpone has tormented them, but they cannot
      bear even the sight of the triumphant Mosca.

78   *basilisk*: A fabulous reptile (also called a cockatrice) alleged to
      be hatched by a serpent from a cock's egg; its breath, and
      even its look, was said to be fatal.

82   *solecism*: a breach of propriety (often a linguistic mistake or
      vulgarism).

83   *biggin*: a skull-cap of lawn or silk worn by lawyers.

84   *Would you have me . . .*: Volpone pretends to be indignant on
      Voltore's behalf.

86   *some familiar*: realising he is being deliberately mocked,
      Voltore surmises that the disguised Volpone is a dependant
      of the household which appears to have fallen to Mosca.

87 *I am mad, a mule . . . should . . . ride an advocate*: I am furious
    that Mosca (the mule) should get the upper hand of Voltore.
    Lawyers customarily rode on mules.

88 *Justinian*: The Emperor Justinian I, who ruled the Eastern
    Roman Empire from 527 to 565, was renowned among other
    things for the code of Roman law, the *Corpus Juris Civilis*,
    which he caused to be drawn up.

89 *quirk*: a trick or quibble – here Volpone is no doubt suggesting
    a legal quibble.

92 *but confederacy to blind the rest*: only a plot to put the other
    legacy-hunters off the scent.

ACT V, SCENE v

 8 *Will he betray himself?*: Voltore has least to lose by making an
    exposure; by claiming that his clients misled him about the
    facts of the case he presented in IV, i he no doubt hopes to
    pass himself off as more sinned against than sinning. On the
    other hand, he no longer has anything to gain from their
    plots since he believes he has lost the inheritance to Mosca.
    He can therefore indulge his strongest desire, to revenge
    himself on Mosca by giving him away to the court.

10 *possessed*: that is, possessed by a devil, the common explanation
    of madness and fits.

13 *I'm caught In mine own noose*: The noose is Volpone's scheme
    of pretending himself dead and Mosca the heir in order to
    torment the vultures; in undertaking this he has cut the ties
    that held Voltore, and has prepared the way for this con-
    fusion.

24 *Dead since*: he died after the events the court is now consider-
    ing.

26 *The parasite, grave fathers*: it is the parasite who is the deceiver,
    your honours. Voltore does not intend to allow the cir-
    cumstantial evidence of Volpone's 'death' to exonerate
    Mosca.

27 *made The thing he gaped for*: given the place he had set his
    heart on – that is, the role of heir.

29 *I'll not justify The other, but he may be some-deal faulty*: I'll not
    exonerate the other party (Mosca), for indeed he may be in

the wrong to some extent. Corvino would be only too pleased to inculpate Mosca if he can do so without incriminating himself.

31　*to your hopes*, etc.: Mosca may have acted at variance with your expectations.

33　*notes*: a dramatic short cut. Jonson does not want Voltore to have to relate what we already know, so provides him with a written account to hand to the judges.

35　*The devil has entered him*: trenchant dramatic comment. The first time any of the vultures has spoken truth in court, his fellow accuses him of being possessed by the devil!

40　*Go you*: We learn from V, vii, 13 that it is the notary who is here dispatched with an obsequious message to Mosca now that the court learns he is a man of substance.

43　*Stand you unto*: Do you still maintain . . .?

44　*are at the stake*: Corvino is saying, 'I stake my wealth, my life, and my reputation on the truth of what I have said.' His report was, of course, totally false.

47　*So is the parasite*: Like Corvino, Corbaccio now wishes in revenge to involve Mosca while escaping himself.

50　Stage direction: *The scene closes*: I have adopted Gifford's phrase here. It is clear that the two court scenes, V, v and V, vii are to be taken as continuous, with the brief V, vi as an inset. We cannot know exactly how this was staged; (in passing it should be emphasised that there is no possibility that this large and important court scene could be squeezed into the obscurity of the tiny inner stage); but it is not difficult to imagine a number of ways in which it could have been readily accomplished.

ACT V, SCENE vi

1　*a snare*: cp. V, v, 13.

2　*with laughter*: gaily, without any misgiving.

4　*Out of mere wantonness*: I have discussed in the Introduction how Volpone enters into his final schemes for the sheer zest of it, with no eye to gain. He here comments on his own folly.

6   *gave it second*: seconded it. As at III, ii, 486, Volpone is again
     ready to complain of Mosca as soon as anything goes
     seriously wrong.

7   *sear up*: cauterise, a way of stemming the flow of blood from a
     wound by scorching.

9   *drown kitlings*: drown kittens; a savage and destructive pastime
     springs naturally to Volpone's mind.

13   *I am farther in*: things look worse and worse for me. This is the
     first intimation Volpone has had that Mosca may be playing
     him false, though this is still only a suspicion: 'His meaning
     may be truer than my fear', that is 'Mosca may not be play-
     ing me false, as I fear'.
     conceits: schemes. This, says Volpone, is where my fine
     schemes have landed me.

14   *I must be merry, with a mischief to me!*: I had to play my prac-
     tical jokes, devil take me!

21   *Unscrew my advocate upon new hopes*: calm down Voltore when
     he again realises he has expectations. 'Unscrew' is used in
     the sense of releasing pressure; and 'upon' in the still current
     sense of following upon.

ACT V, SCENE vii

10   *Obsession*: being controlled by an evil spirit.

12   *invent some other name*: find a better title. With Mosca's new-
     found prosperity, the court no longer accepts his being
     called 'the parasite'.
     sir varlet: 'varlet' ranges in meaning from 'servant' to 'knave'.
     The contemptuous 'sir' here indicates that the commendator
     who has slighted his superior is being put firmly in his place.

13   *the notary*: He was sent to Mosca with a courteous message at
     V, v, 40.

14   *Yet it is misty*: everything is still confused.

17   *You are still the man*: that is, the man chosen as Volpone's heir.

20   *Do I live, sir?*: He's as alive as I am. A nice piece of by-play,
     since Volpone is, of course, discussing himself.

22   *fall down*: Being possessed by a devil involved having fits.

23   *I'll help to make it good*: I'll join in making your act convincing.

24   *Stop your wind hard*: Hold your breath tight.

25   *He vomits crooked pins*: Herford and Simpson quote seven-
       teenth century documents which mention this phenomenon,
       and those referred to in lines 27, 28 and 29, as being in-
       cluded in accounts of actual cases of bewitchment or pre-
       tended bewitchment.

27   *His mouth's running away*: his mouth is working violently.

31   *blue toad*: Herford and Simpson quote the case of a child
       impostor who claimed to see a mouse escape from his mouth
       after a similar fit.

40   *Deny it*: Volpone urges Voltore to deny all remembrance of the
       confession he had submitted to the court, as if he had
       written it while not in his right mind.

49   *make him way*: make way for him.

53   *Had betrayed all*: was on the point of giving the whole thing
       away.

55   *busy knave*: officious rascal. Mosca now braves Volpone to his
       face for the first time.

56   *I sooner had attended your grave pleasures*: I would have been
       here sooner to carry out the wishes of this august court.

60   *Aye, quick, and cozen me of all*: That's right, bury me alive
       (quick) and cheat me of everything.

61   *And come about again*: the whole position has again been
       reversed.

62   *It is a match*: The confirmation of Volpone's death finally
       determines the fourth of the Avocatori to betroth his daughter
       to Mosca.

63   *Will you give me half?*: A crux which is discussed in the Intro-
       duction.

64   *cry not so loud*: keep your voice down. In his excitement
       Volpone has forgotten that what he is saying is for Mosca's
       ear alone.

69   *I cannot now Afford it you so cheap*: I am no longer disposed to
       let you off so lightly. Mosca has offered to 'share' with
       Volpone, as was his first thought at V, iii, 15; but, once

refused, he decided to 'cozen him of all', which he has described (ibid., 16–17) as 'But a cheat well placed'.

75   *If such an insolence as this must pass Upon me*: if I am allowed to be so insulted.

79   *to bear himself*: to show respect.

82   *If I confess, It cannot be much more*: Mosca has not foreseen that Volpone will reason like this, any more than Volpone realised that Voltore would cut his losses and confess in V, v.

85   *Patron!*: Taken by surprise, Mosca at once reverts to the old relationship.

86   *Your match I'll hinder sure*: I'll prevent your marriage, for sure.

87   *my substance shall not glue you*: you shan't marry on my fortune.

88   *Nor screw you into a family*: nor let you worm your way into a good family.

90   *avarice's fool*: one who plays the fool to serve his avarice.

91   *chimera of wittol, fool, and knave*: a monster, part wittol, part fool, and part knave. The original chimera in the Greek myth had a fire-breathing lion's head, a goat's body and a serpent's tail.

93   *Nought but a sentence*: nothing better than the sentence of the court.
     let's not now despair it: let's not despair of gaining our deserts. The tone is sardonic, the bravado characteristic of Volpone.

94   *You hear me brief*: I have wasted no words.

98   *Heaven could not long . . .*: A pious and conventional reaction proper to Bonario's formal role in the structure.

99   *this*: conduct such as Volpone's and Mosca's.

101   *These possess wealth as sick men possess fevers*, etc.: a trenchant close to the powerful analogy in the imagery of the play between wealth and disease.

103   *Disrobe that parasite*: He has wrongly adopted the finery of a magnifico.

105   *And mercy*: It is interesting to compare Celia's brief and ineffectual plea for mercy on behalf of her persecutors with the successful prayers of Isabella which set in train the final reconciliations in Shakespeare's very different comedy, *Measure for Measure*.

111　*And habit of a gentleman of Venice*: and you have also abused
　　　or debased the dress proper to Venetian gentry.

115　*I thank you for him*: Original texts give this speech to Voltore,
　　　which greatly weakens the idea. Modern editors have
　　　followed Gifford in attributing it to Volpone. As Herford
　　　and Simpson point out, it is clearly Volpone's 'retort to
　　　l. 81'.
　　　Bane: destruction; this is an imprecation: 'May destruction
　　　overwhelm . . .'

116　*saffi*: See the note on III, ii, 493.

117　*canst not fall . . .*: social rank offers some protection even to
　　　the criminal, though Volpone's punishment is severe
　　　enough to make the distinction of little consequence.

120　*Incurabili*: Incurables. This building existed.

121　*the most was gotten*: the larger part was procured. This past
　　　participle of 'got' is still current in the United States.

124　*Till thou be'st sick and lame indeed*: The image of disease
　　　is played out to its logical conclusion.

125　*mortifying of a Fox*: Volpone is sardonic and irrepressible
　　　to the last. 'To mortify' is a culinary term meaning to keep
　　　game till it is 'high' so that it shall be more tender and a
　　　greater delicacy.

131　*San Spirito*: an actual monastery in Venice.

133　*what said he?*: Corbaccio is as deaf as ever.

135　*rowed Round about Venice*: Venice, of course, is the city in
　　　which the principal thoroughfares are canals, the most
　　　important being the Grand Canal, nearly two miles long.

136　*Grand Canal*: Jonson uses the then current form 'Canale' (no
　　　doubt influenced by the Italian, since canals were still
　　　rarities in England); this slightly changes the rhythm of the
　　　line.

138　*horns*: again, the cuckold's horns. Celia's innocence has now
　　　been established, so instead of horns Corvino is to wear
　　　ass's ears, the emblem of a fool.

145　*And these are all your judgments*: that is, sentences. Ben
　　　Jonson is summary with his remaining characters, to avoid
　　　anti-climax.

149   *Let all that see these vices thus rewarded Take heart, and love to study them*: a succinct statement of Jonson's conception of didactic comedy.

154   *no suffering due*: the actor hopes that the audience has no cause to punish him in his professional capacity.

156   *doubtful*: uncertain how the audience will react.

157   *fare jovially*: to be compared with 'farewell'.